THE 2004 UNITED METHODIST DIRECTORY

& Index of Resources

GRE

CONTENTS

CONFERENCES

NEWS SERVICES AND PUBLICATIONS

AFFILIATED CAUCUSES AND ECUMENICAL GROUPS

STUDY GROUPS AND COMMITTEES

SCHOOLS, COLLEGES, UNIVERSITIES, SEMINARIES

PROGRAMS AND RESOURCES

INDEX

NOTICES

GENERAL INFORMATION

InfoServ 1-800-251-8140

www.umc.org

COKESBURY INTERNET BOOKSTORE

www. cokesbury.com

This directory includes changes secured from Boards and Agencies through November 2003.

The United Methodist Church

Facts and Figures

MEMBERSHIPS

U.S. **8,298,460**
   Lay. 8,253,606
   Clergy 44,854
   Retired 15,204
   Clergywomen (under appointment). . . . 7,466

BY JURISDICTION

North Central. 1,574,285
Northeastern. 1,530,282
South Central 1,821,197
Southeastern 2,938,111
Western 430,558
Military Service Personnel. 4,027

BY ETHNIC GROUPS (reporting incomplete)

Asian 70,801
African American 419,843
Hispanic. 51,871
Native American. 19,874
Pacific Islander 10,221
White. 7,214,201

LAY MEMBERS OUTSIDE U.S.   1,853,744

Africa. 1,600,964
Europe 73,172
Philippines. 179,608

CLERGY OUTSIDE U.S.   9,358

Africa 6,886
Europe 1,100
Philippines 1,372

PREDOMINANTLY ETHNIC CONGREGATIONS IN U.S. (estimate)

```
Asian .............................. 369
African American.................. 2,468
Hispanic........................... 310
Native American.................... 142
Pacific Islander .................... 39
```

CLERGY MEMBERS OF ANNUAL CONFERENCE-ETHNICITY/GENDER

```
Asian ............................. 976
African American .................. 2,540
Hispanic........................... 535
Native American ................... 192
Pacific Islander.................... 110
Female ............................ 8,623
White ............................. 40,573
```

ACTIVE BISHOPS IN THE U.S. 50

(14 African American, 2 Hispanic, 1 Asian American, 11 Women)
```
Africa ............................ 11
Eurasia ........................... 1
Europe ........................... 3
Philippines........................ 3
Retired bishops (all nations)............ 75
```

MISSION PERSONNEL (GBGM-related)

```
Nations Served ..................... 61
Commissioned ...................... 711
Non-Commissioned .................. 92
PIM............................... 234
IPIM ............................. 13

Total Number of Missionaries ........ 1050
```

EDUCATIONAL INSTITUTIONS 123

```
Seminaries ........................ 13
```

2

Professional School 1
Senior Colleges and Universities 92
Two-year colleges 7
College Preparatory Schools 10

AVERAGE ATTENDANCE AT PRINCIPAL WEEKLY WORSHIP SERVICE IN THE U.S. 3,546,695

AVERAGE ATTENDANCE AT SUNDAY CHURCH SCHOOL IN THE U.S. 1,606,917

PASTORAL CHARGES IN U.S. 26,348

DISTRICTS 520

COUNCIL OF BISHOPS

OFFICERS

President: **Minor, Ruediger R.**, Global Ministries, Box 257, PMB 572 c/o IPS 666 5th Ave., New York, NY 10103 7095 915 1832 FAX: 7095 915 1838 email: rumc@online.ru

President Elect: **Weaver, Peter D.**, POB 820, Valley Forge, PA 19482 610/666-9090 FAX: 610/666-9181 email: bishop@epaumc.org

Secretary: **Rader, Sharon Zimmerman**, 750 Windsor St., Suite #303, Sun Prairie, WI 53590 608/837-8526 FAX: 608/837-0281 email: szrader@aol.com

Assistant to the Secretary: **Tuell, Jack M.**, 816 S. 216th St., #637, Des Moines, WA 98198-6331 206/870-8637 FAX: 206/824-0128 email: marjac92@juno.com

Ecumenical Officer: **Talbert, Melvin G.**, 108 Rausch Dr., Brentwood, TN 37027-4447 615/309-8096 FAX: 615-661-8576 email: bishopmel@netzero.net

Administrative Assistant: **Alford, Joyce L.**, 750 Windsor St., Suite #303, Sun Prairie, WI 53590 608/837-8526 FAX: 608/837-0281 email: JAlford105@aol.com

ACTIVE

Blake, Bruce P., P.O. Box 60467, Oklahoma City, OK 73146-0467 405/530-2025 FAX: 405/530-2040

Bolleter, Heinrich, Badener Strasse 69, POB 2239, CH-8026 Zürich, SWITZERLAND 41-1-299-30-60 FAX: 41-1-299 30 60 email: heinrrich.bolleter@umc-northerneurope.org

Brown, Warner H., Jr., 2200 South University Blvd., Denver, CO 80210-4797 303/733-3736, ext. 601 FAX: 303/733-5047 email: bishop@rmcumc.com

Carder, Kenneth, P.O. Box 931, Jackson, MS 39205-0931 601/948-4561 FAX: 601/948-5981 email: bishop@mississippi-umc.org

Chamberlain, Ray W., 9915 Kingston Pike, Suite C, P.O. Box 32939, Knoxville, TN 37930-2939 865/690-4080 FAX: 865/690-7112 email: bishop@holston.org

Chamness, Benjamin, 464 Bailey, Ft. Worth, TX 76107-2153 817/877-5222 FAX: 817/332-4609 email: bishop@ctcumc.org

Christopher, Sharon A. Brown, 400 Chatham Rd., Suite 100,

Springfield, IL 62704 217/726-8071, ext. 201s FAX: 217/726-8074
email: ILAreaUMC@aol.com

Coyner, Michael J., 3910 25th St. S., Fargo, ND 58104 701/232-2241
FAX: 701/232-2615 email: BISHOPCOYNER@juno.com

Dabale, Done Peter, UMCN Secretariot, Mile Six, Jalingo-Numan
Rd., P.O. Box 155, Jalingo, Taraba State, NIGERIA 871-761-808665 or
234 79 22605 FAX: 871-761-808666 mailing address: c/o Zebediah
Marewangepo, 475 Riverside Rd., New York, NY 10115

Davis, G. Lindsey, P.O. Box 922997, Norcross, GA 30010 678/533-
1360 FAX: 678/533-1361 email: bishop@ngumc.org

Dew, William W., Jr., 1550 E. Meadowbrook Ave., Suite 200, Phoenix,
AZ 85014-4040 602/266-6956 FAX: 602/279-1355
email: Bishop@desertsw.org

Domingos, Gaspar Joao, Caixa Postal 68, Rua de N. S. Da Muxima
12, Luanda Angola 244 2 33 2107 FAX: 244 2 39 0184
email: imuangola@netangola.com

Edwards, Marion M., P.O. Box 10955, Raleigh, NC 27605 919/832-
9560, ext. 243 or 800/849-4433 FAX: 919/832-4721
email: bishopmme@nccumc.org

Fannin, Robert E., 898 Arkadelphia Rd., Birmingham, AL 35204-5011
205/322-8665 FAX: 205/322-8938 email: Rfannin@umcna.bsc.edu

Fisher, Violet., 1010 East Ave., Rochester, NY 14607-2220 585/271-
3400 FAX: 585/271-3404 email: NYWAUMC@frontiernet.net

Galván, Elias G., 2112 Third Ave., #301, Seattle, WA 98121-2333
206/728-7674 FAX: 206/728-8442 email: bishop@pnwumc.org

Goodpaster, Larry M., 312 Interstate Park Dr., Montgomery
AL 36109 334/227-1787 FAX: 334/277-0109
email: bishop.awf@knology.net

Hassinger, Susan W., P.O. Box 249, Lawrence, MA 01842-0449
978/682-7555, ext. 30 FAX: 978/682-9555
email: bishopsoffice@neumc.org

Hopkins, John L., 122 West Franklin Ave., #200, Minneapolis, MN
55404-2472 612/870-4007 FAX: 612/870-3587
email: jhopkins@msn.com

Huie, Janice Riggle, 723 Center St., Little Rock, AR 72201-4399
501/324-8019 FAX: 501/324-8021 email: bishophuie@aristotle.net

Humper, Joseph C., 31 Lightfoot Boston St., P.O. Box 523, Freetown,
SIERRA LEONE, WEST AFRICA 232 22 22665
FAX: 232-22 224439 email: cjhumper77@yahoo.com

Hutchinson, William W., 527 North Blvd., Baton Rouge, LA 70802
225/346-1646 ext. 212 FAX: 225/387-3662
email: enixmore@bellsouth.net

Innis, John G., P.O. Box 10-1010, Tubman Blvd. @ 13th St., Monrovia,

LIBERIA, WEST AFRICA Phone & fax: 231 227 154
email: bishopinnis@hotmail.com or liberiaumc@yahoo.com

Irons, Neil L., 303 Mulberry Dr., Suite 100, Mechanicsburg,
PA 17050-3141 717/766-7871 FAX: 717/766-3210
email: bishop@cpcumc.org

Ives, S. Clifton, 900 Washington St., E., Charleston, WV 25301 Phone
and fax: 304/344-8330 email: wvareaumc@aol.com

Johnson, Alfred, 1001 Wickapecko Dr., Ocean, NJ 07712-4733
732/359-1010 FAX: 732/359-1019 email: Bishop@gnjumc.org

Jokomo, Christopher, UMC-163 Chinhoyi St., P.O. Box 3408, Harare,
ZIMBABWE 263 4 751 508 FAX: 263 4 791 105

Justo, Benjamin A., Methodist Mission Center, 10 Marcos Highway,
P.O. Box 87, 2600 Baguio City, PHILIPPINES 6374 442 2879
FAX: 6374 304 2653 email: bajusto@yahoo.com

Kammerer, Charlene P., P.O. Box 18750, Charlotte, NC 28218
704/535-2260 FAX: 704/535-9160 email: Lkmmrr@aol.com

Katembo, Kainda, 960 Av. Mzee Laurent Kabila, LUMBUMBASHI
DEMOCRATIC REPUBLIC OF CONGO 243 88 47256 FAX: 243 23
41191 Send mail to: P.O. Box 20219, KITWE ZAMBIA
email: bishop-umc-sc@maf.org

Keaton, Jonathan D., POB 2800, North Canton, OH 44720-0800
330/499-3972 FAX: 330/497-4911 email: jonathan@eocumc.com

Kim, Hae-Jong, 1204 Freedom Rd. Send mail to: P.O. box 5002,
Cranberry TWP PA 16066-4914 724/776/1499/776-1599
FAX: 724/776-1683 email: umbishop@umchurch.org

King, James R., Jr., 7400 Floydsburg Rd., Crestwood, KY 40014-8202
502/425-4240 FAX: 502/426-9232 email: jking@kyumc.org

Klaiber, Walter, Wilhelm-Leuschner-Strasse 8, D-60329, Frankfurt,
GERMANY 49 69 24 25 210 FAX: 49 69 24 24 2129
email: emk.kirchenkanzlei@t-online.de

Lee, Linda, P.O.Box 25068, Lansing, MI 48909-5068 517/347-4030
FAX: 517/347-4003 email: mareaumc@tir.com

Lyght, Ernest S., 20 Soundview, White Plains, NY 10606 914/615-
2221 FAX: 914/615-2246 email: Bishop@nyac.com

Machado, Joao Somane, Rua D. Francisco Barreto 229, Caixa Postal
2640, Maputo, MOZAMBIQUE 258 1 49 3568
FAX: 258 1 49 35 68 email: umcmho@zebra.uem.mz

Martinez, Joel N., P.O. Box 781688, San Antonio, TX 78278 210/408-
4500 Toll free 888/349-4191 FAX: 210/408-4501
email: bishop@umc.swtx.org

May, Felton Edwin, 100 Maryland Ave., N.E., Suite 510, Washington,
DC 20002-5611 202/546-3110 FAX: 202/546-3186
email: bishopmay@bwcumc.org

McCleskey, J. Lawrence, 4908 Colonial Dr., #108, Columbia, SC 29203 803/786-9486 FAX: 803/754-9327 email: bishop@umcsc.org

Minor, Ruediger R., Global Ministries, Box 257, PMB 572 c/o IPS 666 5th Ave., New York, NY 10103 7095 915 1832 FAX: 7095 915 1838 email: rumc@online.ru

Moncure, Rhymes H., Jr., 2641 N. 49th St., Lincoln, NE 68504 402/466-4955 FAX: 402/466-7931 email: bishop@umcneb.org or sjeambey@umcneb.org

Morris, William W., 520 Commerce St., Suite 201, Nashville, TN 37203-3714 615/742-8834 FAX: 615/742-3726 email: UMCOFFICE@aol.com

Morrison, Susan Murch, 215 Lancaster St., Albany, NY 12210-1131 518/426-0386 FAX: 518/426-0347 email: AlbEpisArea@worldnet.att.net

Mutti, Albert Frederick, 4201 W. 15th St., P.O. Box 4187, Topeka, KS 66604-0187 785/272-0587 FAX: 785/272-9135 email: Kansasbishop@kansaseast.org

Ndoricimpa, J. Alfred, P.O. Box 64583, Apt. B4 Regent Management, Nairobi, KENYA 254 2 72 5373 or 4133 FAX: 254 2 72 5393 email: Umceaacoff@iconnect.co.ke

Norris, Alfred L., 5215 S. Main St., Houston, TX 77002-9792 713/528-6881 FAX: 713/529-7736 email: ijarratt@methodists.net

Ntambo, Nkulu Ntanda, UMC, Batiment Mokador Avenue Mobutu, Lubumbashi, DEMOCRATIC REPUBLIC OF CONGO 260 22 28 535 FAX: 871 683 02 5522

Oden, William B., 3300 Mockingbird Lane, Suite 316, P.O. BOX 600127, Dallas, TX 75360-0127 214/522-6741 FAX: 214/528-4435 email: dallasbishop@hpumc.org

Olsen, Øystein, Methodistkirkens Biskopskontor, Akersbakken 35A, N-0172 OSLO NORWAY 47 2320 1060 FAX: 47 2320 1410 email: bishop@umc-northerneurope.org or Oystein.olsen@umc-northerneurope.org

Onema, Fama, 2867 Ave. Des Ecuries, Ngaliema, B.P. 472, Kinshasa II, DEMOCRATIC REPUBLIC OF CONGO 243 99 36829 or 243 99 04534 FAX: 243 88 03723 email: Bishopofamaumc@aol.com or hilairepesse@hotmail.com

Ough, Bruce R., 32 Wesley Blvd., Worthington, OH 43085 800/437-0028 614/844-6200 ext. 215 FAX: 614/781-2625 email: bishop@wocumc.org

Palmer, Gregory V., 500 E. Court Ave., Suite C, Des Moines, IA 50309 515/283-1996, ext. 101 FAX: 515/283-8672 email: bishop.palmer@iaumc.org

Paup, Edward W., 1505 SW 18th Ave., Portland, OR 97201

503/226-1530 FAX: 503/228-3189 email: bishop@umoi.org
Pennel, Joe E., Jr., P.O. Box 1719, Glen Allen, VA 23060 804/521-1100, ext. 102 FAX: 804/521-1171 email; estellepruden@vaumc.org
Quipungo, Jose, Rua Comandante Dangereux No. 46, C.P. No 9, MALANGE ANGOLA 244 057 2 0306 FAX: 244 057 2 1497 email: imu-cala@ebonet.net
Rader, Sharon Zimmerman, 750 Windsor St., Suite #303, Sun Prairie, WI 53590 608/837-8526 FAX: 608/837-0281 email: szrader@aol.com
Shamana, Beverly J., P.O. Box 980250, West Sacramento, CA 95798-0250 916/374-1510 FAX: 916/372-9062 email: BISHOP@calnevumc.org
Sherer, Ann, 4800 Santana Circle, Suite 100, Columbia, MO 65203-7138 573/441-1770 FAX: 573/441-0765 email: mo.bishop.office.umc@cunet.org
Soriano, Leo A., Spottswood Methodist Center, 9400 Kidapawan City, Cotobato, PHILIPPINES 63 64 288 5131 FAX: 63 64 278 4150 email: bishopdea@yahoo.com or umcdea@pworld.net.ph
Sprague, C. Joseph, 77 W. Washington St., Suite 1820, Chicago, IL 60602 312/346-9766 ext. 102 FAX: 312/214-9031 email: jsprague@umcnic.org
Swenson, Mary Ann, P.O. Box 6006, Pasadena, CA 91102-6006 626/568-7312 FAX: 626/568-7377 email: calpacbishop@earthlink.net
Toquero, Solito K., United Methodist Headquarters, P.O. Box 756, 900 United Nations Ave., 1000 Ermita, Metro Manila, PHILIPPINES 63 2 523 4136, 63 2 521 1114, 63 2 523 0297 FAX: 63 2 521 2278 email: solbishop@hotmail.com
Vera Mendez, Juan A., P.O. Box 23339, U.P.R. Station, San Juan, PUERTO RICO 00931-3339 787/765-3195 FAX: 787/751-3615 email: Javera@coqui.net
Watson, B. Michael, P.O. Box 13616, Macon, GA 31208-3616 478/475-9286 FAX: 478/475-9248 email: bishopsga@aol.com
Weaver, Peter D., P.O. Box 820, Valley Forge, PA 19482 610/666-9090 FAX: 610/666-9181 email: BISHOP@EPAUMC.ORG
Whitaker, Timothy W., 1122 E. McDonald St., P.O. Box 1747, Lakeland, FL 33802-1747 863/688-4427 FAX: 863/687-0568 email: bishop@flumc.org
White, Woodie W., 1100 W. 42nd St., Suite 210, Indianapolis, IN 46208 317/924-1321 FAX: 317/924-1380 email: ecoleman@inareaumc.org
Whitfield, D. Max, 7920 Mountain Rd., NE, Albuquerque, NM 87110-7805 505/255-9361 FAX: 505-255-8738 email: whitmax@nmconfum.com

RETIRED

Allen, L. Scott, P.O. Box 92281, Atlanta, GA 30314 404/589-9508 FAX: 847/866-9553

Ammons, Edsel A., 1516 Hinman Ave., Unit 201, Evanston, IL 60201
847/869-9866 email: Abishop160@aol.com

Arichea, Daniel C., Jr., Union Theological Seminary, PCU Campus,
Palapla, Dasmarinas, Cavite, 414 PHILIPPINES 63917 506 4066
FAX: 634 6 416 0451 email: aricheajr@yahoo.com

Ault, James Mase, 1 Amoskegan Dr., Brunswick, ME 04011 Phone &
FAX: 207/798-7946 email: jmaorda@gwi.net

Bangura, Thomas S., United Methodist Church, 31 Lightfoot Boston St.,
P.O. Box 523, Freetown, Sierra Leone, WEST AFRICA 232 22 272 602

Bashore, George W., 2409 Broadlawn Dr., Pittsburgh, PA 15241-2407
412/854-2389 FAX: 412/854-2398 email: charis@adelphia.net

Borgen, Ole E., Torvgata 13A, 2000 Lillestrom, NORWAY Tel. and
FAX: 47 63 80 1501 email: borgeno@online.no

Bryan, Monk, 333 Crum Dr., P.O. Box 100, Lake Junaluska, NC 28745-0100
828/452-1999 email: tmbryan@haywood.main.nc.us

Choy, Wilbur W. Y., 23319-53rd Ave., S., Kent, WA 98032-3349
253/852-0964

Clark, Roy C., (Summer: P.O. Box 531, Lake Junaluska, NC 28745
828/456-3142) 4400 Belmont Park Terrace, #192, Nashville, TN
37215-3629 615/383-3047 (phone and FAX) email: Mscrcc@aol.com

Clymer, Wayne K., (May-Oct.) 2850 Inner Rd., Wayzata, MN 55391
952/473-2812 or (Nov.-Apr.) Parkway Villas, 6054 Coral Way,
Bradenton, FL 34207 941/727-7875 email: wclymer2000@yahoo.com

Colaw, Emerson S., 2444 Madison Rd., #201, Cincinnati, OH 45208
513/871-3273 email: Bayviewemer@aol.com

Craig, Judith, 3699 Orchard, Powell, OH 43056 614/761-0855
FAX: 614/761-0858 email: bcraig@ameritech.net

DeCarvalho, Emilio J. M., Rua Oliveira Martins, 29, Bairro de
Alvalade, Caixa Postal 2648, Luanda Angola, AFRICA 244 2 32
4431 FAX: 244 2 32 4629 email: emarcar@netangola.com

DeWitt, Jesse R., 2968 Leslie Park Cir., Ann Arbor, MI 48105
734/322-1477 FAX: 734/332-3854 email: ajdewitt@concentric.net

Dodge, Ralph E., 8581 E. Sweetwater Dr., Inverness, FL 34450
352/726-4751 email: red9198@atlantic.net

Duecker, R. Sheldon, 8625 Sweet Blossom Ct., Fort Wayne, IN 46835-9625
260/485-8255 FAX: 219/485-8255 email: rsduecker@aol.com

Duffey, Paul A., 3643 Fernway Dr., Montgomery, AL 36111-3309
334/284-6341 email: paduffey@mindspring.com

Eutsler, R. Kern, 7090 Covenant Woods Dr., Apt. F-304,
Mechanicsville, VA 23111 804/569-8053 email: uvim@worldnet.att.net

Fernandes, Moises Domingos, Rua de Liberdade, 154 Trasito 156,
DeVila Alice, Luanda, ANGOLA

Finger, H. Ellis, Jr.,Givens Estates, 414 Lady Huntington Lane,
Asheville, NC 28803 828/274-1093

Frank, Eugene M., 10000 Wornall Rd., Apt. 4111, Kansas City, MO 64114-4369 816/942-3436

Gamboa, José C., Jr., Block 5, Lot 21, 72 Virgo St., Camella Homes, Baccor, Cavite, PHILLIPINES 63 46 472 1937

Grove, William Boyd, 109 McDavid Ln., Charleston, WV 25311-9708 304/344-1384 FAX: 304/344-3717 email: WboydGrove@aol.com

Hancock, Charles W., 5300 Zebulon Rd., Apt. 1129, Macon, GA 31210 478/757-0791 email: cwhmacon@msn.com

Hardt, John Wesley, 6309 Crestmont, Dallas, TX 75214 214/696-2370 email: Hardt@flash.net

Hearn, J. Woodrow, (Oct. 26-May 14) 62 Campeche Circle, Galveston, TX 77554-9361 409/741-0350 (May 15-Oct. 25) P.O. Box 25, Friendship, ME 04547 207/832-7518

Hicks, Kenneth W., 3909 South Lookout, Little Rock, AR 72205-2027 501/663-9670 FAX: 501/663-2977 email: KHbishop@aol.com

Hodapp, Leroy C., 1206 Dress Lane, Evansville, IN 47711 812/867-6503

Hughes, H. Hasbrouck, Jr. 113 South Stocker Ct., Williamsburg, VA 23188-6307 757/258-0538 email: H3MGH@aol.com

Hunt, Earl G., Jr., Givens Estates, 100 Wesley Dr., Unit 509, Asheville, NC 28803 828/277-8631

Job, Rueben P., 4900 Huffman Rd., Goodlettsville, TN 37072-9612 615/876-3110 FAX: 615/876-8296 email: dakotajob@aol.com

Jones, L. Bevel, III, 2977 Blackwood Rd., Decatur, GA 30033-1011 404/636-4401

Jordan, Charles Wesley, 1014 Deborah St., Upland, CA 91748 909/946-6785 FAX: 909/946-7357 email: Bishop.Jordan@iaumc.org

Kelly, Leontine T. C., 316 N. El Camino Real #112, San Mateo, CA 94401-3529 650/343-9029 email: Ltckelly@aol.com

Knox, J. Lloyd, 6848-15th St. South, St. Petersburg, FL 33705-6024 727/864-2874 email: Senorobispo@yahoo.com

Kulah, Arthur F., Send mail to the Sierra Leone Area Office in care of Bishop Humper 232-22-229028; 232-22-225106

Lawson, David J., Perkins School of Theology, P.O. Box 750133, Dallas, TX 75275-0133 214/768-4343 FAX: 214/768-1042 email: Dlawso@mail.smu.edu

Lee, Clay F., Jr., 5033 Forest Hill Rd., Byram, MS 39272 601/373-3449 FAX: 601/373-7179 email: 76434.3707@compuserve.com

Lewis, William B., 916 University Dr., Edwardsville, IL 62025-2962 618/656-1357

Looney, Richard C., Foundation for Evangelism, P.O. Box 985, Lake Junaluska, NC 28745 800/737-8333 FAX: 828/456-4313 email: richardclooney@aol.com or P.O. Box 747, Lake Junaluska, NC 23745 828/456-5312 email:r-c.Looney@juno.com

Mathews, James K., Sumner Village #502, 4978 Sentinel Dr., 12-502, Bethesda, MD 20816 301/320-9429 FAX: 301/320-9439 email: EunikenMatthews@aol.com

McConnell, Calvin D., 1630 S.E. River Ridge Dr., Portland, OR 97222 503/353-2754 email: cvmcconnell@comcast.net

McDavid, Joel D., 616 Willow Brook Run, Mobile, AL 36660 334/460-4689

Meadors, Marshall L., Jr., Candler School of Theology, Emory University, Atlanta, GA 30322 404/727-6326 FAX: 404/727-2494 email: jackmeadors@aol.com

Milhouse, Paul W., 1070 W. Jefferson St., Franklin, IN 46131 317/736-1396

Minnick, C. P., Jr., 5101 Coronado Dr., Raleigh, NC 27609-5122 919/787-4066 email: cminn27@aol.com

Morgan, Robert C., 1295 Malibu Pl., Birmingham, AL 35216 205/979-7244 (phone and FAX) Office FAX: must have cover letter: 205/226-4805 email: bmorgan@panther.bsc.edu

Muzorewa, Abel T., P.O. Box 353, Borrowdale Harare ZIMBABWE

Nacpil, Emerito P., #4 Gardenia St., Dona Manuela Subdv., Pamplona Las Pinas, Metro Manila, PHILIPPINES 63 2 872 0309 FAX: 63 2 525 6778 email: pccumc@world.net.ph

Newman, Ernest W., 3636 Carriage Way, East Point, GA 30344 404/768-4808 email: ewnthn@aol.com

Nichols, Roy C., 6314 Whaley Dr., San Jose, CA 95135-1446 408/223-1121

Oliphint, Benjamin R., 8008 Oakwood Bend, Houston, TX 77040 713/896-0252

Ott, Donald A., N22W24040 Cloister Cir., 3D, Pewaukee, WI 53072-4677 262/523-2624 FAX: 262/523-1198 email: BISHDOTT@aol.com

Owen, Raymond, 1824 Craig Blvd., Edmong, OK 73003 405/348-2307 email: randlowen@juno.com

Penicela, Almeida, Rua d. Francisco Barreto 229, Maputo, MOZAMBIQUE, AFRICA 258 1 49 0671

Russell, John W., 8037 Misty Trail, Ft. Worth, TX 76123-1935 817/292-2086

Sanders, Carl J., 4016 Meadowview Cir., Birmingham, AL 35243-5636 205/967-3705 email: carljsanders@aol.com

Sano, Roy I., 400 Elysian Fields Dr., Oakland, CA 94605 510/635-7916 FAX: 510/635-5052 Seminary Tel: 510/848-8202 email: bishoprsano@earthlink.net

Schäfer, Franz W., Drosselstrasse 14, CH-8038 Zurich, SWITZERLAND 41 1 481 64 28 email: f.schaefer@bluewin.ch

Skeete, F. Herbert, 2765 Edgehill Ave., Riverdale, NY 10463 718/549-1784 (Jan. 1-April 1) "Stella" 2nd Ave., Stanmore Crescent,

Black Rock, St. Michael, Barbados, WEST INDIES 246/424-7171 email: FHSBLKRCK@aol.com

Solomon, Dan E., McMurry Station Box 56, Abilene, TX 79697 (H) 325/691-9716 (O) 325/793-4899

Spain, Robert H., 201 Eighth Ave., So., P.O. Box 801, Nashville, TN 37202 615/749-6377 FAX: 615/749-6704 email: rspain@umpublishing.org

Sticher, Hermann L., Untere Wengert-Strasse 16, D-72622 Nuertingen, GERMANY 49 7 022 495 16 FAX: 49 4 403 603 044 508 email: HermSti@aol.com

Stith, Forrest C., 13506 Leesburg Pl., Upper Marlboro, MD 20774 301/249-5584 FAX: 301/249-3785 email: FCPreach@aol.com

Stockton, Thomas B., 1835 Country Club Dr., W., High Point, NC 27262-4584 336/886-1835 email: Livalive@northstate.net

Stokes, Mack B., P.O. Box 497, Waynesville, NC 28726 828/456-8931

Stuart, R. Marvin, 850 Webster St. #223, Palo Alto, CA 94301-2837 650/470-5620

Talbert, Melvin G., 108 Rausch Dr., Brentwood, TN 37027-4447 615/309-8096 FAX: 615/661-8576 email: bishopmel@netzero.net

Thomas, James S., 2148 Briar Glen Lane, Atlanta, GA 30331 404/349-5996

Tuell, Jack M., 816 S. 216th St., #637, Des Moines, WA 98198-6331 206/870-8637 FAX: 206/824-0128 email: marjac92@juno.com

Tullis, Edward L., 510 Crum Dr., Lake Junaluska, NC 28745-9777 828/452-5427 email: etullis@iopener.net

Wertz, Frederick, 1 Longsdorf Way #1, Carlisle, PA 17013 717/240-2515 FAX: 717/243-1883 email: dfwertz@pa.net

Wheatley, Melvin E., Jr., 859A Ronda Mendoza, Laguna Hills, CA 92653-5940 949/837-5338 email: Lmwheatley@webtv.net

White, C. Dale, 117 Eustis Ave., Newport, RI 02840-2865 401/847-3419 email: dwhite12@earthlink.net

Wilke, Richard B., 904 N. Clyde St., Winfield, KS 67156-1517 620/221-0307 (Part Time: P.O. Box 88, Lake Junaluska, NC 28745) 828/452-3068

Wilson, Joe A., 132 Melissa Ct., Georgetown, TX 78628-2769 512/868-2553 email: jwbish@thegateway.net

Yeakel, Joseph H., 14137 Windy Haven Rd., Smithsburg, MD 21783-1126 301/824-7002 FAX: 815/377-9067 email: jhyeakel@erols.com

EPISCOPAL ASSIGNMENTS

Central Conferences

Baguio Area - **Justo, Benjamin A.**
Central and Southern Europe Area - **Bolleter, Heinrich**
Central Congo Area - **Onema, Fama**
Davao Area - **Soriano, Leo A.**
East Africa Area - **Ndoricimpa, J. Alfred**
East Angola Area - **Quipungo, Jose**
Germany - **Klaiber, Walter**
Liberia Area - **Innis, John G.**
Manila Area - **Toquero, Solito Kuramin**
Mozambique Area - **Machado, Joao Somane**
Nigeria Area - **Dabale, Done Peter**
North Katanga Area - **Ntambo, Nkulu Ntanda**
Nordic & Baltic Area - **Olsen, Øystein**
Eurasia Area - **Minor, Ruediger R.**
Sierra Leone Area - **Humper, Joseph Christian**
Southern Congo Area - **Katembo, Kainda**
West Angola Area - **Domingos, Gaspar Joao**
Zimbabwe Area - **Jokomo, Christopher**

Northeastern Jurisdiction

Albany Area - **Morrison, Susan Murch**
  Troy and Wyoming Conferences
Boston Area - **Hassinger, Susan W.**
  Harrisburg Area - **Irons, Neil L.**
  Central Pennsylvania
  New Jersey Area - **Johnson, Alfred**
  Greater New Jersey Conferences
New York Area - **Lyght, Ernest S.**
  New York Conference
New York West Area - **Fisher, Violet L.**
  North Central New York and Western New York Conferences
Philadelphia Area - **Weaver, Peter D.**
  Eastern Pennsylvania and Peninsula-Delaware Conferences
Pittsburgh Area - **Kim, Hae-Jong**
  Western Pennsylvania Conference
Washington Area - **May, Felton Edwin**
  Baltimore-Washington Conference

West Virginia Area - **Ives, S. Clifton**
West Virginia Conference

North Central Jurisdiction

Chicago Area - **Sprague, C. Joseph**
Northern Illinois Conference
Dakotas Area - **Coyner, Michael J.**
Dakotas Conference
Illinois Area - **Christopher, Sharon A. Brown**
Illinois Great Rivers Conference
Indiana Area - **White, Woodie W.**
North Indiana and South Indiana Conferences
Iowa Area - **Palmer, Gregory V.**
Iowa Conference
Michigan Area - **Lee, Linda**
Detroit and West Michigan Conferences
Minnesota Area - **Hopkins, John L.**
Minnesota Conference
Ohio East Area - **Keaton, Jonathan D.**
East Ohio Conference
Ohio West Area - **Ough, Bruce R.**
West Ohio Conference Area
Wisconsin Area - **Rader, Sharon Zimmerman**
Wisconsin Conference

South Central Jurisdiction

Arkansas Area - **Huie, Janice Riggle**
Little Rock and North Arkansas Conferences
Dallas Area - **Oden, William B.**
North Texas Conference
Fort Worth Area - **Chamness, Ben**
Central Texas Conference
Houston Area - **Norris, Alfred L.**
Texas Conference
Kansas Area - **Mutti, Albert**
Kansas East and Kansas West Conferences
Louisiana Area - **Hutchinson, William W.**
Louisiana Conference
Missouri Area - **Sherer, Ann Brookshire**
Missouri East and Missouri West Conferences

Nebraska Area - **Moncure, Rhymes H., Jr.**
Nebraska Conference
Northwest Texas - New Mexico Area - **Whitfield, D. Max**
New Mexico and Northwest Texas Conferences
Oklahoma Area - **Blake, Bruce P.**
Oklahoma and Oklahoma Indian Missionary Conferences
San Antonio Area - **Martinez, Joel N.**
Rio Grande and Southwest Texas Conferences

Southeastern Jurisdiction

Alabama-West Florida Area - **Goodpaster, Larry M.**
Alabama-West Florida Conference
Birmingham Area - **Fannin, Robert E.**
North Alabama Conference
Charlotte Area - **Kammerer, Charlene P.**
Western North Carolina Conference
Columbia Area - **McCleskey, J. Lawrence**
South Carolina Conference
Florida Area - **Whitaker, Timothy W.**
Florida Conference
Holston Area - **Chamberlain, Ray W., Jr.**
Holston Conference
Louisville Area - **King, James R., Jr.**
Kentucky and Red Bird Missionary Conferences
Mississippi Area - **Carder, Kenneth L.**
Mississippi Conference
Nashville Area - **Morris, William W.**
Memphis and Tennessee Conferences
North Georgia Area - **Davis, G. Lindsey**
North Georgia Conference
Raleigh Area - **Edwards, Marion M.**
North Carolina Conference
Richmond Area - **Pennel, Joe E., Jr.**
Virginia Conference
South Georgia Area - **Watson, B. Michael**
South Georgia Conference

Western Jurisdiction

Denver Area - **Brown, Warner H., Jr.**
Rocky Mountain and Yellowstone Conferences

Los Angeles Area - **Swenson, Mary Ann**
  California-Pacific Conference
Phoenix Area - **Dew, William W., Jr.**
  Desert Southwest Conference
Portland Area - **Paup, Edward W.**
  Alaska Missionary and Oregon-Idaho Conferences
San Francisco Area - **Shamana, Beverly J.**
  California-Nevada Conference
Seattle Area - **Galván, Elias G.**
  Pacific Northwest Conference

GENERAL COUNCIL ON FINANCE AND ADMINISTRATION
EXECUTIVE STAFF REPORTING RELATIONSHIPS

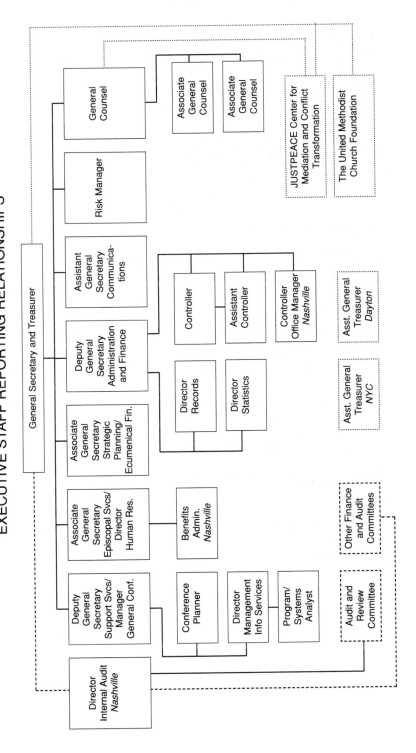

GENERAL COUNCIL ON FINANCE AND ADMINISTRATION
www.gcfa.org

OFFICERS

President: **Norris, Alfred L.**
Vice President: **Fannin, Robert E.**
Recording Secretary: **Mitchell, Connie L.**
General Secretary and Treasurer: **Lackore, Sandra Kelley**

MEMBERS

Bishops
Fannin, Robert E., 898 Arkadelphia Rd., Birmingham, AL 35204
205/322-8665
Norris, Alfred L., 5215 S. Main St., Houston, TX 77002-9792 713/528-6881
Swenson, Mary Ann, POB 6006, Pasadena, CA 91102-6006 626/568-7312

North Central Jurisdiction

Aubuchon, David R., 9634 Brixton Ave., NW, Uniontown, OH 44685
330/497-8706
Hinker, Patricia B., 815 E. University St., Owatonna, MN 55060
507/451-4734
Odle, Samuel L., 1701 N. Senate Ave., Indianapolis, IN 46206
317/962-8641
Sutton, R. Stanley, 32 Wesley Blvd., Worthington, OH 43085-3585
614/844-6200
Ulman, Barbara L., 5600 W. Maple #A-120, West Bloomfield,
MI 48322-3782 248/855-6266
Woodruff, John H., 20 Brompton Ct., Bloomington, IL 61704 309/663-2596

Northeastern Jurisdiction

Dockery, Lucille W., 5 Hill & Hollow Rd., Hyde Park,
NY 12538-2919 845/229-5471
Harris, Patricia Bryant, 211A Phillip Morris Dr., Salisbury,
MD 21804-4310 410/749-3331

Hoover, Clarence C., III, 625 Plum St., Vineland, NJ 08360
856/794-6500
Moseley, Ray, 10004 Village Green Dr., Woodstock, MD 21163
410/922-9962
Scott, Gail F., 621 Leon Dr., Endicott, NY 13760-1359 607/754-1275
Wogaman, J. Phillip, 4620 45th St. NW, Washington, DC 20016
202/363-3093

South Central Jurisdiction

Brim, Jay, 2525 Wallingwood Bldg 14, Austin, TX 78746 512/328-0048
House, Donald R., 3833 Texas Ave., Suite 285, Bryan, TX 77802
979/846-4713
Moore, Marilyn S., 1624 Van Dorn, Lincoln, NE 68502 402/436-1625
Underwood, Donald W., 3101 Coit Rd., Plano, TX 75075-3725
972/596-4303
Waymire, Mona Mae, POB 617, Madill, OK 73446 580/795-7577
Wilbur, Reuben L., 4800 Santana Cir., Suite 500, Columbia,
MO 65203-7138 573/441-1770

Southeastern Jurisdiction

Bullard, John C., 3359 Warrenton Rd., Montgomery, AL 36111-1736
334/264-0325
Holston, L. Jonathan, 1000 Main St., Suite #C, Stone Mountain,
GA 30083 770/879-9016
Mitchell, Connie L., 1705 Leestown Rd. #418, Lexington, KY 40511
859/253-0318
Phillips, J. Taylor, POB 6242, Macon, GA 31208 478/749-6676
Scarborough, Martha A., 126 Langford Dr., Brandon, MS 39047
601/948-8845

Western Jurisdiction

Bulkeley, Jeff, 14418 N. 17th Pl., Phoenix, AZ 85022 602/808-8461
Knudsen, J. Diane, POB 980250, West Sacramento, CA 95798-0250
916/374-1520
Meyers, Robert C., 1505 SW 18th Ave., Portland, OR 97201-2599
503/223-7931

Parrish, Craig A., 2112 3rd Ave. Suite 300, Seattle, WA 98121-2333
206/728-7462
Sewell, Peggy I., 339 Park Dr., Glenwood Springs, CO 81601-4137
970/928-8936
Smith, Robert, 6050 Hayes Ave., Los Angeles, CA 90042 323/256-3657

AT-LARGE MEMBERS

Avery, Donald R., 9375 Highland Rd., Baton Rouge, LA 70810-4024
225/766-4594
Bankurunaze, Lazare, POB 64583, Nairobi, Kenya 254-2-72-761-469
Battle, LaVeeda Morgan, 2101 Sixth Ave., N., #700, Birmingham,
AL 35203 205/254-3216
Hartman, Shawn M., 64 Queen Anne's Ct., Apt. 23, Weymouth, MA
02189 617/236-5417
Hernandez, Andrew R., 6603 Seinfeld Ct., Houston, TX 77069-1723
713/973-5361
Pinson, Mathew Avary, 6 Wilson Dr., Rome, GA 30165 706/234-2022
Sherbrooke, Sue, 2300 N. 43rd St., Seattle, WA 98103 206/461-4854

COMMITTEE CHAIRS

Executive: **Norris, Alfred L.**
Audit and Review: **Sutton, R. Stanley**
Connectional Services: **Woodruff, John H.**
Episcopal Services: **Sewell, Peggy I.**
Financial Services: **Fannin, Robert E.**
Investment: **Wogaman, J. Phillip**
Legal Responsibilities: **Battle, LaVeeda Morgan**
Legislation: **Swenson, Mary Ann**
Nominations: **Hartman, Shawn M.**
Official Forms and Records: **Aubuchon, David R.**
Personnel: **Norris, Alfred L.**
Personnel Policies and Practices: **Brim, Jay**
Property Services: **Waymire, Mona Mae**

STAFF

1200 Davis St., Evanston, IL 60201-4193
847/869-3345 FAX: 847/425-6565
Web site: www.gcfa.org
gcfa@gcfa.org

General Secretary and Treasurer: **Lackore, Sandra Kelley**, 847/425-6501
Deputy General Secretary/Administration and Finance: **Fishel, Robert**, 847/425-6503 email: rfishel@gcfa.org
Associate General Secretary/Strategic Planning and Ecumenical Finance: **Goolsbey, John**, 847/425-6505 email: jgoolsbe@gcfa.org
Assistant General Secretary/Communications: **Zekoff, Steve**, 847/425-6506 email: szekoff@gcfa.org

Director, Records: **Haralson, Cynthia J.**, 847/425-6548
email: charalso@gcfa.org
Director, Statistics: **Borst, Beth Babbitt**, 847/425-6573
email: bbabbitt@gcfa.org

Deputy General Secretary/Support Services/Manager, General Conference: **Bowen, Gary K.**, 847/425-6556 FAX: 847/425-6570
email: gbowen@gcfa.org
Conference Planner: **McKinsey, Linda,** 847/425-6557
email: lmckinse@gcfa.org
Director MIS: **Zhang, Shukai,** 847/425-6541
Program/Systems Analyst: **McGorry, Peter,** 847/425-6540

Associate General Secretary/Episcopal Services and Director, Human Resources: **Okayama, Elizabeth T.**, 847/425-6522
email: lokayama@gcfa.org

Legal Services: FAX: 847/425-6568
General Counsel: **Howard, Irene,** 847/425-6531
email: ihoward@gcfa.org
Associate General Counsel: **Allen, James R.**, 615/329-3393 ext. 17
email: jallen@gcfa.org
Associate General Counsel: **Gary, Dan,** 847/425-6533
email: dgary@gcfa.org

Risk Management: FAX: 847/425-6569

Risk Manager: **Cholak, Linda C.**, 847/425-6558
email: lcholak@gcfa.org

Controller: **Soo Hoo, Frank**, 847/425-6514 email: fsoohoo@gcfa.org
Assistant Controller: **Geier, Petra**, 847/425-6509
Senior Staff Accountant: **Nie, Lily**, 847/425-6512
Staff Accountant: **Saustegui, Nora**, 847/425-6515
Staff Accountant: **Thomas, Dalphin**, 847/425-6516

Executive Director, JUSTPEACE: **Porter, Tom**, 847/425-6526
email: TPorter@JustPeaceUMC.org
Director of Administration, JUST PEACE: **Mancao, Mark**, 847/425-6526 email: mcmancao@justpeaceumc.org

Executive Director, The United Methodist Church Foundation:
Bonner, Byrd, 847/420-1796 email: BBonner@UMCFoundation.org
Director of Development, The United Methodist Church Foundation:
Rivas, John, 615/340-1798 email: jrivas@UMCFoundation.org

Service Centers
Nashville: 1000 17th Ave. S., Nashville, TN 37212
615/329-3393 FAX: 615/329-3394
Controller and Office Manager: **Smith, Brent**, ext. 11,
email: bsmith@gcfa.org
Staff Accountant: **Fusco, Kimberly**, ext. 14 email: kfusco@gcfa.org
Benefits Administrator: **Manous, Rhonda**, ext. 15

Director of Internal Audit: **Belton, Dennis**, ext. 12
Internal Audit Supervisor: **Peña, Alberto L.**, ext. 16 email:
apena@gcfa.org
Senior Internal Auditor: **Thomason, Jennifer**, ext. 19
email: jthomaso@gcfa.org

New York: 475 Riverside Dr., #1439, New York, NY 10115-0111
212/870-3637 FAX: 212/870-3748
Assistant General Treasurer:

Dayton: 601 W. Riverview Ave., Dayton, OH 45406-5543
937/227-9400 FAX: 937/227-9407 Assistant General Treasurer:
Conrad, Lola I.

JUDICIAL COUNCIL

OFFICERS

President: **Corry, John G.,** Box 1702, 1005 D. B. Todd Blvd., Meharry
Medical College, Nashville, TN 37208 615/327-6975
email: jcorry@mmc.edu
Vice-President: **Bevins, C. Rex,** 1201 O Street, Suite 010, Lincoln, NE
68508
Secretary: **Askew, Sally Curtis,** 306 Providence Rd., Athens,
GA 30606 706/548-8107 FAX: 706/548-8108
email: judicialcouncil@charter.net

MEMBERS

Beltran, Rudolfo C., 1071 Del Pilar St., Cabanatuan City,
PHILIPPINES A-3100 463-22-38
Boyette, Keith D., Wilderness Community Church, POB 579,
Locust Grove, VA 22508 540/972-8808
Daffin, Mary A., 1900 St. James Pl., Suite 500, Houston, TX 77056
Geis, Sally, 420 S. Marion Pkwy., #501, Denver, CO 80209
Holsinger, James, 4705 Waterside Ct., Lexington, KY 40513
859/323-5126
Pickens, Larry, First UMC, 216 E. Highland Ave., Elgin, IL 60120
First Clergy Alternate: **Henry-Crowe, Susan,** 316 Cannon Chapel,
Emory University, Atlanta, GA 30322

GENERAL COUNCIL ON MINISTRIES
www.gcom-umc.org

OFFICERS

President: **Paup, Edward W.**
Vice-President: **Barker, Amy Valdez**
Vice-President: **Chiripasi, Solomon**
Secretary: **Langford, Thomas A., III**
Treasurer: **Silva, Mary**

MEMBERS

Alexander, Neil M., United Methodist Publishing House, 201 Eighth
 Ave., S., POB 801, Nashville, TN 37202 615/749-6327
 FAX: 615/749-6510 email: nalexander@umpublishing.org
Allread, Ardith, 1445 Everett Way, Roseville, CA 95747 916/624-5534
 email: aallread@infostations.net
Amon, Darlene V., 5128 Stratford Dr., Suffolk, VA 23435-1437
 757/484-2943 FAX: 757/484-8276 email: dvamon@aol.com
Anderson-Wilkins, Danita R., 21 E. Franklin, Naperville, IL 60540
 630/355-6445 FAX: 630/355-9524 email: danderso@umcnic.org
Arant, A. Turner, 414 Blaine Rd., Sunflower, MS 38778 662/887-6465
 FAX: 662/887-6242 email: tarant@deltaland.net
Baker, Jonathan E., 226 Oakwood Dr., Wilmington, DE 19803
 302/478-2575 FAX: 302/478-1828 email: jonbaker@comcast.net
Barker, Amy Valdez, 750 Windsor St., POB 620, Sun Prairie,
 WI 53590-0620 608/837-7328 FAX: 608/837-8547
 email: amybarker@wisconsinumc.org
Bennett, Jana M., 1116 Iredell St., Durham, NC 27705 919/286-7641
 email: janambennett@hotmail.com
Bledsoe, W. Earl, 2107 Maplewood Ct., College Station, TX 77845
 979/779-1041 email: ebledsoe@cox-internet.com
Burkhart, J. Robert, 1340 3rd Ave., SE POB 2065, Cedar Rapids,
 IA 52406 319/363-2058 FAX: 319/363-6348
 email: Bob.Burkhart@stpaulsumc.org
Byington, Tim, HC30, Box 1125, Lawton, OK 73501 580/492-5636
 email: lakota512000@yahoo.com
Cantor-Orate, Emma A., 41 Sct Castor, Laging Handa (Roces),
 Quezon City, The Philippines 011/632-523-9587

FAX: 011/632-524-5183 email: rmoasia@ph.inter.net

Chamberlain, Ray W., Jr., Holston Area, POB 32939, Knoxville, TN 37930-2939 865/690-4080 FAX: 865/690-7112 email: Bishop@holston.org

Chiripasi, Solomon, The United Methodist Church, 163 Chinhoyi St., POB 3408, Harare, ZIMBABWE 011 263 4 751 508 FAX: 011 263 4 702 028

Day, R. Randy, General Secretary, General Board of Global Ministries, 475 Riverside Dr., Room 350, New York, NY 10115 212/870-3606 FAX: 212/870-3748 email: rday@gbgm-umc.org

deCarvalho, Marilina, Rua Oliveira Martins 29, POB 2648, Luanda, Angola, Africa FAX: 011-2442-324629 email: emarcar@netangola.com

Del Pino, Jerome King, General Board of Higher Education and Ministry, 1001-19th Ave. S., POB 34007, Nashville, TN 37203 615/340-7356 FAX: 615/340-7048 email: jdelpino@gbhem.org

Ellison, Betty G., 4058 Ayers Dr., Kennesaw, GA 30144 770/427-8929 FAX: 770/426-1560 email: BettyEll@ix.netcom.com

Francisco, Raul, 507 Scenic Dr., Ewing, NJ 08628 201/440-6259 email: francis4@tcnj.edu

Frederick, Austin K., Jr., POB 781149, San Antonio, TX 78278-1149 210/408-4500 FAX: 210/408-4515 email: afred@umcswtx.org

Frueh, Henry, 21 Berkshire Dr., East Greenbush, NY 12061 518/477-9693 email: hfrueh@juno.com

Frueh, Abby, 10 Lincoln Ave., Glens Falls, NY 12801 518/793-2103 FAX: 518/793-2103 email: abby10@juno.com

Furr, Steven, 214 Plantation Trail, Jackson, AL 36545 251/246-4446 FAX: 251/246-5111 email: furrs@bellsouth.net

Glenn, Twila M., Director of Connectional Ministries, Iowa Conference, 500 E. Court Ave., Suite C, Des Moines, IA 50309 515/283-1991 FAX: 515/283-0836 email: Twila.Glenn@iaumc.org

Greenwaldt, Karen, General Board of Discipleship, POB 340003, Nashville, TN 37203 615/340-7022 FAX: 615/340-7019 email: kgreenwaldt@gbod.org

Guerra, Jaziel, 1 Macklem Dr., CPO Box 554, Wilmore, KY 40390-1198 956/702-7832 email: jaziel350@aol.com

Gwinn, Alfred W., 3709 Long Meadow Ct., Lexington, KY 40509 859/233-0545 FAX: 859/254-2083 email: awgwinn@aol.com

Harris, Joseph L., General Comission on United Methodist Men, POB 340006, Nashville, TN 37203-0006 615/340-7145 FAX: 615/340-1770 email: jharris@gcumm.org

Hayenga, Mary, 13431 416th Ave., Andover, SD 57422-9703 605/298-5617 FAX: 605/298-5617 email: hayengashop@nvc.net

Helliesen, Øyvind, Alperosev. 5, N-4022, Stavanger, Norway 011-47-51896620 FAX: 011-4751896622
email: oyvind.helliesen@metodistkirken.no

Hollon, Larry, United Methodist Communications, POB 320, Nashville, TN 37202 615/742-5410 FAX: 615/742-5415
email: lhollon@umcom.umc.org

Hopkins, John L., 122 W. Franklin Ave., #200, Minneapolis, MN 55404 612/870-4007 FAX: 612/870-3587 email: jhopkins@msn.com

Hoshibata, Robert T., 2112 Third Ave., Suite 303, Seattle, WA 98121-2333 206/448-6426 FAX: 206/728-8442
email: seadistumc@aol.com

Huntington, Marilynn M., 110 S. Euclid, POB 6006, Pasadena, CA 91102 626/568-7351 FAX: 626/796-7297
email: mhuntington@cal-pac.org

Johnson, Alfred, New Jersey Area, 1001 Wickapecko Dr., Ocean, NJ 07712-4733 732/359-1019 email: umbishopnj@aol.com

Johnson, Carolyn E., 2550 Yeager Rd., 19-2, West Lafayette, IN 47906 765/494-5680 FAX: 765/496-1581 email: cjohnson@sla.purdue.edu

Johnson, Vicki A., 1700 Monroe St., POB 58, Endicott, NY 13760-0058 607/757-0608 FAX: 607/757-0752 email: vjohnson427@aol.com

Jones, Chester R., General Commission on Religion and Race, 100 Maryland Ave. NE, #400, Washington, DC 20002-5680 202/547-4270 FAX: 202/547-0358 email: gcorr@erols.com

Jones, Richard H., Box 407, 2137 Seminole, Grafton, WI 53024 262/376-5397 email: revjones@execpc.com

Ka Bamba, Kazadi, c/o Bishop Nkulu Ntando Ntambo, North Katenga Area, UMC, Batiment Makador Ave., Mobutu, Lubumbashi, Democratic Republic of Congo email: afenk@maf.org

Langford, Thomas A., III, 30 Union St., N., Concord, NC 28025 704/786-4109 FAX: 704/786-4110 email: andy@concordcentral.org

Marubitoba, Peter D., c/o Bishop Done Peter Dabale, UMC-Nigeria, POB 155, Lankaveri Compound, Jalingo, Taraba State, NIGERIA 22525 FAX: 011-873-761-249-653

Mataele, Paea, 4736 W. 149th St., Lawndale, CA 90260 310/970-0513 email: LuHouse2002@yahoo.com

Matthews, Marcus, 324 Alastair St., Kettering, MD 20774 301/218-2951 FAX: 301/218-2957 email: mmtthwsmrc@aol.com

McClendon, W. Timothy, POB 149, Rock Hill, SC 29731 803/327-3113 803/327-3119 email: tmcclendon@stjohnsrh.org

Middleton, Jane Allen, POB 3007, Stamford, CT 06905 203/348-9181 FAX: 203/964-1423 email: cnynyac@aol.com

Moncure, Rhymes H., Jr., 2641 N. 49th St., Lincoln, NE 68504 402/466-4955 FAX: 402/466-7931 email: bishop@umcneb.org

Montoya, Shirley C., Christ UMC, 655 N. Craycroft Rd., Tucson, AZ 85711-1404 520/327-1116 FAX: 520/327-2232 email: xstchurch@aol.com

Mooneyhan, Joel E., 1244 Redemption Dr., Lawrenceville, GA 30045, 678/442-1302 email: jemooneyhan@hotmail.com

Morgan, T. Michael, 898 Arkadelphia Dr., Birmingham, AL 35204 205/226-7982 FAX: 205/226-7996 email: mmorgan@umcna.bsc.edu

Morris, Patricia A., 151 Crosswynds, Beaver, PA 15010 724/775-1330 FAX: 724/775-9727 email: patmor@nauticom.net

Paup, Edward W., 1505 SW 18th Ave., Portland, OR 97201 503/226-1530 FAX: 503/228-3189 email: edward@umoi.org

Perez, Victor, 200 Ave. los Chalets, Apt. G313, Box 51, San Juan, PR 00926 787/763-6700 ext 239 FAX: 787/751-0847 email: visaperez@aol.com

Powell, Larry P., Sr., 7921 Fanciful Ave., Las Vegas, NV 89128 702/494-9678 FAX: 702/363-8173 email: lpowellsr2@aol.com

Rhee, Seong Kwan, 21222 Summerside Ln., Northville, MI 48167 248/362-7160 FAX: 248/348-5261 email: skmkrhee@aol.com

Robbins, Bruce W., General Commission on Christian Unity and Interreligious Concerns, 475 Riverside Dr., Ste. 1300, New York, NY 10115 212/749-3553 FAX: 212/749-3556 email: brobbins@gccuic-umc.org

Roberts, Stella, P.O. Box 31545, Knoxville, TN 37930 865/470-7005 FAX: 865/470-7067 email: stellaroberts@holston.org

Robinson, Burnham A., 2129 Briardale Rd., Fort Worth, TX 76119 817/536-5537 FAX: 817/536-9170 email: theresaburnham@aol.com

Rumph, A. J., 701 Griswold Rd., Fairfield, AL 35064 205/786-7501

Schenck, Carl L., 129 Woods Mill Rd., Manchester, MO 63011 636/394-7506 FAX: 636/394-4662 email: carl.schenck@manchesterumc.org

Shaw, James C., 5229 Leone Place, Indianapolis, IN 46226-1751 317/547-6982 FAX: 317/547-8626 email: jcshaw@iquest.net

Shipman, Namiqa, St. Johns UMC. 1200 Old Pecos Trail, Sante Fe, NM 87501 505/982-5397

Siegrist, Roland, Figulystrasse 32, A-4020, Linz, Austria 011-43-732-657-137 FAX: 011-43-732-657-138

Silva, Mary, 209 Grove St., San Marcos, TX 78666 512/558-4534
FAX: 512/558-4540 email: marcha2000@centurytel.net

Simmons, Laura, MSC 1805, 59 College Ave., Buckhannon, WV 26201
304/473-7797 email: simmons_lh@wvwc.edu

Soriano, Leo A., Spottswood Methodist Center, 9400 Kidapawan,
Cotabato, The Philippines 011-6364-288-5131
FAX: 011-6364-278-4150 email: bishopdea@yahnoo.com

Walker, William A., II, 2171 Glencoe Rd., Winter Park, FL 32789-6034
407/496-2627 FAX: 407/599-0555 email: wwalker787@aol.com

Ward, Hope Morgan, 6201 Godfrey Dr., Raleigh, NC 27612 919/834-
5100 FAX: 919/834-1106 email: hmw@nccumgg.org

Watson, Thomas, 3 Sycamore Pl., Kearney, NE 68847 308/234-1918
FAX: 308/237-3321 email: twatson@kearney.net

Williams, Donald, 5226 Forest View Ct., Hudsonville, MI 49426
616/895-3682 FAX: 616/895-3735 email: williamd@gvsu.edu

Williams, Edna, 2801 Bulls Ave., Tuskegee Institute, AL 36008-2903
334/727-0314 FAX: 334/727-6510 email: elwilli@bellsouth.net

Williams, Gerald, 45 Wall St., Apt. 1422, New York, NY 10005-1947
212/236-1040 FAX: 509/692-6084 email: jaywilliams@post.harvard.edu

Williams, Jared, 2108 Elmwood Dr., Monroe, LA 71201
318/387-2426

Winkler, James, 100 Maryland, NE, Suite 300, Washington, DC 20002
202/488-5629 FAX: 202/488-5619 email: jwinkler@umc-gbcs.org

Young, Carl W., 417 Kenswick Ct., Edmond, OK 73034 405/340-9200
FAX: 405/340-9233 email: carl.w.young@worldnet.att.net

Yrigoyen, Charles, Jr., General Commission on Archives and History,
36 Madison Ave., POB 127, Madison, NJ 07940 973/408-3189
FAX: 973/408-3909 email: cyrigoyen@gcah.org

Zeiders, G. Edwin, 1810 Harvard Blvd., Dayton, OH 45406
937/278-5817 FAX: 937/278-1218 email: ezeiders@united.edu

WORK AREAS AND OTHER GROUP LEADERS

Agency Relationships Work Area
Team Leader: **Amon, Darlene V.**
Associate Team Leader: **Perez, Victor**
Secretary: **Shipman, Namiqa**

Conference Relationships Work Area
Team Leader: **Johnson, Carolyn E.**
Associate Team Leader: **Soriano, Leo A.**
Secretary: **Johnson, Vicki A.**

The Advance for Christ and His Church
Team Leader: **Johnson, Alfred**
Associate Team Leader: **Simmons, Laura**
Secretary: **Cantor-Orate, Emma A.**

Cooperative Parish Ministries
Team Leader: **Anderson, Danita R.**
Associate Team Leader: **Hayenga, Mary**
Secretary: **Ellison, Betty G.**

Ethnic Local Church Concerns
Team Leader: **Moncure, Rhymes H., Jr.**
Associate Team Leaders: **Guerra, Jaziel**
Secretary: **Williams, Edna**

Elimination of Institutional Racism
Team Leader: **Shaw, James C.**
Associate Team Leader: **Middleton, Jane Allen**
Secretary: **Baker, Jonathan E.**

Faith and Order
Team Leaders: **Allread, Ardith; Francisco, Raul; Jones, Richard H.**

Legislation
Team Leader: **Baker, Jonathan E.**
Associate Team Leader: **Middleton, Jane Allen**
Secretary: **Bledsoe, Earl**

Native American Forum
Team Leader: **Montoya, Shirley C.**
Associate Team Leader: **McClendon, W. Timothy**
Secretary: **Frederick, Austin K., Jr.**

STAFF

601 W. Riverview Ave., Dayton, OH 45406
937/227-9400 FAX: 937/227-9407; email: gcom@gcom-umc.org
Web site: gcom-umc.org

General Secretary: Church, Daniel K.
email: dchurch@gcom-umc.org

Associate General Secretary: Hayashi, Donald L.
email: dhayashi@gcom-umc.org

Associate General Secretary: Silva-Netto, Benoni
email: bsnetto@gcom-umc.org

Director of the Advance for Christ and His Church: Carter,
William T., 475 Riverside Dr., New York, NY 10115 212/870-3790
FAX: 212/870-3775 email: wcarter@gbgm-umc.org

Conciliar Officer: Long, Cecelia M., email: clong@gcom-umc.org

Chief Operating Officer: Conrad, Lola I.
email: lconrad@gcom-umc.org

Director of Research: This, Craig email: cthis@gcom-umc.org

Strengthening the Black Church for the 21st Century
Stevenson, Cheryl email: cstevens@gcom-umc.org

GENERAL BOARD OF CHURCH AND SOCIETY

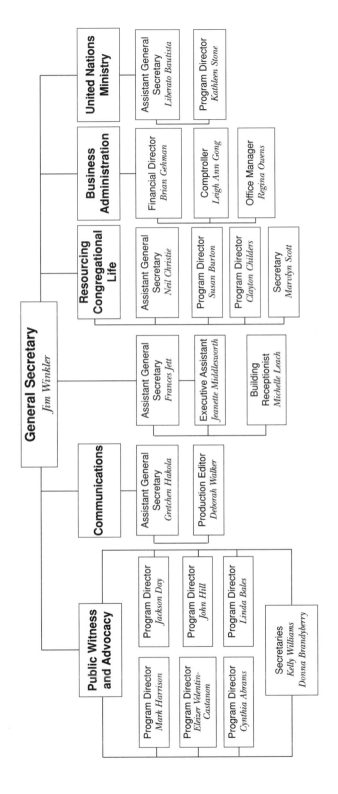

General Secretary
Jim Winkler

Public Witness and Advocacy

Program Director
Mark Harrison

Program Director
Jackson Day

Program Director
Eleizer Valentin-Castanon

Program Director
John Hill

Program Director
Cynthia Abrams

Program Director
Linda Bales

Secretaries
Kelly Williams
Donna Brandyberry

Communications

Assistant General Secretary
Gretchen Hakola

Production Editor
Deborah Walker

Assistant General Secretary
Frances Jett

Executive Assistant
Jeanette Middlesworth

Building Receptionist
Michelle Leach

Resourcing Congregational Life

Assistant General Secretary
Neil Christie

Program Director
Susan Burton

Program Director
Clayton Childers

Secretary
Marvlyn Scott

Business Administration

Financial Director
Brian Gehman

Comptroller
Leigh Ann Gong

Office Manager
Regina Owens

United Nations Ministry

Assistant General Secretary
Liberato Bautista

Program Director
Kathleen Stone

GENERAL BOARD
OF CHURCH AND SOCIETY
www.umc-gbcs.org

OFFICERS

President: **Ives, S. Clifton**
Vice-Chair: **Shamana, Beverly J.**
Secretary: **Wendland, Barbara**
Asst. Secretary: **Newcomer, Helenmae**
Treasurer: **Redmond, John A.**

MEMBERS

Bishops
Goodpaster, Larry M., 312 Interstate Park Dr., Montgomery, AL 36109 334/277-1787 FAX: 334/277-0109 email: awfbishop@aol.com
Hutchinson, William W., 527 North Blvd., Baton Rouge, LA 70802-5720 255/346-1646 ext. 212 FAX: 225/387-3662 email: enixmore@bellsouth.net
Ives, S. Clifton, 900 Washington St., E, Charleston, WV 25301 304/344-8331 FAX: 304/344-8330 email: wvareaumc@aol.com
Katembo, Kainda, AV. De l'Etoile #960, Centre Methodiste, Lubumbashi, Congo DR email: bishop-umc-sc@maf.org
Lee, Linda, POB 25068, Lansing, MI 48909-5068 517/347-4030 FAX: 517/347-4003 email: mareaumc@tir.com
Shamana, Beverly J., POB 980250, West Sacramento, CA 95798-0250 916/374-1500 FAX: 916/372-9062 email: bishop@calnevumc.org

Adamu, Napoleon, c/o Mr. Shelu Thomas, Dental Unit Specialist Hospital, Jalingo, Tarabo State, Nigeria 011-073-462911 email: grummetti@yahoo.com
Ahn, Eusook, 51 Tenby Chase Dr., Newark, DE 19711 302/239-3100 email: eusook@yahoo.com
Batie, Larry, 1400 41st St. W., Birmingham, AL 35208 205/929-1517
Caballero, Louis, 3401 W. Hwy 4, Century, FL 32535 850/327-4933 email: hispmin@bellsouth.net
Curtin, C. Pat, 27205 Paula Ln., Conroe, TX 77385 281/367-5092 FAX: 281/367-6330 email: pat.curtin@choctawsales.com
Deal, Patricia M., 4627 Willow Bend Dr., Wichita Falls, TX 76310 940/691-1899 FAX: 940/691-3432 email: patmdeal@aol.com

Delamater, W. Alan, POB 560, Saratoga Falls, NY 12866
518/584-8295 ext. 116 FAX: 518/584-8378
email: adirondackdist@troyac.org

Dial, Karen A., 324 Apple St., Hazard, KY 41701
email: karendial@yahoo.com

Djamba, Mumba, 2867 Ecuries Ave., Ngaliema, Kinshasa, Democratic
Republic of Congo, P.B. 4727 Kiushasa II FAX: 011/243-88-03723

Dowell, John, 1120 W. Kennedy Blvd., Tampa, FL 33606
813/251-6458 FAX: 813/254-1984 email: jdowellumm@aol.com

Extrum-Fernandez, Renae, 1543 Sunny Vale Ave., Walnut Creek, CA
94596 925/934-4208 FAX: 925/934-1492 email: wcumcpastor@halls.net

Fisher, Deborah L., 1032 Maple Ave., Downer Grove, IL 60515
630/968-7120 ext. 102 email: Debmattil@aol.com

Fowler, Les O., 181 E. Ward St., Asheboro, NC 27203 336/629-6464
FAX: 336/629-9737 email: lof@ashboro.com

Fukumoto, JoAnn Yoon, 1796 Hoolehua St., Pearl City, HI 96782
808/454-2855 FAX: 808/454-2955 email: joumc@aol.com

Garcia, Barbara P., 520 Commerce St., Suite 201, Nashville, TN 37203
615/742-8834 FAX: 615/742-3726 email: bpgoffice@aol.com

Granger, Philip R., 6243 Crooked Creek Rd., Norcross, GA 30012
770/446-1381 FAX: 770/446-3044 email: pgranger@msum.org

Holt, Gloria E., 6740 Clear Creek Cir., Trussville, AL 35173
205/661-9292 FAX: 205/856-8788 email: Gholt@umcna.bsc.edu

Johnson, Teri, 625 Fifth St., Brookings, SD 57006 605/692-4345
FAX: 605/692-0909 email: firstum@itctel.com

Kaleuati, K. F., 1600 West E St., North Platte, NE 69101 308/532-1478
FAX: 308/532-5237 email: npfumc@inebraska.com

Kwak, Cheol, 12741 Main St., Garden Grove, CA 92840 714/539-1053
FAX: 714/636-6409 email: cheolkwak@hotmail.com

Little, Laura, 217 King George Rd., Greenville, NC 27858 252/756-
5704 email: LLITTLE217@aol.com

Livingston, David, 5519 Meade Rd., Cummings, KS 66018 913/367-
0014 FAX: 913/262-1041 email: DSL2@juno.com

Lovelace, Helen Byholt, Kiev 150, a/c 225, 03150 Kiev Ukraine 011/380-
44-202-1591 FAX: 011/44-227-4885 email: whlovelace@aol.com

Martin, Delores, 16505 Magnolia Ct., Silver Spring, MD 20905
301/421-9441 FAX: 301/879-7301
email: litteone_martin@yahoo.com

Mason, Howard J., 406 Shipley St., Seaford, DE 19973-1226 302/629-8141 FAX: 302/629-0425

Mattox, Michael L., 715 Center St., Suite 203, Little Rock, AR 72201 501/324-8022 FAX: 501/324-8018 email: mmattox@arumc.org

May, Joe Willie, POB 931, Jackson, MS 39205-0931 601/948-4561 FAX: 601/948-5981 email: joemay@mississippi-umc.org

McHenry, Eli, POB 64, Homing, OK 74305 918/885-6478

Meisel, Ulrich, Mittelbreite 46, D-06849, Dessau, GERMANY 011/49.341-585-2209 (T/F) email: familie.meisel@gmx.de

Moffatt, Jessica, 77 E. Breckenridge, Bixby, OK 74008 918/366-4463 FAX: 918/366-4465 email: jmoffatt@olp.net

Moore, J. Harris, POB 3177, Fayetteville, AR 72702 479/619-2270 FAX: 479/619-4346 email: jhmoore@NWACC.edu

Moreland, Pat, 814-16th St., West Des Moines, IA 50265 515/223-7822 FAX: 515/221-9570 email: PpMore@aol.com

Newcomer, Helenmae, 1132 Moltke Ave., Scranton, PA 18505 570/479-3200 email: maeyung@yahoo.com

Orphe, Martha M., 5401 Centre Ave., Pittsburgh, PA 15232 412/681-3770 FAX: 412/681-3775 email: Marthaorphe@aol.com

Paulsmeyer, Jason A., 1133 Aghland Rd., Apt. 1301, Columbia, MO 65201 573/447-1388 email: jpaulsmeyer@aol.com

Pina, Michael J., 78500 Frazier Ln., Covelo, CA 95438 707/983-6126 FAX: 707/983-6128 email: mjp32@humboldt.edu

Pinto, Argentina, Rua George Dimitrov, 12 Luanda 68, Angola 011/244-233-0782 FAX: 011/244-239-0515 email: argentinapinto@yahoo.com.br'

Porterfield, Charles, 5708 Wallingwood Dr., Indianapolis, IN 46225-1341 317/549-2209 FAX: 317/849-8595 email: chuckmin@aol.com

Puslecki, Edward, UL Mokotowska 12/9, Warsaw 00-561, POLAND 011/48.22.628.53.28 email: E.Puslecki@metodysci.pl

Quick, Elizabeth, 51 Salyes St., Oneida, NY 13421 315/363-1921 email: elizabeth.quick@owu.edu

Rapisora, Ricarte R., 039 Mt. Apo Village, Corner Lamban & Narra Sts., Kidapawan City 9400, PHILIPPINES 011/63-64-278-4096 (phone and FAX) email: ricarterapisora@hotmail.com

Redmond, John A., Box 26, Greenville, SC 29602-0026 864/233-0763 FAX: 864/233-7632 email: johnaredmond@aol.com

Rivera, Lizet, 400 Butter Cird, El Paso, TX 79902 915/544-0841 email: LizetDreamerGirl@cs.com

Robinson, Willard A., 191 Summer St., Andover, MA 01810 978/475-2055 email: ET2Robinson@worldnet.att.net

Scott, William D., III, 566 N. Swaney, Holly Springs, MS 38635 662/252-2144 FAX: 662/915-7300 email: chscott@olemiss.edu

Shelton, Henry C., III, 80 Monroe, Suite 700, Memphis, TN 38103 901/524-4941 FAX: 901/524-4936 email: hshelton@armstrong.allen.com

Sikes, Marget, 205 Jordan St., Tunnel Hill, GA 30755 706/673-5811 email: gakidsmom@charter.net

Soto-Velez, Hector, POB 10727, Caparra Heights, San Juan, PR 00922 787/782-3352 email: sotovel@hotmail.com

Sprecher, Steven J., 1855 South Shore Blvd., Lake Oswego, OR 97304 503/636-8423 email: srpastor@teleport.com

Sublette, Jean S., 135 Hillcrest Dr., Titus, AL 36080 334/567-4046 FAX: 334/567-6156 email: roysublette@aol.com

Swanson, James E., Sr., 106 Lee Blvd., Savannah, GA 31405 912/352-7867 FAX: 912/354-4597 email: sdofffice@bellsouth.net

Taryor, Elena, 303 W. Coventry Ct., Apt. 108, Glendale, WI 53217 414/352-4156 email: Anastasia_77@email.com

Trimble, Julius C., 2495 Edgerton Rd., University Heights, OH 44118 216/664-1602 FAX: 216/664-1744 email: DSTrimble@clevedumc.org

Tshimwang, Muzangish, UMC POB 20219, Kitwe, Zambie email: AFENK@maf.org

Wendland, Barbara, 505 Cherokee Dr., Temple, TX 76504-3629 254/773-2625 FAX: 254/773-2923 email: bcwendland@aol.com

Wright, Varlyna D., 118 Alexander Rd., Beverly, NJ 08010 732/359-1041 FAX: 732/359-1049 email: VDWright@GNJUMC.ORG

STAFF

100 Maryland Ave., NE, Washington, DC 20002
All Washington phone numbers have the prefix 202/488
FAX: 202/488-5619
Web site: www.umc-gbcs.org

*Church Center for The United Nations, 777 UN Plaza, New York, New York 10017 212/682-3633 FAX 212/682-5354

General Secretary's Office

General Secretary: **Winkler, James,** 5623 email: jwinkler@umc-gbcs.org

Assistant General Secretary for Administrative Coordinator and Management/Human Resources, **Jett, Frances,** 5658 email: fjett@umc-gbcs.org

Executive Assistant: **Middlesworth, Jeanette,** 5629 email: jmiddlesworth@umc.gbcs.org

Service Department—ORDERS@umc-gbcs.org

Director of Information Technology, **Weimer, Stephen,** 5635, sweimer@umc-gbcs.org

Receptionist: **Leach, Michelle,** 5600 email: mleach@umc-gbcs.org

Business Administration

Chief Financial Officer: **Gehman, Brian,** 5625 email: bgehman@umc-gbcs.org

Controller: **Gong, Leigh Ann,** 5627 email: lgong@umc-gbcs.org

Accounts Payable/Office Manager: **Owens, Regina D.** 5624 email: rowens@umc-gbcs.org

Ministry of Public Witness and Advocacy

Program Director: **Bales, Linda,** 5649 email: lbales@umc-gbcs.org

Program Director: **Hill, John,** 5654 email: jhill@umc-gbcs.org

Program Director: **Day, Jackson,** 5608 email: jday@umc-gbcs.org

Program Director: **Valentin-Castañon, Eliezer,** 5657 email: evalentin@umc-gbcs.org

Program Director: **Abrams, Cynthia,** 5636 email: cabrams@umc-gbcs.org

Program Director: **Harrison, Mark,** 5645 email: mharrison@umc-gbcs.org

Secretary: **Brandyberry, Donna,** 5641 email: dbrandyberry@umc-gbcs.org

Secretary: **Williams, Kelly,** 5655 email: kwilliams@umc-gbcs.org

Ministry of Resourcing Congregational Life

Assistant General Secretary: **Christie, Neal,** 5611 email: nchristie@umc-gbcs.org

Program Director for Seminar Designer: **Burton, Susan,** 5609 email: sburton@umc-gbcs.org

Program Director for Annual Conference Relations: **Childers, Clayton,** 5642 email: cchilders@umc-gbcs.org

Secretary: **Scott, Marvlyn,** 5643 email: mscott@umc-gbcs.org

Communications

Assistant General Secretary: **Hakola, Gretchen,** 5630
  email: ghakola@umc-gbcs.org
Production Editor: **Walker, Deborah,** 5632
  email: dwalker@umc-gbcs.org

United Nations Office

Assistant General Secretary: **Bautista, Liberato C.,** 212/682-3633
Program Director: **Stone, Kathleen,** 212/682-3633

GENERAL BOARD OF DISCIPLESHIP

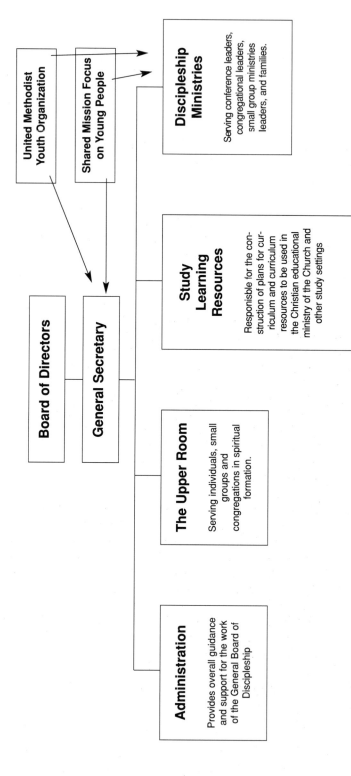

Board of Directors

General Secretary

United Methodist Youth Organization

Shared Mission Focus on Young People

Administration

Provides overall guidance and support for the work of the General Board of Discipleship

The Upper Room

Serving individuals, small groups and congregations in spiritual formation.

Study Learning Resources

Responsibile for the construction of plans for curriculum and curriculum resources to be used in the Christian educational ministry of the Church and other study settings

Discipleship Ministries

Serving conference leaders, congregational leaders, small group ministries leaders, and families.

GENERAL BOARD OF DISCIPLESHIP
www.gbod.org

OFFICERS

President: **Carder, Kenneth L.**
Vice President: **Coyner, Michael J.**
Secretary: **Park, Sonja**
Treasurer: **Webb, Foye**

MEMBERS

Bishops

Brown, Warner H., Jr., 2200 S. University Blvd., Denver, CO 80210
303/733-3736 FAX: 303/733-5047 email: bishop@rmcumc.com

Carder, Kenneth L., POB 931, Jackson, MS 39205-0931 601/948-4561
FAX: 601/948-5981 email: bishop@mississippi-umc.org

Coyner, Michael J., 3910 25th St. S., Fargo, ND 58104 701/232-2241
FAX: 701/232-2615 email: bishopcoyner@juno.com

Hassinger, Susan W., POB 249, Lawrence, MA 01842-0449
978-682-7555 FAX 978/682-9555

Jokomo, Christopher, UMC-163 Sinoia St., POB 3408, Harare, ZIM-
BABWE 011 263 4 751 508 FAX: 011 263 4 791 105

Sherer, Ann Brookshire, 870 Woods Mill Rd., Suite 100, Ballwin, MO
63011 314/491-8001 FAX: 314-891-8003 email: sherer@ecunet.org

Alsted, Christian, Stokhusgade, 2, DK-1317 Copenhagen K,
DENMARK 45 33 1296 06 FAX: 45 33 1296 04
email: ca@jerusalemskirken.dk (CENTRAL CONFERENCE)

Atuma, Eunice, c/o Rev. Daniel Wandabula, U.M.C., Baumann
House, Paraliament Ave., Ste. B-101, Kampala, Africa
email: atumaeunice@yahoo.com (CENTRAL CONFERENCE)

Archibald, Julius A., Jr., 90 Park Ave., Plattsburgh, NY 12901
518/561-4395 FAX: 518/561-6455
email: julius.archibald@plattsburgh.edu (TROY CONFERENCE)

Bagwell, Timothy J., 192 Barrington Hall Dr., Macon, GA 31220
478/471-7087 email: TBagwell@cox.net (SOUTH GEORGIA
CONFERENCE)

Banks, Kendra, 3886 S. Upper Terry Rd., Eden, MD 21822
410/548-9862 FAX: 410/548-9862 email: kendra@ezy.net
(PENINSULA DELAWARE CONFERENCE)

Barto, Suella C., 303 Mulberry Dr., Mechanicsburg, PA 17055-2053 717/766-7441 ext. 3604 email: sbarto@cpcumc.org (CENTRAL PENNSYLVANIA CONFERENCE)

Bowdan, Melvin R. (Mel), Jr., 2236 Clear Creek Rd., Nicholasville, KY 40356-8757 859/885-7712 FAX: 859/887-9755 email: mbowdanjr@aol.com (KENTUCKY CONFERENCE)

Champion, Dr. Willie (Pan Methodist Member), 102 Pearly Top Dr., Glenn Heights, TX 75154 email: champ_dr@msn.com

Crump, Anita, 7321 Dalewood Rd., New Orleans, LA 70126-1831 504/246-4735 FAX: 504/246-4901 email: ahele@aol.com (LOUISIANA CONFERENCE)

DeVance, Celestyne, 4700 SW 14th St., Des Moines, IA 50315 515/285-3983 email: stjumc@msn.com or pastor_ceeumc@aol.com (IOWA CONFERENCE)

Dicks, J. Jeannette Cooper, 165 S. Coit St., Florence SC 29502 843/662-2904 FAX: 843/669-3792 email: jcdicks@umcsc.org (SOUTH CAROLINA CONFERENCE)

Easley, Ida, 1295 Ft. Wayne, Rushville, IN 46173 765/938-1556 or 800/919-8167 email: rushds@lightbound.com (SOUTH INDIANA CONFERENCE)

Ehlers, Don, 549 W. Fourth, Maryville, MO 64468 660/582-2211 FAX: 660/582-4863 email: m500275@mail.nwmissouri.edu (MISSOURI WEST CONFERENCE)

Etter, Martha B., 4905 Hodges Dr., San Antonio, TX 78238 210/684-2212 FAX: 210/684-2212 email: mbesge@hotmail.com (SOUTHWEST TEXAS CONFERENCE)

Euper, Leilani, Wesley Theological Seminary, Campus Box 43, 4500 Massachusetts Ave., NW, Washington, DC 20016 202/885-8765 (DETROIT CONFERENCE)

Franklin, V. Leon, Jr., Gammon Theological Seminary, Atlanta, GA 615/310-4784 email: victor1978@thetruth.com (TENNESSEE CONFERENCE)

Gordon, Tyrone, POB 150425, Dallas, TX 75315 214/887-3906 FAX: 214/827-8432 email: Pastorg@slcumc.org (NORTH TEXAS CONFERENCE)

Greenway, Jeffrey E., 733 South Ave., Pittsburgh, PA 15221-2939 412/371-4772 FAX: 412/371-4788 email: jeffgrnway@aol.com (WESTERN PA CONFERENCE)

Harnish, James A., 500 W. Platt St., Tampa, FL 33606 813/253-5388 FAX: 813/251-3145 email: jharanish@hydeparkumc.org (FLORIDA CONFERENCE)

Henderson, Jean, 3475 Willow Oak Cr. NW, Cleveland, TN 37312 423/472-6428 email: Jeanhendersonj@aol.com (HOLSTON CONFERENCE)

Hodges, Larry, Rt. 1 Box 3, Forgan, OK 73938 580/487-3589 FAX: 580/487-3775 email: lehodg@ptsi.net (OKLAHOMA CONFERENCE)

Howard, George G., 32 Wesley Blvd., Worthington, OH 43085
800/437-0028 FAX: 614/781-2642 email: ghoward@wocumc.org
(WEST OHIO CONFERENCE)

Hwang, In-Sook, 906 S. Hickory St., Pana, IL 62557 217/562-2823
email: insookhwang@hotmail.com (ILLINOIS GREAT RIVERS
CONFERENCE)

Jones, Arthur D., 1530 Massachusetts St., Lawrence, KS 66044
785/865-1647 email: jones@ku.edu (NORTH TEXAS CONFERENCE)

Jones, Cynthia A., 729 Franklin Ave., Charleston, IL 61920 214/243-
3917 email: cynthiajones@charlestonwesley.org
(ILLINOIS GREAT RIVERS CONFERENCE)

Justice, Jean Fitch, 10025 Amsden Way, Eden Prairie, MN 55347
651/641-3434 email: JFJUSTICE@aol.com or jjustice@luthersem.edu
(MINNESOTA CONFERENCE)

Kilimbo, Kajoba, POB 2237, Kitwe, Zambia, AFRICA
011-260-2-889-9295 (CENTRAL CONFERENCE)

LaBarr, Joan G., POB 516069, Dallas, TX 75251-6069
email: LaBarr@ntcumc.org (NORTH TEXAS CONFERENCE)

Lindo, Osmond A., Sr., 4300 Bellflower Blvd., Lakewood, CA 90713
562/429-1441 (CAL-PAC CONFERENCE)

Ling, Daniel H., 3700 Rath Ave., Endwell, NY 13760 607/748-3228
FAX: 607/797-4331 email: dling1125@aol.com (WYOMING
CONFERENCE)

Middleton, John H., 41 Pine Tree St., Lexington, TN 38351 731/217-
6119 (MEMPHIS CONFERENCE)

Moreno-Rivas, Rafael, Urb. Rio Padras Heights, 1668 Calle San
Lorenzo, San Juan, PUERTO RICO 00926-3244 787/767-0955
FAX: 787/751-3615 email: rafaelmoreno64@hotmail.com (PUERTO
RICO CONFERENCE)

Murphy, Sandra Lee, 3875 Dune Dr., Avalon, NJ 08202 609/967-4290
email: slcmurpy@hotmail.com (SOUTHERN NEW JERSEY
CONFERENCE)

Mustoe, Adam, 810 Alta Vista Dr., Cape Giradeau, MO 63701-4704
573/332-1069 email: mustoman@mail.com
(MISSOURI EAST CONFERENCE)

Norris, Elizabeth (Beth), 3625 Alleghany Dr., Raleigh, NC 27609
919/787-2616 FAX: 919/786-0648 email: bnorris@nccumc.org
(NORTH CAROLINA CONFERENCE)

Park, Sonja, POB 6006, Pasadena, Ca 91102-6006 626/568-7354 FAX:
626/796-6297 email: songjapark@earthlink.com or sjpark
@cal-pac.org(CALIFORNIA-PACIFIC CONFERENCE)

Parker, Myrtis, 4725 Flat Rock, Ft. Worth, TX 76132 817/922-6850
(CENTRAL TEXAS CONFERENCE)

Phillips, Anita, POB 987, Atoka, OK 74525 580/889-6449
FAX: 580/889-6449 (OKLAHOMA INDIAN MISSIONARY
CONFERENCE)

Ponce, Philip I., 130 W. Madison St., Mohnton, PA 19540
610/775-4150 FAX: 610/775-4154 email: vze2t6p4@verizon.net
(ALASKA MISSIONARY CONFERENCE)

Puloka, Sia, 4137 B. Delridge Way, SW., Sea, WA 98106 206/937-3662
FAX: 206/296-0191 email: SIA.PULOKA@metroke
(PACIFIC NORTHWEST CONFERENCE)

Ramirez, Nohemi V., 2575 Delk Rd., Apt. 1550H, Marietta, GA 30067
770/580-1366 FAX: 770/850-1366 email: pray4me@yahoo.com

Razon, Arturo, Isabela State University, Echague, Isabela
PHILIPPINES Ve3lasco Subd., San Fabian, Echague 3309 Isabela,
Philippines 63 919 675-4059 FAX: 63 78 672 2119
email: doc jong@yahoo. com (CENTRAL CONFERENCE)

Saafi, Lupe, POB 241681, Anchorage, AK 99524 907/272-6928
FAX: 907/274-5739 email: ilsaafi@hotmail.com (ALASKA MIS-
SIONARY CONFERENCE)

Sankonkoro, Haruna, c/oBishop Done Dabale, UMCN Secretariot,
Mile Six, Jalingo-Numan Rd., POB 155, Jalingo, Taraba State, Nigeria
871/761-808-665 FAX: 871/761-808-66 (CENTRAL CONFERENCE)

Shuler, Albert, POB 1662, Elizabeth City, NC 27906
252/335-2415 email: ashuler@nccumc.org
(NORTH CAROLINA CONFERENCE)

Sizemore, Joyce, PO Box 4, Roark, KY 40979 606/599-0313 email:
joycesizemore@yahoo.com (RED BIRD MISSIONARY CONFERENCE)

Stabler, Monty, 3538 Victoria Rd., Birmingham, AL 35223
205/967-4189 FAX: 205/879-9866 email: MSG1936@aol.com
(NORTH ALABAMA CONFERENCE)

Titoce, Isaias Paulo, Rua D Francisco Barreto 229, POB 2640, Maputo,
Mozambique 258 1 49 06 71 FAX: 258 1 49 35 68 email:
Isapault@yahoo.com (MOZAMBIQUE CONFERENCE)

Whitaker, Asa, 160 Ottinger St., Batesville, AR 72501 870/793-3007
FAX: 870/793-9398 email: asa@ipa.net

Wildrick-Cole, Dawn, 116 Minnesota St., Rochester, NY 14609
716/482-0049 email: dwildrick cole@yahoo.com
(WESTERN NEW YORK CONFERENCE)

Windham, James C., Jr., POB 995, Gastonia, NC 28053-0995
704/864-3425 FAX: 704/864-0478 (WESTERN NORTH CAROLINA
CONFERENCE)

Yoost, Charles D., 3157 Morley Rd., Shaker Heights, OH 44122-2861
216/295-2389 FAX: 216/321-3019 email: cdyoost@aol.com

STAFF

1908 Grand Ave., POB 340003
Nashville, TN 37203-0003
615/340-7200 or 877/899-2780 FAX: 615/340-7006
Web site: www.gbod.org

Administration

General Secretary: **Greenwaldt, Karen,** ext. 7022
  email: kgreenwaldt@gbod.org
Executive Assistant to the General Secretary: **Shepler, Joyce,** ext. 7022
  email: jshepler@gbod.org
Treasurer: **Webb, Foye,** ext. 7032 email: fwebb@gbod.org

Human Resources and Staff Services

Administrator: **Mastin, Kathryn,** ext. 7101, email: kmastin@gbod.org
Benefits & Employee Relations Administrator: **Jordan, Joyce,** ext. 7102
Employment/Compensation: **Farmer, Tina,** ext. 7108
  email: tfarmer@gbod.org
Employment Coordinator: **James, Maria,** ext. 7100
  email: mjames@gbod.org

Building Services

Manager: **Elliott, Terry,** ext. 7133 email: telliot@gbod.org
Maintenance Supervisor: **Melton, Glenn,** ext. 7112
  email: gmelton@gbod.org

Communications

Chief Communications Officer: Kimberly Pace,
ext. 7017, email: kpace@gbod.org

Learning Center

Director: **Gaither, Donna,** ext. 7567 email: dgaither@gbod.org
Technology Specialist, **Roop, Jeff,** ext. 7568 email: jroop@gbod.org

Discipleship Resources

Non-Stock Editor & Online Bookstore Manager: **Bonnet, J. Lee,**
  ext. 7064 email: jbonnet@gbod.org
Business Operations: **Gregory, Mary,** ext. 7067 email:
  mgregory@gbod.org
Production: **Bock, Gail,** ext. 7061 email: gbock@gbod.org

Acquisitions Editor, **Whited, Linda,** ext. 7078 email: lwhited@gbod.org
Production Editor: **Harris, Cindy,** ext. 7130 email: charris@gbod.org
Procuction Editor: **Whitworth, David,** ext. 1790
　email: dwhitworth@gbod.org
On Line Bookstore: www.discipleshipresources.org

Information on Technology

Team Leader: **Johnson, Robert,** ext. 1711 email: bjohnson@gbod.org
Telephone Systems Support Administrator: **Wilson, Patty,** ext. 7088
　email: pwilson@gbod.org
System Support Administrator: **Wooding, Nadina,** ext. 7585
　email: nwooding@gbod.org
Network Administrator: **Lawson, Stephen,** ext. 7092
　email: slawson@gbod.org
Database Developer: **Little, Shaun,** ext. 7037 email: slittle@gbod.org
IT/PC Support Technician: **Payne, Antoniette,** ext. 7027
　email: tpayne@gbod.org

Discipleship Ministries

Staff Leader: **Ross, Vance,** ext. 7132 email: vross@gbod.org
Administrative Assistant: ext. 7166

Teams

Conference Leader Formation Team: ext. 7142
Congregational Leader Formation Team: ext. 7079
Family and Life-Span Ministries Team: ext. 7170
Mission Initiatives Team: ext. 7050

Centers

Center on Aging and Older Adult Ministries, ext. 7173
Center for Christian Stewardship and Fund Development, ext. 7077
Center for Ministries with Young People, ext. 7174
Center for Worship Resourcing, ext. 7072
Center on Evangelism through New Congregational Development,
　ext. 7081

Specialties

Accountable and Covenant Discipleship:
Manskar, Steve, ext. 7165 email: smanskar@gbod.org

African-American Congregational Development:
Taylor-Thirus, Francine, ext. 7167 email: ftaylorthirus@gbod.org

Age-Level Ministries:
Carty, Terry (Youth/Young Adult), ext. 7174 email: tcarty@gbod.org
Crenshaw, Bill (Young Adult), ext. 7005 email: bcrenshaw@gbod.org
Gentzler, Richard (Aging and Older Adult), ext. 7173 email: rgentzler@gbod.org
Gran, Mary Alice (Children), ext. 7143 email: mgran@gbod.org
Hay, Susan (Youth), ext. 7069 email: shay@gobd.org
Miller, Craig (Generational Studies), ext. 7081 email: cmiller@gbod.org
Norton, MaryJane Pierce (Family), ext. 7170 email: mnorton@gbod.orgs
Sa, Soozung (Family and Singles), ext. 7169 email: ssa@gbod.org

Camping & Retreat Ministries:
Witt, Kevin, ext. 7082 email: kwitt@gbod.org

Christian Education:
Carty, Terry, ext. 7174 email: tcarty@gbod.org
Crenshaw, Bill, ext. 7005 email: bcrenshaw@gbod.org
Gentzler, Richard, ext. 7173 email: rgentzler@gbod.org
Gran, Mary Alice, ext. 7143 email: mgran@gbod.org
Hay, Susan, ext. 7069 email: shay@gbod.org
Heavner, Betsey, ext. 7295 email: bheavner@gbod.org
Hynson, Diana, ext. 7053 email: dhynson@gbod.org
Krau, Carol, ext. 7171 email: ckrau@gbod.org
Norton, MaryJane Pierce, ext. 7170 email: mnorton@gbod.org
Smith, Debra, ext. 7135 email: dsmith@gbod.org
Wallace, Julia Kuhn, ext. 7086 email: jwallace@gbod.org

Distinguished Evangelist in Residence:
(Contracted evangelism consultant for the General Board of Discipleship and the Foundation for Evangelism) 740/743-2780

Ethnic Local Church Concerns/Resources and Training:
Chamberlain, Marigene, ext. 1706 email: mchamberlain@bgod.org
Choi, Sungnam, ext. 7050 email: schoi@gbod.org
Pérez, Alma, ext. 7118 email: aperez@gbod.org
Taylor-Thirus, Francine, ext. 7167 email: ftaylorthirus@gbod.org

Evangelism:
Daniel, Wesley S. K., ext. 7049 email: wdaniel@gbod.org
Choi, Sungnam, ext. 7050 email: schoi@gbod.org
Miller, Craig, ext. 7081 email: cmiller@gbod.org

Sa, Soozung, ext. 7169 email: ssa@gbod.org
Taylor-Thirus, Francine, ext. 7167 email: ftaylorthirus@gbod.org

Family Ministries:
Norton, MaryJane Pierce, ext. 7170 email: mnorton@gbod.org
Sa, Soozung, ext. 7169 email: ssa@gbod.org

Hispanic Ministries Congregational Development:
Chamberlain, Marigene, ext. 1706 email: mchamberlain@gbod.org
Pérez, Alma, ext. 7118 email: aperez@gbod.org
Longhurst, Blanca, ext. 7139 email: blonghurst@gbod.org

International Ministries/Leadership Development/Resourcing:
Daniel, Wesley S. K., ext. 7049 email: wdaniel@gbod.org

Korean/Asian American and Pacific Islanders Ministries:
Choi, Sungnam, ext. 7050 email: schoi@gbod.org

Large Membership Church:
Daniel, Wesley S. K., ext. 7049 email: wdaniel@gbod.org

Meeting Planning/Discipleship Ministries Unit Events:
Whitehurst, Lori, ext. 7176 email: lwhitehurst@gbod.org

Ministry of the Laity:
Ziegler, Sandy, ext. 7169 email: sziegler@gbod.org

New Congregational Development:
Miller, Craig, ext. 7081 email: cmiller@gbod.org

Preaching:
Fosua, Safiyah, ext. 7084 email: sfosua@gbod.org

Electronic Publishing:
Capshaw, Cheryl, ext. 7056 email: ccapshaw@gbod.org
Teague, Martha, ext. 1796 email: mhutchinson@gbod.org

Revitalization in Racial Ethnic Congregations:
Taylor-Thirus, Francine, ext. 7167 email: ftaylorthirus@gbod.org
Daniel, Wesley S. K., ext. 7049 email: wdaniel@gbod.org

Shared Ministries:
Wallace, Julia Kuhn, ext. 7086 email: jwallace@gbod.org

Shared Mission Focus on Young People:
Rouse, Ciona, ext. 7058 email: crouse@gbod.org

Small Group Ministries:
Hynson, Diana, ext. 7053 email: dhynson@gbod.org
Krau, Carol, ext. 7171 email: ckrau@gbod.org
Manskar, Steve, ext. 7165 email: smanskar@gbod.org

Small Membership Church
Wallace, Julia Kuhn, ext. 7086 email: jwallace@gbod.org

Spiritual Leadership Formation:
Ruach, Susan, ext. 7142 email: sruach@gbod.org
Dick, Dan, ext. 7049 email: ddick@gbod.org
Heavner, Betsey, ext. 7295 email: bheavner@gbod.org

Stewardship and Fund Development:
Bell, David, ext. 7077 email: dbell@gbod.org
Joiner, Rev. Donald W., ext. 7080 email: djoiner@gbod.org

United Methodist Youth Organization:
Seibert, Ronna, ext. 7181 email: rseibert@gbod.org

Worship Resourcing:
Benedict, Dan, ext. 7072 email: dbenedict@gbod.org
Fosua, Safiyah, ext. 7084 email: sfosua@gbod.org
McIntyre, Dean (music), ext. 7073 email: dmcintyre@gbod.org

CHURCH SCHOOL PUBLICATIONS DEPARTMENT
Administrative Offices

Executive Editor of Church School Publications: **Olson, Harriett Jane,** 615/749-6403
Administrative Assistant: **Emily, Susan,** 615/749-6404

Editorial Staff
Adult Resources

Senior Editor: **Chamberlain, Charles D.,** 615/749-6036
    FAX: 615/749-6512 email: dchamberlain@umpublishing.org

Children's Resources

Senior Editor: **Stickler, LeeDell B.,** 615/749-6216 FAX: 615/749-6061
    email: lstickler@umpublishing.org

Korean and Spanish Language Resources

Director: **Won, Dal Joon,** 615/749-6768 FAX: 615/749-6061
    email: djwon@umpublishing.org

Youth Resources

Senior Editor: **Zinkiewicz, Crys,** 615/749-6220 FAX: 615/749-6061
    email: czinkiewicz@umpublishing.org

THE UPPER ROOM

POB 340004, Nashville, TN 37203-0004
615/340-7200; toll free 877/899-2780
Upper Room Web site: www.upperroom.org
Standing Orders/Books 800/972-0433
Upper Room Subscriptions - English 800/925-6847
Upper Room Subscriptions - Spanish 800/964-3730
Upper Room Subscriptions - Canadian 800/757-9877
Upper Room Living Prayer Center - 800/251-2468
Editor/Publisher: **Bryant, Stephen D.,** ext. 7235
    email: sbryant@upperroom.org
Administrative Services: **Waymack, Dale Rust,** ext. 7236
    email: dwaymack@upperroom.org
International Ministries: **Floyd, Joan,** ext. 7251
    email: jfloyd@upperroom.org

Publishing

Executive Director of Publishing: **vacant**

Books

Executive Editor: **Miller, JoAnn,** ext. 7239 email: jmiller@upper-room.org

Managing Editor: **Collett, Rita B.,** ext. 7530 email: rcollett@upper-room.org

Associate Editor: **Crawford-Lee, Jeannie,** ext. 7244 email: jcrawford-lee@upperroom.org

Associate Editor: **Trudel, Anne,** ext. 7241 email: atrudel@upper-room.org

Library/International Rights and Permissions: **Schaller-Linn, Sarah,** ext. 7204 email: slinn@upperroom.org

Magazines

ALIVE NOW: Tidwell, Melissa, ext. 7216
    email: mtidwell@upperroom.org
    Fisher, Eli, ext. 7217 email: efisher@upperroom.org
DEVO'ZINE: Miller, Sandy, ext. 7089 email: smiller@upperroom.org
    Corlew, Nicole, ext. 1778 email: ncorlew@upperroom.org
EL APOSENTO ALTO: Gaud, Carmen M., ext. 7246
    email: cgaud@upperroom.org
Berrios, Jorge, ext. 7109 email: jberrios@upperroom.org
POCKETS: Gilliam, Lynn, ext. 7238 email: lgilliamt@upperroom.org
THE UPPER ROOM: Redding, Mary Lou, ext. 7237
    email: mredding@upperroom.org
    Stafford, James T., ext. 7259 email: jstafford@upperroom.org
    Hines, Vicki, ext. 7016 email: vhines@upperroom.org
    King, Susan, ext. 7203 email: sking@upperroom.org
WEAVINGS: Mogabgab, John S., ext. 7249
    email: jmogabgab@upperroom.org
    Hawkins, Pamela, ext. 7248 email: phawkins@upperroom.org

Electronic Publishing

Richardson, Beth A., ext. 7242 email: brichardson@upperroom.org
Stephens, Kathleen, ext. 1779 email: kstephens@upperroom.org
Massey, Jane, ext. 1782 email: jmassey@upperroom.org
Treadway, Bill, ext. 1792 email: btreadway@upperroom.org

Production

Gregory, Debbie, ext. 7224 email: dgregory@upperroom.org

McCanner, Sally, ext. 7225 email: smccanner@upperroom.org

Program

Team Leader & Emmaus Walk: **Albin, Tom,** ext. 7110
email: talbin@upperoom.org
Chapel/Museum: **Kimball, Kathryn,** ext. 7206
email: kkimball@upperroom.org

Emmaus Walk: Gilmore, Dick, ext. 7288
email: dgilmore@upperroom.org
Johnson-Green, Jean, ext. 7222 email: jjohnson@upperroom.org
Academy for Spiritual Formation: **Haas, Jerry,** ext. 7232
email: jhaas@upperroom.org
Living Prayer Center: ext. 7214 Prayer Line: 800/251-2468
Pathways Center for Spiritual Leadership: **Thompson, Marjorie,**
ext. 7226 email: mthompson@upperroom.org
Chrysalis: **vacant**

Business Operations

Team Leader of Business Development & Operations: **Brown, John F.,**
ext. 7520 email: jbrown@upperroom.org
Director of Financial Services: **Runyan, Jeff,** ext. 7282
email: jrunyan@upperroom.org
Director of System Software Support: **Bass, Patrick,** ext. 7039
email: pbass@upperroom.org
Associate Team Leader & Fulfillment & Distribution Manager:
Johnson, James, ext. 7243 email: jajohnson@upperroom.org
Accounts Receivable Manager: **Patton, Monique,** ext. 1705
email: mpatton@upperroom.org
Call Center Manager: **Flemmings, Teresa,** ext. 1787
email: tflemmings@upperroom.org
Credit Collections Officer: **Webster, Brenda,** ext. 7040
email: bwebster@upperroom.org
Development: **Saus, Frances** email: fsaus@upperroom.org
McCormick, Chris email: cmccormick@upperroom.org
Subscription Fulfillment: **Eubank, Charlene,** ext. 7255
email: ceubank@upperroom.org
Manager of Mail Services: **Patterson, Alice,** ext. 7115
email: apatterson@upperroom.org

Marketing

Associate Team Leader & Director of Marketing: **Elliott, Sherry,** ext. 7220
email: selliott@upperroom.org

Director of Marketing: **Helms, Cynthia,** ext. 7219
email: chelms@upperroom.org
Promotion Coordinator: **Rainer, Rie,** ext. 7138
email: rrainer@upperroom.org
Promotion Coordinator: **Perry, Trenay,** ext. 7165
email: tperry@upperroom.org
Marketing Project Coordinator: **Dyce, Brandon,** ext. 7287 email:
bdyce@upperroom.org
Director of Trade and Event Marketing: **Donigian, George,** ext. 7172
email: gdonigian@upperroom.org
Customer Resource Information: 800/491-0912

GENERAL BOARD OF GLOBAL MINISTRIES

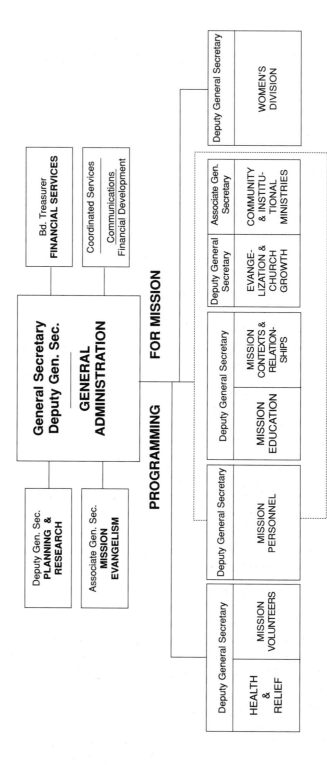

General Secretary
Deputy Gen. Sec.
GENERAL ADMINISTRATION

Deputy Gen. Sec.
PLANNING & RESEARCH

Associate Gen. Sec.
MISSION EVANGELISM

Bd. Treasurer
FINANCIAL SERVICES

Coordinated Services
Communications
Financial Development

PROGRAMMING   **FOR MISSION**

Deputy General Secretary
MISSION VOLUNTEERS
HEALTH & RELIEF

Deputy General Secretary
MISSION PERSONNEL

Deputy General Secretary
MISSION EDUCATION
MISSION CONTEXTS & RELATIONSHIPS

Deputy General Secretary
EVANGE-LIZATION & CHURCH GROWTH

Associate Gen. Secretary
COMMUNITY & INSTITU-TIONAL MINISTRIES

Deputy General Secretary
WOMEN'S DIVISION

PROGRAM AREAS

GENERAL BOARD OF GLOBAL MINISTRIES
www.gbgm-umc.org

OFFICERS

President: Martinez, Joel N.
Vice Presidents:
  Bank, Genie
  Humper, Joseph Christian
  Keaton, Jonathan D.

Standing Committee Chairs
Finance: **Evans, Jr., Cashar W.**
Mission Development: **Black, Charlene R.**
Nominations & Legislation: **Soliz, Daniel**
Personnel: **Dyck, Sally**
Policy & Bylaws: **Ferguson, Phyllis**

Women's Division
President: **Bank, Genie**

Health & Relief
Chairperson: **Davis, G. Lindsey**

Committee to Eliminate Institutional Racism
Chairperson: **Newton, Florise M. Jackson**

DIRECTORS

Bishops
Davis, G. Lindsey, United Methodist Center, P.O. Box 922997, Norcross, GA 30010
Dew, William W., Jr., 1550 E. Meadowbrook Ave., Suite 200, Phoenix, AZ 85014-4040
Humper, Joseph Christian, UMC House, P.O. Box 523, 31 Lightfoot Boston St., Freetown, SIERRA LEONE
Justo, Benjamin A., Sienna Hill #97, Campo Sioco, Baguio City 2600, PHILIPPINES
Keaton, Jonathan D., 8800 Cleveland Ave., NW, P.O. Box 2800, North Canton, OH 44720

Kim, Hae-Jong, P.O. Box 5002, Cranberry Township, PA 16066-4914
Martinez, Joel N., P.O. Box 781688, San Antonio, TX 78278-1688
Minor, Ruediger R., #257, c/o IPS, PMB 572, 666 Fifth Avenue, New York, NY 10103

Ames, III, Guy C., 2717 W. Hefner Rd, Oklahoma City, OK 73120,
Arni, Rita, P.O. Box 135, Marshall MO 65340
Ashcraft, Ann G., 209 Morningstar Drive, Malvern, AR 72104-8953
Baldridge, Mary A., 716 Mattawa Court, Millersville, MD,21108
Bank, Genie, 6551 S. Lakeshore Road, Lexington, MI 48450
Baptista, Paixao, 3316 3rd Avenue, Kearney, NE 68845
Bilog, Francisco B., The UMC, 30 Osmena Street, 8100 Tagum City, PHILIPPINES
Black, Charlene R., 720 Captola Road, Sylvania, GA 30467
Boayue, Jr., Charles, Second Grace UMC, 18700 Joy Rd, Detroit, MI 48228
Brown, Brenda B., 1606 Dolphin Drive, Spring Lake, NC 28390
Carrington, John E., 143-22 109th Avenue, Jamaica, NY 11435
Chijika, Kongolo, Diocese Du Sud-Congo, Katanga, P.O. Box 22037, Kitwe, ZAMBIA
Clark, Joyce S., 2410 Chapman Drive Nashville, TN 37206
Clingenpeel, Myrtle F., 8324 NW 35th St. Bethany, OK 73008
Davis, Jean, 185 W. Nicklaus Ave. Kalispell, MT 59901
Deemer, Julia, 16671 Fewins Road Interlochen, MI 49643
Diaz, Luisa A., Cond. Coral Beach 1, Apt. 204,5869 Isla Verde Avenue,Carolina, PR 00979-5711
Dyck, Sally, 210 Meadowhill Lane, Moreland Hills, OH 44022
Eubanks, Nancy, 426 Eubanks Rd, Brownsville, TN 38012
Evangelista, Ramon A., P.O. Box 86, Northfield, NJ 08225
Evans, Jr., Cashar W., 69 Poteskeet Trail Kitty Hawk, NC 27949-3510
Faulk, Sylvia M., 623 San Fernando Ave. Berkeley, CA 94707
Fenner, Elizabeth, 514 South 13th St. Lexington, MO 64067
Ferguson, Phyllis, 10050 43rd Place, NE Seattle, WA 98125-8112
Ferguson, Sandra, 7178 Columbia Gateway Dr., Columbia, MD 21046-2132
Fooshee, Dale L., 3015 SW Randolph Ave., Apt. 106, Topeka, KS 66611-1770
Garcia, Dolores L., 315 Regency Lane, Apt. 5, Weslaco, TX 78596
Gates, Mary H., 3420 Skycroft Circle Minneapolis, MN 55418-1719
Gibson, Mildred, P.O. Box 66, 44339 Hwy 52 Richfield, NC 28137
Goss, Patricia Ann, 5108 E. Emerald Ave. Mesa, AZ 85206

Gregory, Guinevere P., 7920 Hamilton Ave. Pittsburgh, PA 15208-2107

Henderson, Curtis J., P.O. Box 700 Andalusia, AL 36420-0700

Hinson, William H., 264 Terry Drake Road Owens Crossroads, AL 35763

John, Emmy Lou, 1541 Kenilworth Place Aurora, IL 60506-5353

Johnson, Margaret W., 364 Lake St. - College Manor Dallas, PA 18612-1031

Kabete, Irene, 156 Harare Street Harare ,ZIMBABWE

Kalema, Odimba, 2867 Ecuries, Ngaliema, Kinshasa , DEM. REP. OF THE CONGO

Kelemeni, Eddie, Jefferson Avenue UMC, 4425 Kipling St., Wheat Ridge, CO 80033-2810

Kemper, Thomas, Hollandische Heide 13 42113 Wuppertal ,GERMANY

Kreamer, C. William, 6 Kilkenny Hill Pacific, MO 63069

Leathrum, Nancy H., P. O. Box 479, Townsend, DE 19734

Lister, Georgia R., 226 Heritage Hills Dr. Greeneville, TN 37745

Luecke, Patricia, P.O. Box 149, 140 S. Roosevelt Mission, SD 57555

Lux, William, 101 Rays Court Manchester, IA 52057

Mariano, Liz, 28 M. Jocson St. Varsity Hills, Loyola Heights, Quezon City, PHILIPPINES

McKonly, Melinda, 1533 Springhouse Rd Allentown, PA18104

Meeks, Donald, Living Waters UMC,1041 Woods Way, O'Fallon, IL 62269

Melvin, Mary M., 7302 St. Vincent Street Tampa, FL 33614

Miller, Randolph, 4015 Adeline St. Emeryville, CA, 94608

Mooneyhan, James, P.O. Box 1064, Dalton, GA 30722-1064

Morales, Nelida Mora, 1931 SW 82nd Place Miami, FL 33155-1211

Newton, Florise M. Jackson, 410 Oxford St. Piscataway, NJ 08854

Nutter, Judy, HC39, Box 123B St. Marys, WV 26170

Odland, Tove, The United Methodist Church in Norway, Akersbakken 37, P.O. Box 2744, St. Hanshaugen, N0131 Oslo, NORWAY

Olusiji, Leah, c/o Bishop D.P. Dabale, UMCN, P.O. Box 155, Mile Six, Jalingo, Numan Rd, Taraba State, NIGERIA

Owen, David V.W., 4783 Harrington Court Bloomington, IN 47404-9122

Park, Mee Sue, 2222 N. Beachwood Dr., #207, Hollywood Hills, CA 90068

Peterson, John D., c/o Warren Wilson College, CPO #7281, P.O. Box 9000, Asheville, NC, 28815-9000

Phillips, Cheryl, 5222 Dumfries, Houston, TX 77096

Poindexter, Mary A., 4027 Meadowlane Dr., Jackson, MS 39206-4604

Ratcliff, Billy, 6324 Everglade Rd., Dallas, TX 75227

Rathod, Ella, 323 North Shore Dr., Hastings, NE 68901

Redding, Lavada, P.O. Box 308, Ovid, CO 80744-0308

Rhodehamel, Wendy, 28 Main Street, Postdam, NY 13676

Sarazin, Duane, 11100 River Hills Dr., Burnsville, MN 55337-3281

Schramm, Linda A., 244 S. Elk St., Sandusky, MI 48471

Shinhoster, Richard, 14310 Coffee Bluff Road, Savannah, GA 31419

Siaba, Judith, 2256 N. Lamon Ave., Chicago, IL 60639

Simeon, Rachel Lieder, P.O. Box 670909, Chugiak, AK 99567

Soliz, Daniel, 3727 Falls Drive, Dallas, TX 75211

Staempfli, Andreas, EMK- Missionssekretariat, Badenerstrasse 69, P.O. Box 1344, CH8026 Zurich, SWITZERLAND

Steely, Hazel, 208 Shawnee St., Hiawatha, KS 66434

Tombaugh, Dianne M., P.O. Box 174, Clay Center, KS 67432

Torres, H. Ulises, 148 Rounds St., New Bedford, MA 02740

Villanueva, Lina D., Spottswood Methodist Center, Kidapawan City, Cotabato 9400, PHILIPPINES

Vogler, Diane Clark, 7016 Comanche Drive, North Little Rock, AR 72116

Ward, Gary Thomas, P.O. Box 281, Chelsea, AL 35043

Wilson, David M., 3020 S. Harvey St., Oklahoma City, OK 73109

Wilson, Jr., George D., c/o Liberia Annual Conf., Tubman Blvd at 13th Street Sinkor,1000 Monrovia, LIBERIA

Woodworth, Frances J., 79 Birch Fork Road, P.O. Box 119, Roark, KY 40979

Yohan, Shan, 4028 Sue Lane, Decatur, GA 30035-1075

STAFF

475 RIVERSIDE DRIVE, NEW YORK, NY 10115
212/870-3600 FAX: 212/870-3748
Mission Information Line: 800/UMC-GBGM or 862-4246
Web site: www.gbgm-umc.org

MANAGEMENT AND GENERAL ADMINISTRATION

BOARD CABINET FAX: 212/870-3748
General Secretary: **Day, R. Randy,** 212/870-3606
email rday@gbgm-umc.org
Deputy General Secretary/Administration: **Bass, Deborah E.,**
212/870-3608 email: dbass@gbgm-umc.org

Deputy General Secretary/Women's Division: **Sohl, Joyce D.,**
212/870-3752 email: jsohl@gbgm-umc.org
Deputy General Secretary/Assigned by the General Secretary:
Dirdak, Paul R., 212/870-3816 email: pdirdak@gbgm-umc.org
Deputy General Secretary/Assigned by the General Secretary:
Dixon, Sam W., Jr., 212/870-3856 email: sdixon@gbgm-umc.org
Deputy General Secretary/Assigned by the General Secretary:
Gleaves, Edith L., 212/870-3662 email: egleaves@gbgm-umc.org
Deputy General Secretary/Assigned by the General Secretary: **Kang,**
Youngsook C., 212/870-3885 email: ykang@gbgm-umc.org
Deputy General Secretary/Assigned by the General Secretary: **Rivas,**
Michael G., 212/870-3609 email: mrivas@gbgm-umc.org
General Treasurer: vacant 212/870-3637

OFFICE OF THE GENERAL SECRETARY FAX: 212/870-3748

Associate General Secretary, Mission Evangelism: **Kimbrough, ST,**
Jr., 212/870-3914 email: SKimbrou@gbgm-umc.org
Assistant General Secretary/Special Assignment: **Lee, Christine C.,**
212/870-3681 email: clee@gbgm-umc.org
Assistant General Secretary/Special Assignment: **Njuki, Caroline**
W., 212/870-3702 email: cnjuki@gbgm-umc.org
Assistant General Secretary/Director of Development: **Byrd, Lynda**
R., 212/870-3916 email: lbyrd@gbgm-umc.org

Coordinator/National Plan for Hispanic Ministries: **Rivera, Eli S.,** 212/870-3820 email: erivera@gbgm-umc.org

Executive Assistant to the General Secretary: **Lemon, Melba,** 212/870-3606 email: mlemon@gbgm-umc.org

Business Manager/Global Praise: vacant, 212/870-3633 email:

Program Coordinator/Global Praise: **Lockward, Jorge A.,** 212/870-3967 email: jlockwar@gbgm-umc.org

Manager/Copyright Services: **Scott, Catherine M.,** 212/870-3783 email: CScott@gbgm-umc.org

Staff/Conference Relations: **Moore, Vera T.,** 800/UMC-GBGM email: vmoore@gbgm-umc.org

NETWORK SERVICES

Network Administrator: **Ojeda, Benjamin,** 212/870-3941 email: bojeda@gbgm-umc.org

Network Administrator: **Jolly, Donovan C.,** 212/870-3646 email: djolly@gbgm-umc.org

Network Administrator: **Joseph, Elias,** 212/870-3646 email: ejoseph@gbgm-umc.org

Network Administrator: **Jackson, Richard M.,** 212/870-3646 email: rjackson@gbgm-umc.org

Trainer/Helpline Administrator: **Johnson, Fred M.,** 212/870-3625 FAX: 212/870-3748 email: fjohnson@gbgm-umc.org

COORDINATED SERVICES

Financial Development FAX: 212/870-3775

Assistant General Secretary: **Carter, William T.,** 212/870-3790 email: wcarter@gbgm-umc.org

Field Representative/Financial Development: **Conklin, Elizabeth "Brooke",** 518/884-8456 email: econklin@gbgm-umc.org

Field Representative/Financial Development: **Hawkins, Rick L.,** 214/373-1554 email: rhawkins@gbgm-umc.org

Field Representative/Financial Development: **Magnus, M. Joy,** 404/584-6222 email: jmagnus@gbgm-umc.org

Field Representative/Financial Development: **Rhodes, Wayne, Jr.,** 630/357-0170 email: wrhodes@gbgm-umc.org

Field Representative/Financial Development: **Wilson, Heather C.,** 213/386-5335 email: hwilson@gbgm-umc.org

Executive Secretary/Advance Coordination: **Scott, Russell H.,** 212/870-3796 email: rscott@gbgm-umc.org

Executive Secretary/Special Constituencies: **Carey, Abraham R.,** 954/978-6442 email: acarey@gbgm-umc.org

Director/Current and Deferred Giving: **Bibbee, Barbara J.,** 440/816-1270 email: bbibbee@gbgm-umc.org

Director/Current and Deferred Giving: **Conner, Mark A.,** 603/863-8357 email: mconner@gbgm-umc.org

Director/Current and Deferred Giving: **Park, James N.,** 213/386-5335 email: jpark@gbgm-umc.org

Director/Current and Deferred Giving: **Simmons, Anna Beth,** 704/527-2106 email: asimmons@gbgm-umc.org

Communications FAX 212/870-3654

Assistant General Secretary/Mission Communications: Whiteside, Wendy L., 212/870-3785 email: wendyw@gbgm-umc.org

Coordinator/Language Interpretation Services: **Reasoner, Donald D.,** 212/870-3713 email: dreasone@gbgm-umc.org

Staff Photographer/Photo and Audio-Visual Librarian: **Winn, Lane C.,** 212/870-3811 email: lwinn@gbgm-umc.org

Design Services

Director/Design Services: **DeGregorie, Frank,** 212/870-3778 email: fdegrego@gbgm-umc.org

Assistant Art Director: **Fletcher, Gilbert D.,** 212/870-3779 email: gfletche@gbgm-umc.org

Production Coordinator: **Carr, Brenda L.,** 212/870-3778 email: bcarr@gbgm-umc.org

Promotion and Marketing

Director/Production, Promotion & Marketing: **Moultrie, Edward A.,** 212/870-3779 email: emoultri@gbgm-umc.org

Coordinator/Literature Marketing: **Braithwaite, Gloria,** 212/870-3761 email: gbraithw@gbgm-umc.org

Technical/Information Services

Web Site Manager/Administrator: **Obando, Jorge,** 212/870-3533 email: jobando@gbgm-umc.org

Web Site Programmer: **Kerman, Svetlana (Lana),** 212/870-3782 email: skerman@gbgm-umc.org

Web Systems Operator: **Carey, Sally J.,** 518/356-0650 email: Scarey@gbgm-umc.org

Web Systems Operator: **Wilbur, Margaret B.,** 802/865-2130
email: mwilbur@gbgm-umc.org

Writing/Editorial Services

Editor/*New World Outlook:* **House, Christie R.,** 212/870-3765
FAX: 212/870-3758 email: chouse@gbgm-umc.org
Editor/Multilingual Resources: **Ferrari, Nilda,** 212/870-3763
email: nferrari@gbgm-umc.org
Editor/Korean Language Resources: **Chung, Jungrea H.,** 212/870-
3812 email: jchung@gbgm-umc.org
Writer/Program Areas: vacant 212/870-3692 email:

ADMINISTRATIVE SERVICES FAX: 212/870-3748
Deputy General Secretary: **Bass, Deborah E.,** 212/870-3608
email: dbass@bgm-umc.org
Office Manager: **Soto, Margarita,** 212/870-3705
email: msoto@gbgm-umc.org

Records Management
Board Recording Secretary: **Francisco, Francia L.,** 212/870-3607
email: ffrancisc@gbgm-umc.org
Manager/Central Records: , 212/870-3620 email: musherke@gbgm-
umc.org
Assistant Manager/Records: **Smith, Sheila T.,** 212/870-3722
email: ssmith@gbgm-umc.org
Assistant Manager/Records: **Valle, Lillian,** 212/870-3858
email: lvalle@gbgm-umc.org

Human Resources Department
Director/Human Resources: **Robinson, George M.,** 212/870-3663
email: grobinso@gbgm-umc.org
Manager/Benefits and Staff Development: **Williams, Kerri-Ann,**
212/870-3664 email: kwilliams@gbgm-umc.org

General Services
Director/General Services: **Rodriguez, Raoul J.,** 212/870-3669
email: rrodrigu@gbgm-umc.org
Manager/Central Services: **Kong, Christopher W.,** 212/870-3655
email: ckong@gbgm-umc.org

PLANNING AND RESEARCH FAX: 212/870-3876
Deputy General Secretary: **Rivas, Michael G.,** 212/870-3609
email: mrivas@gbgm-umc.org
Research Director (Interim): **Southwick, John H.,** 212/870-3839
email: jsouthw@gbgm-umc.org
Information Services Associate: **Castaneda, Marion,** 212/870-3609
email: mcastane@gbgm-umc.org

FINANCIAL SERVICES FAX: 212/870-3668
General Treasurer: **vacant.,** 212/870-3637
Associate Treasurer: **Fernandes, Roland,** 212/870-3716
email: rfernand@gbgm-umc.org
Associate Treasurer: **Francisco, Edwin C.,** 212/870-3679
email: efrancis@gbgm-umc.org
Associate Treasurer: **Takamine, Connie J.,** 212/870-3740
email: ctakamin@gbgm-umc.org
General Comptroller: **Edwards, Betty J.,** 212/870-3616
email: bedwards@gbgm-umc.org

Treasury
Assistant Comptroller: **Mui, Halina,** 212/870-3925
email: hmui@gbgm-umc.org
Assistant Comptroller: **Ogando, Sebastian A.,** 212/870-3617
email: sogando@gbgm-umc.org
Assistant Comptroller/Supervisor of Cash Management: **Walfall,
Trevor R.,** 212/870-3627 email: twalfall@gbgm-umc.org
Director/Gifts Processing: **Fongyit, Marjorie E.,** 212/870-3611
email: mfongyit@gbgm-umc.org
Manager/Payroll: **Tharian, Kuriakose P.,** 212/870-3907
email: Ktharian@gbgm-umc.org
Supervisor/Cash Receipts/Cash Management: **Rodriguez, Alicia,**
212/870-3917 email: arodrigu@gbgm-umc.org
Internal Auditor/Software Specialist: **Mehta, Harsha,** 212/870-3714
email: hmehta@gbgm-umc.org
Executive for Treasury Relations: **Paulate, Elfrido,** 212/870-3894
email: epaulate@gbgm-umc.org
Senior Accountant: **Hernandez, Anita N.,** 212/870-3905
email: ahernand@gbgm-umc-org

Insurance, Property, Legal

Risk Management Administrator: **vacant,** 212/870-3636
email:
Estate Planning Associate: **Antone, Xenon U.,** 212/870-3631 email:
xantone@gbgm-umc.org

Data Processing

Programmer Analyst: **Silva, Malkanthi,** 212/870-3647
email: msilva@gbgm-umc.org
Programmer Analyst: **Suslovich, Anatoly,** 212/870-3648
email: asuslovi@gbgm-umc.org

Mission Programming Areas

COMMUNITY AND INSTITUTIONAL MINISTRIES FAX: 212/870-3948

Associate General Secretary: **Scott, Jerald L.,** 212/870-3843
email: jscott@gbgm-umc.org

Community Ministries

Executive Secretary/Community Ministries/Development: **vacant,** 212/870-3821 email:
Executive Secretary/Town & Country Ministries: **Thompson, Carol J.,** 212/870-3684 email: cjthomps@gbgm-umc.org
Executive Secretary/Urban Ministries: **Johnson, Diane H.,** 212/870-3832 email: dhjohnson@gbgm-umc.org
Executive Secretary/Women, Children & Families Ministries: **Reich, Joanne,** 212/870-3833 email: jreich@gbgm-umc.org
Substance Abuse & Related Violence Program:
Director: **Fuentes, Noemi M.,** 212/870-3699
email nfuentes@gbgm-umc.org
Office Manager: **Norfleet, Wilma,** 202/548-2712
email: wnorflee@gbgm-umc.org

Institutional Ministries

Executive Secretary/Institutions: **Jun, Nam-Jin,** 212/870-3697
email: njun@gbgm-umc.org
Executive Secretary/Institutions: **Knudsen, Ellen,** 212/870-3846
email: eknudsen@gbgm-umc.org
Executive Secretary/Institutions: **Triplett, Carlene,** 212/870-3847
email: ctriplet@gbgm-umc.org

Executive Secretary/Institutions: **Tyrell, Hortense A.**, 212/870-3887
email: htyrell@gbgm-umc.org
Executive Secretary/ Technical Assistance: **Nair, Chandrasekharan,**
212/870-3859 email: cnair@gbgm-umc.org

EVANGELIZATION AND CHURCH GROWTH FAX: 212/870-3948

Deputy General Secretary: **Dixon, Sam W., Jr.**, 212/870-3856
email: sdixon@gbgm-umc.org

Congregational Mission Initiatives

Assistant General Secretary, Mission Initiatives: **Wu, David C.,**
212/870-3955 email: dwu@gbgm-umc.org
Executive Secretary/Asian American & Pacific Islanders Ministries:
Kim, Jong Sung, 212/870-3829 email: jskim@gbgm-umc.org
Executive Secretary/Special Initiatives: **Rabb, Clinton,** 212/870-3860
email: crabb@gbgm-umc.org
Specialist/Russian Ministries: **Shaporenko, Vladimir A.**, 703/723-
1307 email: vshapore@gbgm-umc.org

Resources and Services

Assistant General Secretary/Resources and Services: **vacant,**
212/870-3689
Program Associate: **Hinton, Josephine C.**, 212/870-3864
email: jhinton@gbgm-umc.org
Executive Secretary/Transformation Training and Leadership
Development: **vacant**
Executive Secretary/Church Development: **Rae, Keith D.**, 212/870-
3862 email: krae@gbgm-umc.org
Executive Secretary/Church Development: **Rivera, Eli S.**, 212/870-
3820 email: erivera@gbgm-umc.org
Assistant General Secretary/United Methodist Development Fund:
Dixon, Sam W., Jr., 212/870-3856 email: sdixon@gbgm-umc.org
Administrator/UMDF Investment Services: **Webb, Gloria**, 212/870-
3856 email: gwebb@gbgm-umc.org
Administrator/Loan Office: **McMahon, Denise**, 212/870-3865
email: dmcmahon@gbgm-umc.org
Associate/Loan Director: **Herrera, Rhina L.**, 212/870-3865
email: rherrera@gbgm-umc.org

Africa Radio Program

Senior Producer: **Mbading, Raphael,** 212/870-3934
email: rmbading@gbgm-umc.org

Assistant Producer: **Murray, Kai S.,** 212/870-3934
email: kmurray @gbgm-umc.org

Africa Radio Program Engineer: **Tricomi, Christopher,** 212/870-3549
email: ctricomi@gbgm-umc.org

Africa Radio Program Engineer: **Wilson, Stevland,** 212/870-2851
email: swilson@gbgm-umc.org

MISSION CONTEXTS AND RELATIONSHIPS

FAX: 212/870-3932

Deputy General Secretary: **Kang, Youngsook C.,** 212/870-3885
email: ykang@gbgm-umc.org
Assistant General Secretary/Administration: **Domingues, Jorge L.F.,**
212/870-3873 email: jdomingu@gbgm-umc.org
Executive Director/Native American Comprehensive Plan:
Saunkeah, Ann A., 918/747-3660 email: asaunke@gbgm-umc.org
Executive Director/UM Council on Korean American Ministries:
Cho, Brandon I., 626/568-7309 email: bcho@gbgm-umc.org

Connectional Relations

Assistant General Secretary: **Acevedo-Delgado, German,** 212/870-
3689 email: gacevedo@gbgm-umc.org
Executive Secretary/Connectional Relations: **Avitia, Edgar,** 915/593-
1178 email: eavitia@gbgm-umc.org
Executive Secretary/Connectional Relations: **Coulson, Gail V.,**
212/870-3597 email: gcoulson@gbgm-umc.org
Executive Secretary/Connectional Relations: **Guerrero, Franklin,**
212/870-3588 email: fguerrer@gbgm-umc.org
Executive Secretary/Connectional Relations: **Kent, Cynthia A.,**
212/870-3830 email: ckent@gbgm-umc.org
Executive Secretary/Connectional Relations: **Perez-Salgado, Lyssette**
N., 212/870-3768 email: lperez@gbgm-umc.org
Executive Secretary/Connectional Relations: **Siegfried, Peter,**
212/870-3889 email: psiegfri@gbgm-umc.org
Program Associate: **Terrero, Reyna M.,** 212/870-3689 email: rter-
rero@gbgm-umc-org

Global Networks and Ecumenical Relations

Assistant General Secretary: **Hutchison, Peggy J.**, 212/870-3998
email: phutchis@gbgm-umc.org
Executive Secretary/Ecumenical & Interfaith Ministries: **Asedillo, Rebecca C.**, 212/870-3694 email: rasedill@gbgm-umc.org
Executive Secretary/Human Rights & Racial Justice: **Lopez, Eddie, Jr.**, 212/870-3685 email: elopez@gbgm-umc.org
Executive Secretary/Human Rights & Racial Justice: **Wildman, David L.**, 212/870-3735 email: dwildman@gbgm-umc.org
Executive Secretary/Women and Children: **vacant**, 212/870-3707
email:
Executive Secretary/Youth/Young Adults: **Walker, Tamara L.**, 212/870-3690 email: twalker@gbgm-umc.org
Administrator/Scholarships & Leadership Development Grants: **Katzenstein, Lisa H.**, 212/870-3787 email: lkatzens@gbgm-umc.org
Program Associate: **Persaud, Sandra**, 212/870-3998
email: spersaud@gbgm-umc.org

MISSION EDUCATION FAX: 212/870-3932

Deputy General Secretary: **Kang, Youngsook C.**, 212/870-3885
email: ykang@gbgm-umc.org
Executive Secretary/Mission Leadership Development: **Jones, Una R.**, 212/870-3792 email: ujones@gbgm-umc.org
Executive Secretary Emerging Churches' Resources: **Wu, Shirley A.**, 212/870-3615 email: swu@gbgm-umc.org
Project Manager/Mission Studies: **Gould, Ivan (Toby)**, 631/728-7689
email: revtg@aol.com

MISSION PERSONNEL FAX: 212/870-3774

Deputy General Secretary: **Gleaves, Edith L.**, 212/870-3662
email: egleaves@gbgm-umc.org
Assistant General Secretary: **Goldstein, Stephen**, 212/870-3793
email: sgoldste@gbgm-umc.org
Benefits Coordinator: **McCoy, Audrey**, 212/870-3661
email: amccoy@gbgm-umc.org
Coordinator/Personnel Information Management: **Wilson, Antonietta A.**, 212/870-3659 email: awilson@gbgm-umc.org

Missionary Assignment

Executive Secretary/Church & Community Workers: **vacant (Connelly, Brenda)**, 212/870-3819 email: ccworker@gbgm-umc.org
Executive Secretary/Deaconesses: **Dodson, Doris R. (Becky)**, 212/870-3850 email: bdodson@gbgm-umc.org
Missionaries in Residence: **Markay, David & Kristen**, 212/870-3687 email: mir@gbgm-umc.org
Missionaries in Residence, Youth & Young Adult Program: **Wheeler, Barbara**, 212/870-3660 email: MIRYAP1@gbgm-umc.org
Executive Secretary/Selection & Development: **Zaragoza-De Leon, Jeanette**, 212/870-3659 email: jdeleon@gbgm-umc.org
Missionaries: **Garrison, Mark & Nancy**, 212/870-3660 email: mgarriso@gbgm-umc.org or ngarriso@gbgm-umc.org
Missionaries: **Masters, Kathleen K.**, 212/870-3687 email: masters@gbgm-umc.org
Missionaries: **Savuto, Bill & Jerri**, 212/870-3612 email: bsavuto@gbgm-umc.org or jsavuto@gbgm-umc.og

Itineration/Cultivation

Executive Secretary/Missionary Support & Itineration: **Nuessle, John E.**, 212/870-3797 email: jnuessle@gbgm-umc.org

MISSION VOLUNTEERS FAX: 212/870-3624

Deputy General Secretary: **Dirdak, Paul R.**, 212/870-3816 email: pdirdak@gbgm-umc.org
Assistant General Secretary/Mission Volunteer Development: **Blankenbaker, Jeanie**, 212/870-3825 email: lblanken@gbgm-umc.org
Manager/Volunteer Network Services: **DeBorja, Michael R.**, 212/870-3825 email: mdeborja@gbgm-umc.org
Program Coordinator: **Lehmann, Kimberley L.**, 212/870-3825 email: klehmann@gbgm-umc.org

HEALTH AND RELIEF FAX: 212/749-2641 or 212/870-3904

Deputy General Secretary: **Dirdak, Paul R.**, 212/870-3816 email: pdirdak@gbgm-umc.org

Office Manager: **Goldstein, Edward F.**, 212/870-3816 email: egoldste@gbgm-umc.org

Executive Secretary/Financial Resources Development/Promotions:
Luetchens, Melvin H., 212/870-3814
email: mluetche@gbgm-umc.org
Executive Secretary/Communications: **Beher, Linda K.**, 212/870-3815
email: lbeher@gbgm-umc.org
Web Systems Operator: **Carter, Nancy A.**, 212/870-3814
email: ncarter@gbgm-umc.org

Health and Welfare

Executive Secretary/Congregational Health Ministries: **vacant,**
212/870-3870 email: nfuentes@gbgm-umc.org
Executive Secretary/Hospital Revitalization Program: **Thomas,**
Cherian, 212/870-3871 email: cthomas@gbgm-umc.org

United Methodist Committee on Relief

Assistant General Secretary/UMCOR Program: **Sachen, Kristin L.,**
212/870-3909 email: ksachen@gbgm-umc.org

NGO Program FAX: TBD

Emergency Services FAX: 202/544-4116

Executive Secretary/Disaster Network: **Hazelwood, F. Thomas,**
202/548-4002 email: thazelwo@gbgm-umc.org
Coordinator/Volunteers: **Knight, Luz M.** , 202/548-4002
email: lknight@gbgm-umc.org
Emergency Services/Field Staff: **Saddoo, David,** 212/870-3909
email: dsadoo@gbgm-umc.org
Program Coordinator/Emergency Services: **Thompson, Carol R.,**
212/870-3909 email: cthompso@gbgm-umc.org

Refugee Ministries FAX: 212/749-2641

Executive Secretary/Refugees: **Wersan, Susan,** 212/870-3807
email: swersan@gbgm-umc.org
Coordinator/Refugee Ministries: **Daleney, Nancy,** 212/870-3805
email: ndelaney@gbgm-umc.org

Hunger and Poverty

Executive Secretary/World Hunger and Poverty: **Kim, June H.,**
212/870-3877 email: jkim@gbgm-umc.org

UMCOR@Sager Brown FAX: 337/923-4849

Executive Director: **Redding, Gwen E.**, 337/923-6283
email: gredding@sagerbrown.org

WOMEN'S DIVISION
General Administration FAX: 212/870-3736

Deputy General Secretary: **Sohl, Joyce D.,** 212/870-3752
  email: jsohl@gbgm-umc.org
Assistant General Secretary/Administration: **Salter, Andris Y.,**
  212/870-3745 email: mbase@gbgm-umc.org
Executive Secretary/Communications: **Martini, Kelly,** 212/870-3749
  email: kmartini@gbgm-umc.org
Staff Recording Secretary/Office Manager: **Mairena, Judith C.,**
  212/870-3845 email: jmairena@gbgm-umc.org
Assistant Starr Recording Secretary: **Douglas, Linca C.,** 212/870-3753
  email: ldouglas@gbgm-umc.org
Executive Secretary/International Ministries: **Prudente, Karen G.,**
  212/870-3911 email: kprudent@gbgm-umc.org

Response:
Editor: **Jones, Dane E.,** 212/870-3755 email: ejones@gbgm-umc.org
Managing Editor/*Response*: **Moore, Yvette L.,** 212/870-3822
  email: ymoore@gbgm-umc.org
Senior Writer/*Response*: **Hunter, A. Victoria,** 212/870-3757
  email: ahunter@gbgm-umc.org
Service Center: FAX: 513/761-3722
Director: **Stewart, Jacqueline L.,** 513/761-2100
  email: jstewart@gbgm-umc.org
Executive Assistant to the Director: **Bray, Robert E.,** 513/761-2100
  email: rbray@gbgm-umc.org

SECTION OF FINANCE FAX: 212/870-3736
Treasurer: **Takamine, Connie J.,** 212/870-3740
  email: ctakamin@gbgm-umc.org
Assistant Treasurer: **vacant,** 212/870-3739 email: nlee@gbgm-umc.org
Comptroller: **Chung, Fookyin Dawn,** 212/870-3743
  email: dchung@gbgm-umc.org
Executive Secretary/Mission Opportunities: **Coudal, Mary Beth,**
  212/870-3738 email: mbcoudal@gbgm-umc.org

SECTION OF CHRISTIAN SOCIAL RESPONSIBILITY
FAX: 212/870-3736
Assistant General Secretary: **Dauway, Lois M.,** 212/870-3734
  email: ldauway@gbgm-umc.org

Executive Secretary/Community Action: **Lee, Mary Sungok,**
212/870-3766 email: slee@gbgm-umc.org
Executive Secretary/Racial Justice: **vacant**
Executive Secretary/Spiritual & Theological Development: **Craig, J.
Ann,** 212/870-3737 email: acraig@gbgm-umc.org
Reading Program Specialist: **Thompson, Brenda A.**, 212/870-3733
email: bathomps@gbgm-umc.org
United Methodist Office for the United Nations:
Executive Secretary/Global Concerns: **Adjali, Else M.**, 212/870-3874
email: eadjali@gbgm-umc.org
Executive Secretary/Justice Education: **Dharmaraj, Glory E.**,
212/682-3633 FAX: 682-5354 email: gdharmar@gbgm-umc.org
Executive Secretary/Research & Hospitality Centers, **Gittens, Betty,**
212/682-3633 email: bgittens@gbgm-umc.org
Resource Center Specialist: **Brown, Esmeralda V.**, 212/682-3633
email: ebrown@gbgm-umc.org
Resource Center Specialist: **Nadjibulla, Parvina,** 212/682-3633
email: pnadjibu@gbgm-umc.org
Seminar Designer: **Anderson, Lisa A.**, 212/682-3633
email: landerso@gbgm-umc.org
Washington, DC Office:
Executive Secretary/Children, Youth, & Family Advocacy: **Taylor,
Julie A.,** 202/488-5660 ext 102 email: jtaylor@gbgm-umc.org
Executive Secretary/Public Policy: **Johnson, Susie,** 202/488-5660
ext 103 email: johnsons@gbgm-umc.org

SECTION OF MEMBERSHIP & ORGANIZATIONAL DEVELOPMENT
FAX: 212/870-3736
Assistant General Secretary: **Trent, Cheryl E.**, 212/870-3723
email: ctrent@gbgm-umc.org
Executive Secretary/Membership: **vacant**
Executive Secretary/Leadership Education: **Tulloch, Julia R.,**
212/870-3769 email: jtulloch@gbgm-umc.org
Executive Secretary/Organizational Development: **Rodriguez, Diana
M.,** 212/870-3727 email: drodrigu@gbgm-umc.org
Executive Secretary/Mission Education: **Villarreal, Marisa,** 212/870-
3726 email: mvillarr@gbgm-umc.org
Executive Secretary/Resource Development: **Simms, Carolyn R.,**
212/870-3728 email: csimms@gbgm-umc.org

Executive Secretary/Mission Team Training: **Johnson, Sue C.,**
615/320-4601 email: sjohnson@gbgm-umc.org
Executive Secretary/Mission Team Training: **Williams, Lizzie,**
214/373-0070 email: lwilliam@gbgm-umc.org

Executive Secretary/Mission Team Training: **Winfield, Janet W.,**
404/377-4815 email: jwinfield@gbgm-umc.org
Pre-Retirement Assignment/Indianapolis, IN: **Ruby, Sandra K.,**
765/361-1714 email: sruby@gbgm-umc.org
Pre-Retirement Assignment/Denver, CO: **Saul, Jean L.,** 303/756-3501
email: jsaul@gbgm-umc.org

GENERAL BOARD OF HIGHER EDUCATION AND MINISTRY

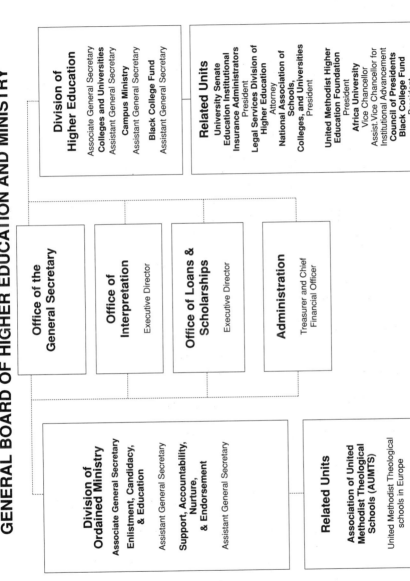

Office of the General Secretary

Office of Interpretation
Executive Director

Office of Loans & Scholarships
Executive Director

Administration
Treasurer and Chief Financial Officer

Division of Higher Education
Associate General Secretary
Colleges and Universities
Assistant General Secretary
Campus Ministry
Assistant General Secretary
Black College Fund
Assistant General Secretary

Related Units
University Senate
Education Institutional Insurance Administrators
President
Legal Services Division of Higher Education
Attorney
National Association of Schools, Colleges, and Universities
President
United Methodist Higher Education Foundation
President
Africa University
Vice Chancellor
Assist.Vice Chancellor for Institutional Advancement
Council of Presidents
Black College Fund
President

Division of Ordained Ministry
Associate General Secretary
Enlistment, Candidacy, & Education
Assistant General Secretary
Support, Accountability, Nurture, & Endorsement
Assistant General Secretary

Related Units
Association of United Methodist Theological Schools (AUMTS)
United Methodist Theological schools in Europe

GENERAL BOARD OF HIGHER EDUCATION AND MINISTRY
www.gbhem.org

OFFICERS

President - **Huie, Janice Riggle**
Secretary - **Crawford, Timothy D.**
Assistant Secretary - McCumons, Brent L.

MEMBERS

Bishops
Edwards, Marion M., POB 10955, Raleigh, NC 27605 919/832-9560
FAX: 919/832-4721 email: bishopmme@nccumc.org
Huie, Janice Riggle, 723 Center St., Little Rock, AR 72201-4399
501/324-8019 FAX: 501/324-8021 email: bishophuie@aristotle.net
May, Felton Edwin, 100 Maryland Ave., NE, Suite 510, Washington,
DC 20002-5611 202/546-3110 FAX: 202/546-3186
email: bishopmay@bwcumc.org
Ntambo, Nkulu Ntanda, United Methodist Church, B.P 11237,
Chingola, Zambia, AFRICA 011 260 22 28535 FAX: 871-683-025522
TGMETHO@MWANGAZA.CD email: nkulu@hotmail.com
Palmer, Gregory V., 500 E. Court Ave., Suite C, Des Moines,
IA 50309-2019 515/283-1996 FAX: 515/283-8672
email: Bishop.Palmer@iaumc.org
Rader, Sharon Zimmerman, 750 Windsor St., Suite 303, Sun Prairie,
WI 53590 608/837-8526 FAX: 608/837-0281 email: szrader@aol.com

Aldridge, Geneva J., 2433 Alpena Ave., Dayton, OH 45406
937/275-4650 FAX: 937/276-4380 email: GAldr52991@aol.com
Alexander, Betty Masters, 147 Allen Dr., Hendersonville, TN 37075
615/822-4932 FAX: 615/824-8784
Amstutz, Allen W., 11634 Boone Dr., Indianapolis, IN 46229
317/359-9651 FAX: 317/359-1318 email: aamstutz@gabrielmail.com
Anderson, Otis, 1144 Cedar View Dr., Minneapolis, MN 55405
612/377-0797 email:otis_anderson@mnumc.org
Bergdoll, James R., 4500 Pinebrook Ct., Virginia Beach, VA 23462
804/521-1120 FAX: 804-521-1174 email: jimbergdoll@vaumc.org
Boone, Ruth H., 8 Walberta Dr., Rochester, IL 62563 217/498-9577
email: ruthboone@msn.com
Bowles, Albert J., POB 80353, Chattanooga, TN 37414-7353
423/629-0333 FAX: 423/622-8360 email: chatdist@umc.holston.org

Briscoe, Carolyn, POB 1825, Clemson, SC 29633 864/654-5547
FAX: 864/654-6540 email: carolynb@clemsonumc.org

Chaviano, Emilio, 400 Biscayne Blvd., Miami, FL 33132 305/371-4706
FAX: 305/371-4707 email: eachaviano@msn.com

Cobb, Michelle A., 404 N. 6th St., Suite 201, West Lafayette, IN 47901-
1127 765/742-4114 FAX: 765/742-4333 email: ladisumc@indy.net

Cole, Thomas W., Jr., Clark Atlanta University, 1852 Simpson Rd.,
Atlanta, GA 30314 404/799-5155 FAX: 404/799-5882
email: tcole@cau.edu

Couch, Bill, 4701 82nd St., Lubbock, TX 79424 806/794-4015
FAX: 806/794-2266 email: bcouch@lakeridgeumc.org

Crawford, Timothy D., POB 205, Frakes, KY 40940 606/337-3613
FAX: 606/337-2225 email: timcrawford@hendersonsettlement.info

Doyle, Lin, Lane 2100, Hyattville, WY 82428 307/469-2253
email: ldoyle@tectwest.net

Eberhart, Diane W., 916 5th Ave., Grinnell, IA 50112 641/236-3757
FAX: 641/236-5755 email: DeaconDiane@IowaTelecom.net

Edwards, Marion M., POB 10955, Raleigh, NC 27605 919/832-9560 ext.
243 FAX: 919-832-4721 email: bishopmme@nccumc.org

Fowler, F. Cole, 5410 Corby St., Omaha, NE 68104 402/556-2433 FAX:
402/556-2372 email: scd-umc@computer-concepts.com

Good, Stephen H., 1134 W. High Point, Springfield, MO 65810
417/873-7225 FAX: 417/873-7568 email: sgood@lib.drury.edu

Goodwin, Galen L., 246 Millbrook Ave., Randolph, NJ 07869-2108
973/538-1299 FAX: 973-292-7584 email: glgoodwin@att.net

Gregory, Anna D., 2709 N. 8th, Independence, KS 67301 620/331-
6059 email: annadimmit@hotmail.com

Haden, William R., West Virginia Wesleyan, 59 College Rd.,
Buckhannon, WV 26201 304/473-8181 FAX: 304/473-8187
email: haden@wvwc.edu

Henderson, Ronald D., 14841 Coit Rd., Suite 310, Dallas, TX 75248-
5701 972/788-4114 FAX: 972/788-4805 email: dne@ntcumc.org

Hopson, Roger A., 24 Corporate Blvd., Jackson, TN 38305-2315
731/664-8480 FAX: 731/660-5712 email: rhopson@memphis-umc.org

Huie, Janice Riggle, 723 Center St., Little Rock, AR 72201-4399
501/324-8019 FAX: 501/324-8021 email: bishophuie@aristotle.net

Jackson, Maggie, 23256 Shurmer Dr., Warrensville Heights, OH 44128
216/687-4599 FAX: 216/687-5590 email: mag.jackson@csuohio.edu

Jackson, Zella D., 2413 Oakleigh Dr., Mobile, AL 36617 334/457-5838
FAX: 334/457-6726 email: zdjackson@juno.com

Johnson, Charles L., Sr., 4908 Colonial Dr., Suite 101, Columbia, SC 29203 803/735-8792 FAX: 803/691-0220 email: cjohnson@umcsc.org

Lacaria, John F., POB 2313, Charleston, WV 25328 304/344-8331 ext. 27 FAX: 304/344-2871 email: jayeph@aol.com

Layman, Karen Engle, 240 Old Stonehouse Rd., Carlisle, PA 17013 717/243-5962 FAX: 717/249-1136 email: layman@comcast.net

Lucero, Rody A., University of Mindanao, Research and Planning, Bolton St., Davao City 8000, PHILIPPINES 011-63 82 227 5456 FAX: 011-63 82 226 3526 email: rhodie@davao.fapenet.org

Maldonado, David, Jr., Iliff School of Theology, 2201 S. University Blvd., Denver, CO 80210 303/765-3102 FAX: 303/777-3387 email: dmaldonado@iliff.edu

May, Felton Edwin, 100 Maryland Ave., N.E., Suite 510, Washington, DC 20002-5611 202/546-3110 FAX: 202/546-3186 email: bishopmay@bwcumc.org

McCumons, Brent L., 315 W. Larkin St., Midland, MI 48640 517/835-6797 ext. 17 email: bmccumons@fumcmid.org

Meinhardt, Heinrich, Tessenowstr. 51 D-13437 Berlin, GERMANY 49-30-414-1236 FAX: 49-30-409-14879 email: berlin.nord@emk.de

Monga, Kalamba Kabonze, c/o pastor Disu/Tresorerie Generale Eglise, Methodiste Unie, Av. Likaski, Lubumbashi, Democratic Republic of the Congo, 260/22-28535 FAX: 871/683-025522 email: afenk@maf.org

Moreno, David J., 123 N. Sugar Rd., Edinburg, TX 78539 956/381-4463 FAX: 956/381-1728 email: applenow@aol.com

Navas, Hector M., POB 1736, Tarpon Springs, FL 34688-1736 727/641-5749 FAX: 727/934-1600 email: hec-no@worldnet.att.net

Ngaue, Renei, 788 W. 94th St., Los Angeles, CA 90044 323/757-8637 FAX: 310/970-1713

Ntambo, Nkulu Ntanda, United Methodist Church, B.P 11237, Chingola, Zambia 260-22-28535 FAX: 871-683-025522 email: TGMETHO@MWANGAZA.CD

Owan, Kasap T., c/o Jeff Hoover, 1313, Ave. Ndjamena, Lubumbashi, Democrratic Republic of the Congo email: mulungwishi@maf.org

Palmer, Gregory V., 500 E. Court Ave., Suite C, Des Moines, IA 50309-2019 515/283-1996 FAX: 515-283-8672 email: Bishop.Palmer@iaumc.org

Palmer, Ruth G., 2001 Holcombe Blvd., #1206, Houston, TX 77030 713/223-8131 FAX: 713-225 3449 email: rpalmer@wesleyhousehouston.org

Peabody, Joe P., 500 South Thornton Ave., Dalton, GA 30720 706/278-8494 email: joepeabod@alltel.net

Peters, Rhoda A., 1911 Hurstbourne Cir., Louisville, KY 40220 502/491-0809 email: RGPtrs@aol.com

Rader, Sharon Zimmerman, 750 Windsor St., Suite 303, Sun Prairie, WI 53590 608/837-8526 FAX: 608/837-0281 email: szrader@aol.com

Randall, Beth, PO Box 316, Leesburg, GA 31763 229/759-6506 email: beth@randall.us

Richardson, Gerald, 1217 Delaware Ave., #902, Buffalo, NY 14209 716/885-0701 FAX: 716/887-3365 email: geraldrichardson@oasas.state.ny.us

Rodriguez, Leonardo, POB 143491, Villa Serena, PUERTO RICO 00622-3491 787/879-4132 email: eagle2258@yahoo.com

Rohlfs, Erika, 3401 Amherst Circle, #111, Bedford, TX 76021 817/247-1846 email: supererika@yahoo.com

Saunkeah, Ann A., 5332 South Columbia Ave., Tulsa, OK 74105 918/747-3660 FAX: 918/747-3664 email: asaunke@gbgm-umc.org

Schnase, Robert, POB 2558, McAllen, TX 78502 956/686-3784 FAX: 956/664-0204 email: rsmcfirst@aol.com

Sheldon, Barbara P., 304 East Mulvane, Mulvane, KS 67110 316/777-4197 FAX: 316/777-4197 email: bsheldon@prodigy.net

Sherrill, William N., 3231 Blenheim Pl., Winston-Salem, NC 27106 336/765-6186 email: drnugz27@yahoo.com

Shumake-Keller, Michele Sue, 4240 Blue Ridge Blvd., Suite 700, Kansas City, MO 64133-1708 816/743-9098 FAX: 816/743-0782 email: mshumake-keller@swbell.net

Stanovsky, Elaine J., United Methodist Office, 2112 Third Ave., Suite 300, Seattle, WA 98121-2333 206/728-7462 FAX: 206/728-8442 email: elainejws@pnwumc.org

Stepanova, Elena, 4-142 Voevodina St., Ekaterinburg 620014, RUSSIAN FEDERATION 734-32-714255 FAX: 734-32-761784 email: sea@ekt.ru

Stouffer, Sarah, 40 Orchard St., Hanover, PA 17331 717/632-1626 email: basyouth@aol.com

Streiff, Patrick, Plaenkestrassee 17a, Neuchatel CH-2502 Bvel., SWITZERLAND 41-32-725-2850 FAX: 41-32-725-2850 email: patrick.streiff@umc-europe.org

Tan, Rev. Wee-Li, 10 Bricketts Mill Rd., Suite 5, Hampstead, NH 03841 603/329-4444 FAX: 603/329-4430 email: wee-li@umfne.org

Thompson, Lenora, 45 E. City Line Ave., No. 422, Bala Cynwyd, PA 19004 215/473-8219 FAX: 215/473-3333 email: lenorathompson@hotmail.com

Wolfe, Thomas V., Syracuse Univ., Hendricks Chapel, Syracuse, NY 13244 315/443-2902 FAX: 315/443-4128 email: tvwolfe@syr.edu
Yoshino, Mariellen Sawada, 566 N. 5th St., San Jose, CA 95112 408/295-0367 email: msawada@flash.net

STAFF

1001 Nineteenth Avenue, South
POB 340007
Nashville, TN 37203-0007
615/340-7400 FAX: 615/340-7048
Web site: www.gbhem.org

General Secretary's Office: 615/340-7356
General Secretary: **Del Pino, Jerome King**
 email: jkdelpino@gbhem.org
Executive Assistant to General Secretary: **vacant,** 615/340-7356

Office of Administration 615/340-7400

Treasurer and Chief Financial Officer: **vacant,** 615/340-7359
Human Resources Manager: **Stacker, Cheryl,** 615/340-7360
 email: cstacker@gbhem.org

Division of Ordained Ministry (DOM): 615/340-7389 email:
 dom@bghem.org
Associate General Secretary: **Moman, Mary Ann,** 615/340-7357
 FAX: 615/340-7048 email: mmoman@gbhem.org
Assistant General Secretary: **Barrett, Patricia,** 615/340-7397
 FAX: 615/340-7358 email: pbarrett@gbhem.org
Assistant General Secretary: **Kohler, Robert F.,** 615/340-7388
 FAX: 615/340-7337 email: bkohler@gbhem.org

DOM Administration Team: 615/340-7389 FAX: 340-7048
Team Leader: **Lane, Susan,** 615/340-7357
 email: slane@gbhem.org

DOM Education Team: 615/340-7388 FAX: 615/340-7377
Team Leader/Director of Professional Development: **Wood, Anita,**
 615/340-7371 email: awood@gbhem.org

Course of Study Coordinator: **Daye, Lynn,** 615/340-7416
  email: ldaye@gbhem.org
Deacon & Cert. Studies Coordinator: **Heist, Linda,** 615/340-7335
  email: lheist@gbhem.org

DOM/United Methodist Endorsing Agency, 615/340-7411
  FAX: 615/340-7358
Team Leader/Director of Endorsement: **Hill, Greg,** 615/340-7363
  email: ghill@gbhem.org

DOM/Enlistment/Candidacy Team: 615/340-7374 FAX: 615/340-7395
Team Leader/Director of Conference Relations: **Rubey, Sharon,**
  615/340-7372 email: srubey@gbhem.org
Director of Enlistment: **Hartley, Harold V., III,** 615/340-7405
  email: hhartley@gbhem.org
Candidacy Coordinator: **Kinslow, Rebecca,** 615/340-7374
  email: rkinslow@gbhem.org
Assessment Coordinator: **Howe, Debbe,** 615/340-7394
  email: dhowe@gbhem.org

DOM/Support/Accountability/Nurture Team: 615/340-7392 FAX:
  615/340-7395
Team Leader/Director of Recruitment & Retreats: **Espino, Saul,**
  615/340-7366 email: sespino@gbhem.org
Director of Continuing Education: **Jackson, Marion,** 615/340-7391
  email: mjackson@gbhem.org
Director of Clergy Supervision & Accountability: **Purushotham,**
  Gwen, 615/340-7393 email: gpurushotham@gbhem.org

Division of Higher Education
  615/340-7402 FAX: 615/340-7379

Associate General Secretary: **Yamada, Ken,**
  email: kyamada@gbhem.org
Assistant General Secretary/Schools, Colleges and Universities:
  Bigham, Wanda D., email: wbigham@gbhem.org
Assistant General Secretary/Campus Ministry: **Felder, Luther B.,**
  email: lfelder@gbhem.org
Assistant General Secretary Black College Fund: **Capers, Joreatha M.,**
  email: jcapers@gbhem.org

77

Director, Campus Ministry: **Hartley, Harold V., III,**
  email: hhartley@gbhem.org
Director, Campus Ministry: **Smith, Lillian,** email: lsmith@gbhem.org

Office of Interpretation 615/340-7383

Interim Executive Director: **Hiers, Terri J.**
Art Director: **Haines, Bret**
Editor, *Quarterly Review:* **Pieterse, Hendrik R.**

Office of Loans and Scholarships 615/340-7342
Executive Director: **Current-Felder, Angella P.**

RELATED UNITS

Africa University Development Office
POB 340007, Nashville, TN 37203-0007
615/340-7438 FAX: 615/340-7290 email: audevoffice@gbhem.org

Associate Vice-Chancellor for Institutional Advancement: **Salley,**
  James H., email: jsalley@gbhem.org
Director of Development: **Rollins, F. Lloyd,** 703/333-5246
  email: flrollins@msn.com
Director of Planned Giving: **Jenkins, Elaine,** 615/340-7428
  email: ejenkins@gbhem.org

Africa University
Mutare, Zimbabwe Web site: www.africau.edu

United Methodist Higher Education Foundation
  615/340-7386 800/811-8110 FAX: 615/340-7330

President/CEO: **Miller, George M.** email: gmiller@gbhem.org
Executive Vice President: **Davis, Cheryl B.**
  email: cdavis@gbhem.org
Vice President of Development: Historically Black Colleges and
  Universities Endowment: **Hemphill, Rhonnie**
  email: rhemphill@gbhem.org

GENERAL BOARD OF PENSION AND HEALTH BENEFITS

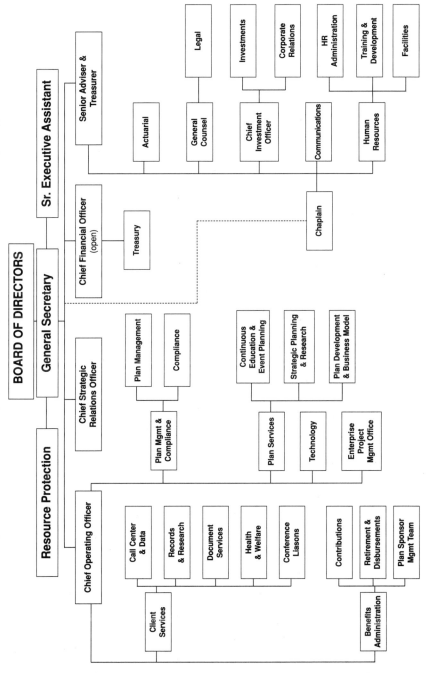

BOARD OF DIRECTORS

Sr. Executive Assistant

Resource Protection	General Secretary	Senior Adviser & Treasurer

Senior Adviser & Treasurer
- Actuarial — Legal
- General Counsel — Investments
- Chief Investment Officer — Corporate Relations
- Communications
- Chaplain
- Human Resources — HR Administration
  - Training & Development
  - Facilities

Chief Financial Officer (open)
- Treasury

Chief Strategic Relations Officer
- Plan Mgmt & Compliance
  - Plan Management
  - Compliance
- Plan Services
  - Continuous Education & Event Planning
  - Strategic Planning & Research
- Technology
- Enterprise Project Mgmt Office
  - Plan Development & Business Model

Chief Operating Officer
- Client Services
  - Call Center & Data
  - Records & Research
  - Document Services
  - Health & Welfare
  - Conference Liasons
- Benefits Administration
  - Contributions
  - Retirement & Disbursements
  - Plan Sponsor Mgmt Team

GENERAL BOARD OF PENSION AND HEALTH BENEFITS
www.gbophb.org

EXECUTIVE COMMITTEE
Chairperson: **Morris, William W.**
Vice Chairperson: **Blake, Bruce P.**
Recording Secretary: **Peak, Diane**
Chairperson, Asset/Liability, **Green, William**
Chairperson, Pension & Welfare Benefits: **O'Neill, Dan**
Chairperson, Board Life and Work: **Garn, Cyndy L.**
Chairperson, Health Benefits: **Huffman, Joel**
Chairperson, Resources: **Williams, Idalene R.**
Chairperson, Social Responsibility: **Wilson, Peary**

DIRECTORS

Bishops
Blake, Bruce P., POB 60467, Oklahoma City, OK 73146 405/530-2025
   FAX: 405/530-2040 email: cnoble@okumc.org
Chamness, Ben, 464 Bailey, Fort Worth, TX 76107-2153 817/877-5222
   FAX: 817/332-4609 email: bishop@ctcumc.org
Morris, William W., 520 Commerce St., Suite 201, Nashville, TN
   37203-3714 615/742-8834 FAX: 615/742-3726
   email: umoffice@aol.com

Addison, Rubielee, 76 Highway, New Hope Rd., Clemson, SC 29633
   864/654-1107 FAX: 864/653-8032 email: addison2@mindspring.com
Brackey, Donald, 518 Davis St., Evanston, IL 60201 847/492-1640
   FAX: 847/492-1683 email: BrackeyConsulting@compuserve.com
Branscome, James L., 10330 Staples Mill Rd.,Glen Allen, VA 23060
   804/521-1100 FAX: 804/521-1172 email: jimbranscome@vaumc.org
Butler, Monica, Frank Russell Co., 909 A St., Tacoma, WA 98402
   253/596-2417 FAX: 253/594-1885 email: mbutler@russell.com
Colbert, J. D., 1517 NW 37th St., Oklahoma City, OK 73118 405/946-
   2265 FAX: 405/528-4391 email: nanba@ionet.net
Ewing, E. Keith, POB 1747, Lakeland, FL 33802-1747 863/688-5563,
   ext. 152 FAX: 863/688-5563, ext. 152 email: ekewing@flumc.org
Garn, Cyndy L., 471 E. Broad St., Suite 1108, Columbus, OH 43215
   614/222-0602 FAX: 614/326-1586 email: cyndylg@aol.com

Gebhardtsbauer, Ron, 2804 27th St., N.W., Washington, DC 20008-4102 202/785-7868 202/872-1948 email: gebhardtsbauer@actuary.org

Green, William, 750 Washington Blvd., 6th Floor, Stamford, CT 06901, 203/961-0408 ext. 313 FAX: 203/961-0424 email: wlg@federal-street.com

Huffman, Joel, 1550 E. Meadowbrook Ave., Ste. 200, Phoenix, AZ 85014-4040 602/266-6956, ext. 712 FAX: 602/266-5343 email: joel@desertsw.org

Lee, B. Lum, 179 Hunting Ridge Rd., Stamford, CT 06903 203/322-0514 email: bowlumlee@aol.com

McGarvey, Gregory, 621 South Range Line Rd., Carmel, IN 46032-2182 317/844-7275 FAX: 317/848-8790 email: gmcgarvey@carmelumc.org

Murapa, Rukudzo, Africa University, POB 1320, Mutare, Zimbabwe, Africa 011/263-20-61611 FAX: 011/263-20-63284 email: vc@syscom.co.zw

Nixon, Harold, 15 Cobblestone Lane, Abilene, TX 79606 325/692-2255 FAX: 325/692-2295 email: abifarm1@aol.com

Nord, Carl O., 302 Pattie, Wichita, KS 67211-1721 316/263-4961 FAX: 316/263-5012 email:wichitacpa@aol.com

Ogden, David, 15800 Bluemound Rd., Suite 400, Brookfield, WI 53005 262/796-3419 FAX: 262/784-9572 email: dave.ogden@milliman.com

O'Neill, Dan, 2200 S. University Blvd., Denver, CO 80210-4797 303/733-3736, ext. 205 FAX: 303/733-1730 email: dan@rmumc.com

Outslay, Marilyn, 8762 SW Firview Pl., Aloha, OR 97007 503/649-9801 FAX: 503/649-2651 email: XTUC2@aol.com

Paul, Doris Brown, 751 Channing Dr., NW, Atlanta, GA 30318-2504 404/892-1776 FAX: 404/892-1089

Peak, Diane, 276 Essex St., POB 249, Lawrence, MA 01842-0449 978/682-8055 ext. 14 FAX: 978/682-1171 email: dlp@neumc.org

Reistroffer, Dianne, Louisville Presbyterian Seminary, 1044 Alta Vista Rd., Louisville, KY 40205-1798 800/264-1839 FAX: 502/895-1096 email: dreistroffer@lpts.edu

Rhoads, Carl E., III, 527 North Blvd., Baton Rouge, LA 70802 225/346-1646 FAX: 225/383-2652 email: crhoads@bellsouth.net

Schoener, Sue Wolfe, Franklin County Sheriff, Assistant Human Resource Director, 370 S. Front St., Columbus OH 43215 614/462-5758 FAX: 614/462-3560 email: swschoener@aol.com

Schwab, Penney, 1052 C Rd., Copeland, KS 67837 620/275-1766 ext. 225 FAX: 620/275-4729 email: pschwab@ummam.org

Stegall, Karl K., First UMC, 2416 W. Cloverdale Park, Montgomery, AL 36106 334/834-8990 FAX: 334/834-4333
email: kstegall@fumcmontgomery.org
Thornton, Randall, 2516 Boyce Fairview Rd., Alvaton, KY 42122 270/842-6667
Velez, Samuel, Zion UMC, POB 305, 1 N. Main St., E. Prospect, PA 17317-0305 717/252-1800 FAX: 717/252-0531
email: zionep@juno.com
Williams, Idalene R., 13421 Larimore Ave., Omaha, NE 68164 402/457-2669 FAX: 402/457-2256
email: iwilliams@metropo.mccneb.edu
Wilson, Peary, 5552 Limelight Ln., Rapid City, SD 57702 605/343-3172 FAX: 605/343-4684 email: swds1@juno.com
Wyman, William C., Jr., POB 18005, Charlotte, NC 28218 704/535-2260, ext. 129 FAX: 704/537-7710 email: bwyman@wnc-cumc.org

AT-LARGE MEMBERS

Holland, Lou, Holland Capital Management, One N. Wacker Dr., Suite 700, Chicago, IL 60606 312/553-4836 FAX: 312/553-4848
email: lholand@hollandcap.com
Kottke, Emmett, 455 S. Fourth Ave., Suite 1400, Louisville, KY 40202 502/587-8851 FAX: 502/587-8855 email: cdkottke@aye.net
Mann, Jessica, 2511 Orleans Ave., Lakeland, FL 33803-1747 863/683-1313 FAX: 863/683-1913 email: jmann911@aol.com
Pinkerton, Jerry, 9327 Canter Dr., Dallas, TX 75231 214/812-4729 FAX: 214/812-5722 email: J.Pinkerton@sbcglobal.net
Walker, Donna, Twin Quest Advisors, Three Greenich Office Park, Five Weaver St., 3rd Floor, Greenich, CT 06830 203/422-0120 FAX: 203/422-0125 email: dwalker@barbnet.com
Wrisley, Norton L. (Bud), 29360 Pamoosa Ln., Valley Center, CA 92082 858/759-2995 FAX: 858/759-1334
email: lnwrisley@hotmail.com

STAFF

1201 Davis Street, Evanston, IL 60201
847/869-4550 FAX 847/475-5061
Web site: www.gbophb.org

AGENCY MANAGEMENT STAFF

General Secretary: **Boigegrain, Barbara A.**, 847/866-4200
email: bboigegrain@gbophb.org
Senior Executive Assistant: **Neal, Christine,** 847/866-4201
email: cneal@gbophb.org
Senior Advisor to the General Secretary and Treasurer: **Whitson-Schmidt, Gale,** 847/866-4218 email: gwhitson-schmidt@gbophb.org
Chief Operating Officer: **Donaghey, Kevin,** 847/866-4300
email: kdonaghey@gbophb.org
Chief Strategic Relations Officer: **Bedell, Woody,** 847/866-2734
email: wbedell@gbophb.org
Managing Director, Client Services: **Evans-Vantrease, Kimberly,**
email: kevans@gbophb.org
Chief Investment Officer: **Zellner, Dave,** 847/866-4698
email: dzellner@gbophb.org
General Counsel: **Hirsen, Sarah,** 847/866-4644
email: shirsen@gbophb.org
Manager, Benefits Administration: **Reid, Debbie,** 847/866-4576
email: dreid@gbophb.org
Managing Director, Human Resources: **Livernois, Gertrude,**
847/866-4579 email: glivernois@gbophb.org
Director of Actuarial: **Schilling, Lisa,** 847/866-5276
email: l schilling@gbophb.org
Director of Corporate Relations: **Bullock Mixon, Vidette,** 847/866-5293 email: vmixon@gbophb.org
Senior Communications Strategist: **Lee, Mike,** 847/866-4561
email: mlee@gbophb.org

BOARD OF
THE UNITED METHODIST PUBLISHING HOUSE

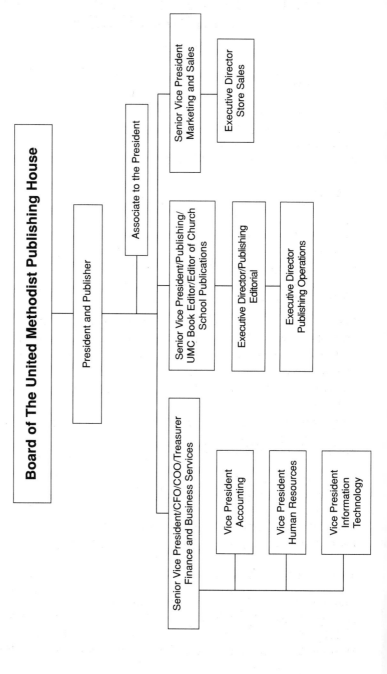

Board of The United Methodist Publishing House

President and Publisher

Associate to the President

Senior Vice President/CFO/COO/Treasurer
Finance and Business Services

Vice President
Accounting

Vice President
Human Resources

Vice President
Information
Technology

Senior Vice President/Publishing/
UMC Book Editor/Editor of Church
School Publications

Executive Director/Publishing
Editorial

Executive Director
Publishing Operations

Senior Vice President
Marketing and Sales

Executive Director
Store Sales

BOARD OF THE UNITED METHODIST PUBLISHING HOUSE
www.umph.org

OFFICERS

Chair: **McCoy, Myron F.**
Vice Chair: **Hatcher, William**
Secretary: **Davis, Judy K.**
President and Publisher: **Alexander, Neil M.**

MEMBERS

Bishops
Christopher, Sharon A. Brown, 400 Chatham Rd., Suite 100, Springfield, IL 62704
Pennel, Joe E., Jr., POB 1719, Glen Allen, VA 23060

North Central Jurisdiction

Lutz, Benis, 641 W. Main St., Ashville, OH 43103
McCoy, Myron F., 5123 Truman Rd., Kansas City, MO 64127
McRee, Edward B., 123 North East St., Eaton Rapids, MI 48827
Streiff, Fritz C., P.O. Box 631, Akron, OH 44309
Walker, Katharine Lehman, 102 N. Chauncey Ave., West Lafayette, IN 47906
Womeldorff, Porter, 735 Country Manor Dr., Decatur, IL 62521

Northeastern Jurisdiction

Daugherty, Ruth, 1936 N. Eden Rd., Lancaster, PA 17601
Hershberger, Nyle M., 318 Kerr Dr., Johnstown, PA 15904
Hope, Garey, 23109 Columbus Rd., Columbus, NJ 08022
Keels, Bernard, 69 E. Main St., Newark, DE 19711-4645
Pritts, Deborah L., 25 Academy St., Windsor, NY 13865

South Central Jurisdiction

Bodenhamer, Pat D., 715 Center St., Little Rock, AR 72201
Branton, L. Ray, 10026 Ferry Creek Dr., Shreveport, LA 71106-8406
Heare, Jerry, 7320 Mopac No., Suite 101, Austin, TX 78731
Holmes, Lucinda S., 807 West 132nd Terrace, Kansas City, MO 64145

Holmes, Zan W., Jr., 6910 Robin Rd., Dallas, TX 75209
Howard, J. N., 3865 Fiery Gizzard Rd., South Pittsburg, TN 37380
Matherson, Thalia F., 1750 Windmill Hill Lane, DeSoto, TX 75115
Smith, Hiram, 400 Comanche Dr., DeLeon, TX 76444

Southeastern Jurisdiction

Alford, Ben R., 4643 Goodman Rd., Adams, TN 37010
Dixon, J. D., POB 117, 315 Hartford Rd., Hawesville, KY 42348
Finger, James M., 24 Corporate Blvd., Jackson, TN 38305
Kilpatrick, Joe W., 10 Perimeter Park Dr., Suite 100, Atlanta, GA 30341
Mathison, John Ed, 6000 Atlanta Hwy., Montgomery, AL 36117
McAlilly, Stephen L., 109 S. Broadway, Tupelo, MS 38804
McGuirt, Betty Moss, POB 444, Pawley Island, SC 29585
Toney, Carol, POB 6654, Huntsville, AL 35824

Western Jurisdiction

Davis, Judy K., 545 W. 10th St., Broomfield, CO 80020
Goto, Shinya, 1798 Scenic Ave., #400, Berkeley, CA 94709

Central Conference

Fuentes, Vilma May A., Marlboro Drive—Tahimik Ave., Km. 6, Matina, 8000 Davao City, PHILIPPINES

ADDITIONAL MEMBERS

Carcaño, Minerva G., Metropolitan District Ofc., 1505 SW 18th, Portland, OR 97201-2524
Hatcher, William, 104 Dumbarton Dr., Statesboro, GA 30458
Job, Rueben P., 4900 Huffman Rd., Goodlettsville, TN 37072
Kimbrough, Walter, 3144 Cascade Rd., SW, Atlanta, GA 30311
Smith, Donna Strickland, Grace UMC, 846 Faith Road, Salisbury, NC 28146
Tribble, Jefferey L., Sr., 9544 S. Leavitt St., Chicago, IL 60643
Wheless, Kim, 7710 Woodway, Houston, TX 77063
Yoon, Dae-Sob, 241 Townsend Ave., Conneaut, OH 44030

STAFF

201 Eighth Avenue South, Nashville, TN 37203
615/749-6000 FAX: 615/749-6079
Web site: www.umph.org

Administrative Staff of The United Methodists Publishing House

President and Publisher: **Alexander, Neil M.,** 615/749-6327
    FAX: 615/749-6510 email: nalexander@umpublishing.org
Associate to the President & Publisher/CAO: **Smith, Judith E.,**
    615/749-6034 FAX: 749-6510 email: jesmith@umpublishing.org
Administrative Assistant: **Jenkins, Velma,** 615/749-6328 FAX: 749-
    6510 email: vjenkins@umpublishing.org
Communications Coordinator: **Wyatt, Kimberly,** 615/749-6329
    FAX: 749-6510 email: kwyatt@umpublishing.org
Executive Director of Communications & Strategic Projects: **Allen,**
    Fred, 615/749-6331 FAX: 749-6510 email: fallen@umpublishing.org
Senior Vice President, Publishing/UMC Book Editor/Editor of
    Church School Publications: **Olson, Harriett Jane,** 615/749-6403
    FAX: 615/749-6512 email: holson@umpublishing.org
Executive Director of Publishing Operations, **Gilbert, Thomas A.,**
    615/749-6933 FAX: 615/749-6512 email: tgilbert@umpublishing.org
Executive Director/Publishing - Editorial: **Dean, Mary Catherine,**
    615/749-6792 FAX: 615/749-6512
    email: mdean@umpublishing.org
Senior Vice President, Finance and Business Services/CFO/COO/
    Treasurer, **Wallace, Larry L.,** 615/749-6214 FAX: 615/749-6236
    email: lwallace@umpublishing.org
Vice President, Accounting: **Gaines, Tammy,** 615/749-6271
    FAX: 615/749-6236 email: tgaines@umpublishing.org
Vice President, Human Resources, **Meadors, Alyce,** 615/749-6367
    FAX: 615/749-6704 email: ameadors@umpublishing.org
Vice President, Information Technology/CIO Information
    Technology: **Linville, Larry,** 615/749-6005 FAX: 615/749-6967
    email: llinville@umpublishing.org
Executive Director of Technology: **Cunningham, Mike,** 615/749-6554
    FAX: 615/749-6966 email: mcunningham@umpublishing.org
Senior Vice President, Marketing and Sales: **Kowalski, Edward,**
    615/749-6044 FAX: 615/749-6417
    email: ekowalski@umpublishing.org
Executive Director of Store Sales: **Recio, Michael,** 615/749-6059
    FAX: 615/749-6056 email: mrecio@umpublishing.org

Finance and Business Services

Senior Vice-President/CFO/COO/Treasurer, Finance and Business
Services: **Wallace, Larry L.,** 615/749-6214
FAX: 615/749-6236 email: lwallace@umpublishing.org
Administrative Office Manager: **Acuff, Barbara,** 615/749-6215
FAX: 615/749-6236 email: bacuff@umpublishing.org
Vice President, Accounting: **Gaines, Tammy,** 615/749-6271
FAX: 615/749-6236 email: tgaines@umpublishing.org
Administrative Assistant: **Smith, Rachel,** 615/749-6263
FAX: 615/749-6236 email: rasmith@umpublishing.org
Inventory and Distribution Services Director: **Loggins, Robert,**
615/749-6203 FAX: 615/749-6078
email: rloggins@umpublishing.org
Production and Property Services Director: **Murphy, Billy,** 615/749-
6326 FAX: 615/749-6313 email: bmurphy@umpublishing.org
Risk & Operations Services Director: **Dillard, Michael K.,** 615/749-
6270 FAX: 615/749-6050 email: kdillard@umpublishing.org
Customer Care Director: **Jones, Daniel A.,** 615/749-6838 FAX
615/749-6417 email: djones@umpublishing.org

Human Resources

Vice President: **Meadors, Alyce,** 615/749-6367 FAX: 615/749-6704
email: ameadors@umpublishing.org
Administrative Services Manager: **Manning, Cherri,** 615/749-6368
FAX: 615/749-6704 email: cmanning@umpublishing.org
Compensation Manager: **Hahn, Kevin,** 615/749-6495
FAX: 615/749-6366 email: khahn@umpublishing.org
Employment Manager: **Knight, Cindy,** 615/749-6443
FAX: 615/749-6366 email: cknight@umpublishing.org
Benefits Manager/Health & Safety Officer: **Thorpe, Robbie,** 615/749-
6339 FAX: 615/749-6415 email: rthorpe@umpublishing.org
Training & Development Manager: **Robinson, Cathy,** 615/749-6887
FAX: 615/749-6366 email: crobinson@umpublishing.org

Information Technology

Vice President/CIO Information Technology: **Linville, Larry,**
615/749-6005 FAX: 615/749-6967 email: llinville@umpublishing.org
Executive Director/IT: **Cunningham, Mike,** 615/749-6554 FAX:
615/749-6966 email: mcunningham@umpublishing.org
Planning and Projects Mgt. Coordinator: **Hunter, Angela,**
615/749-6006 FAX: 615/749-6970 email: ahunter@umpublishing.org
Applications Director: **Cashion, Steve,** 615/749-6547
FAX: 615/749-6984 email: scashion@umpublishing.org
Customer Support Director: **Hill, Linda,** 615/749-6143
FAX: 615/749-6986 email: lhill@umpublishing.org

Database Management Director: **Heile, Dan,** 615/749-6566
FAX: 615/749-6985 email: dheile@umpublishing.org

Marketing and Sales

Senior Vice President, Marketing and Sales: **Kowalski, Edward,**
615/749-6044 FAX: 615/749-6417 email: ekowalski@umpublishing.org
Product Database & Adm. Manager: **Stacy, Connie,** 615/749-6409
FAX: 615/749-6417 email: cstacy@umpublishing.org
Executive Director of Store Sales: **Recio, Michael,** 615/749-6059 FAX:
615/749-6056 email: mrecio@umpublishing.org
Cokesbury Stores (see listing under Cokesbury)
Direct Sales Director: **Handy, Stephen E.,** 615/749-6640
FAX: 615/749-6578 email: shandy@umpublishing.org
e-Commerce Director: **Booher, Jody,** 615/749-6735 FAX: 615/749-
6725 email: jbooher@umpublishing.org
Director - Store Operations and Events: **Barnes, Jeff,** 615/749-6682
FAX: 615/749-6056 email: jbarnes@umpublishing.orgs
Creative Director: **Chalfant, Kim,** 615/749-6144 FAX: 615/749-6417
email: kchalfant@umpublishing.org
Special Projects/Products Director: **Heinlein, John,** 615/749-6803
FAX: 615/749-6172 email: jheinlein@umpublishing.org
Strategic Alliances/Business & Marketing Services: **Bruner, Linda,**
615/749-6155 FAX: 615/749-6417 email: lbruner@umpublishing.org
Wholesale Sales Director: **Williams, Carol,** 615/749-6451
FAX: 615/749-6372 email: cwilliams@umpublishing.org
Customer Database/Promotion Planning Director: **Blair, Alan,**
615/746-6466 FAX: 615/746-6417 email: ablair@umpublishing.org

Publishing

Senior Vice President, Publishing (UMC Book Editor and Editor of
Church School Publications: **Olson, Harriett Jane,** 615/749-6403
FAX: 615/749-6512 email: holson@umpublishing.org
Administrative Assistant: **Emily, Susan,** 615/749-6404
FAX: 615/749-6512 email: semily@umpublishing.org
Executive Director/Publishing - Editorial: **Dean, Mary Catherine,**
615/749-6792 FAX: 615/749-6512
email: mdean@umpublishing.org
Executive Director Publishing Operations: **Gilbert, Thomas A.,**
615/749-6933 FAX: 615/749-6512 email: tgilbert@umpublishing.org
Copy Editing Manager: **Johnston, Mada,** 615/749-6375
FAX: 615/749-6128 email: mjohnston@umpublishing.org
Marketing Research Manager: **Smith, Amy,** 615/749-6860

FAX: 615/749-6056 email: asmith@umpublishing.org
Rights & Permissions Contact: **Porter, Barb,** 615/749-6268
FAX: 615/749-6128 email: bporter@umpublishing.org

Market Business Units

Academic/Professional Resources Director: **Kutsko, John,** 615/749-6302 email: jkutsko@umpublishing.org
Adult and General Interest Resources Director: **Dean, Mary Catherine,** 615/749-6792 email: mdean@umpublishing.org
Children's Resources Director: **Pon, Marjorie,** 615/749-6219 email: mpon@umpublishing.org
Congregational Resources Director: **Johannes, Mary,** 615/749-6191 email: mjohannes@umpublishing.org
Disciple Director: **Deming, Lynne,** 615/749-6334 email: ldeming@umpublishing.org
Bible, ePublishing and Reference Director: **Franklyn, Paul,** 615/749-6733 email: pfranklyn@umpublishing.org
Korean and Spanish Language Resources Director: **Won, Dal Joon,** 615/749-6768 email: djwon@umpublishing.org
Music Resources Director: **Gnegy, Bill,** 615/749-6181 email: bgnegy@umpublishing.org
New Ventures Director: **Salley, Susan,** 615/749-6736 FAX: 615/749-6152 email: ssalley@umpublishing.org
Church School Publications Editor: **Olson, Harriett Jane,** 615/749-6403
Youth Resources Director: **Shell, Bob,** 615/749-6265 email: bshell@umpublishing.org
Disciple Director: **Deming, Lynne,** 615/749-6334 email: ldeming@umpublishing.org

Cokesbury Telephone and Mail Orders— National Service Center

201 Eighth Avenue, South, POB 801, Nashville, TN 37202-9931, 800/672-1789 FAX: 1-800/445-8189 TDD/TT: 800/227-4091
Internet Store www.cokesbury.com

Cokesbury Retail Stores

Atlanta (Decatur), GA, 2495 Lawrenceville Hwy., Decatur, GA 30033, 866/211-9322 or 404/320-1034 FAX: 404/320-1201
Manager, **Haverfield, Beth**
Atlanta (NW) GA, Akers Mill Square, 2969 M Cobb Pkwy., Atlanta, GA 30339 866/222-6027 or 770/988-8023 FAX: 770/988-8365
Manager, **Huston, Jim**

Atlanta Presbyterian (The Bookstore), GA, First Presbyterian Church of Atlanta, 1328 Peachtree St., NE. Atlanta, GA 30309 404/897-3382 FAX: 404/897-1495 Assist. Manager, **Sparks, Robert**

Aurora, IL, Yorkshire Plaza, 4358 E. New York St., Aurora, IL 60504 800/552-0823 or 630/585-0996 FAX: 630/585-0997 Manager, **Blumer, Martha**

Austin, TX, Lake Hills Shopping Center, 4211 South Lamar Blvd., Suite B-3, Austin, TX 78704 800/436-3518 or 512/447-5558 FAX: 512/447-5633 Manager, **Pruitt, Rebecca**

Baltimore, MD, Rolling Road Plaza, 1102 N. Rolling Rd., Baltimore, MD 21228 877/758-7134 or 410/788-1900 FAX: 410/747-8093 Manager, **Hostetter, Virginia**

Birmingham, AL, Vestavia Hills Shopping Ctr., 632 Montgomery Hwy, Suite. 100, Birmingham, AL 35216 888/380-6233 or 205/822-5190 FAX: 205/823-1374 Manager, **Jones, Drew**

Blackstone, VA, The Virginia United Methodist Assembly Center, 707 4th St., Blackstone, VA 23824 866/267-4872 or 434/292-7662 FAX: 434/292-7674 Manager, **Wolf, Susie**

Canton, OH, 5110 Whipple Ave., NW, Canton, OH 44718 800/830-9516 or 330/493-0079 FAX: 330/493-8067 Manager, **Sipe, Freda**

Charleston, WV, 612 E. Washington St., Charleston, WV 25301 877/848-9031 or 304/345-9377 FAX: 304/345-2503 Manager, **Roberts, Steve**

Charlotte, NC, 726 Tyvola Rd., Charlotte, NC 28217 866/863-9713 or 704/525-4543 FAX: 704/521-9428 Manager, **Busby, James E.**

Chesapeake, VA, Knell's Ridge Shopping Center, 805 N. Battlefield Blvd., Suite 119, Chesapeake, VA 23320 800/334-1878 or 757/312-0084 FAX: 757/312-0460 Manager, **Fahrig, Rebecca**

Cincinnati, OH, 9180 Winton Rd., Cincinnati, OH 45231 866/277-5101 or 513/521-5111 FAX: 513/521-5157 Manager, **Harris, Brenda**

Clearwater, FL, Clearwater East Shopping Ctr, 2781 Gulf-to-Bay Blvd., Clearwater, FL 33759 877/865-5669 or 727/797-7303 FAX: 727/797-7644 Manager, **Thomas, Gary**

Columbia, SC, 2730 Broad River Rd., Columbia, SC 29210 888/211-5628 or 803/798-3220 FAX: 803/798-2542 Manager, **Richardson, Lizzie**

Columbus, OH, 5520 N. High St., Columbus, OH 43214 866/255-7856 or 614/436-5636 FAX: 614/436-5670 Manager, **Snarr, Natalie J.**

Dallas, TX, 19200 Preston Rd., Ste. 101, Dallas, TX 75252
866/784-5673 or 972/964-5777 FAX: 972/964-5676 Manager,
Whittington, Whit

Denver (Englewood), CO, 730 W. Hampden Ave., Englewood, CO
80110 877/222-1439 or 303/761-5070 FAX: 303/761-6381
Manager, **Friedman, Su**

Des Moines, IA, 3528 Merle Hay Rd., Des Moines, IA 50310
877/231-1594 or 515/278-1631 FAX: 515/276-7929 Manager,
Peterson, Dawn

Detroit (Livonia), MI, Sheldon Place Shopping Center, 15175
Sheldon Place, Plymouth, MI 48170 877/382-8794 Manager,
Mueller, Joan

Fort Worth, TX, 6333 Camp Bowie Blvd., Suite 207, Ft. Worth, TX
76116 866/784-5674 or 817/763-9560 FAX: 817/763-8045 Manager,
Field, Carol

Harrisburg, PA, The Point, 4223 Union Deposit Rd., Harrisburg, PA
17111 877/577-8541 or 717/564-2212 FAX: 717/564-5270 Manager,
Zurcher, Joan

Houston, TX, 3502 W. Alabama at Edloe, Houston, TX 77027
866/784-5672 or 713/621-1755 FAX: 713/621-6201
Manager, **Dillahunty, Gordon**

Indianapolis (Fishers), IN, 8808 E. 116th St., Fishers, IN 46038 800/914-
9934 or 317/849-1551 FAX: 317/578-3960 Manager, **Cross, Bill**

Jackson (Ridgeland), MS, Center Park Shopping Ctr., 1060 E. County
Line Rd., Ste. 1, Ridgeland, MS 39157 877/300-7608 or 601/978-
3827 FAX: 601/978-3724 Manager, **Ingram, Alicia Beam**

Kansas City, MO, 6501 E. 87th St., Kansas City, MO 64138 877/690-
8146 or 816/765-4422 FAX: 816/763-0833 Manager, **Hines, Nancy**

Knoxville, TN, 9915 Kingston Pk., Knoxville, TN 37922 888/279-3715
or 865/693-6750 FAX: 865/693-7926 Manager, **Boring, Clarinda**

Lake Junaluska, NC, 710 Lakeshore Dr., Lake Junaluska, NC 28745
866/439-7684 or 828/456-8746 FAX: 828/452-5983 Manager,
Rathbone, Laura

Leesburg, FL, (Fruitland Park) (Life Enrichment Center) FL
04991 Picciola Rd., Fruitland Park, FL 34731 866/878-4977 or
352/365-0775 FAX: 352/365-1792 Manager, **Stewart, Della**

Lexington, KY, Woodhill Circle Plaza, 1555 E. New Circle Rd.,
Lexington, KY 40509 877/260-0573 or 859/268-0274
FAX: 859/268-1395 Manager, **Adamson, Dinah**

Little Rock, AR, 715 Center St. at Seventh, Little Rock, AR 72201
877/653-7113 (Arkansas Only) or 501/372-4901 FAX: 501/372-7236
Manager, **Albright, Sam**

Lubbock, TX, 4414 82nd at Quaker, Lubbock, TX 79424 800/331-9153 (West Texas & New Mexico Only) or 806/799-0940 FAX: 806/799-3440 Manager, **Cole, Carolyn**

Memphis, TN, Regalia Shopping Ctr., 6150 Poplar Ave., Suite 111, Memphis, TN 38119 877/221-8638 or 901/683-8271 FAX: 901/682-9439 Manager, **Windsor, Brandon**

Mobile, AL Cokesbury Connection at Crossroads Bks & Gifts, 1401 Hillcrest Rd., Mobile, AL 36695 251/776-1515 FAX: 251/639-0752 Assist. Manager, **Reynoso, Lori**

Mt. Sequoyah (Fayetteville), AR, Conference Center, 150 NW Skyline Dr., Fayetteville, AR 72701 888/989-6363 (Arkansas Only) or 479/442-9832 FAX: 479/444-7683 Supervisor, **Bryant, Nora**

Nashville, TN, 301 Eighth Ave. S., Nashville, TN 37203 615/749-6123 FAX 615/749-6072 Manager, **Carty, Anne**

Oklahoma City, OK, Lakewood Shopping Ctr., 6907 N. May Ave., Oklahoma City, OK 73116 866/647-1634 or 405/858-5195 FAX: 405/858-0801 Asst. Manager, **Wise, Julie**

Orlando, FL, Herndon Village Shoppes, 4900 E. Colonial Dr., Orlando, FL 32803 866/283-6113 or 407/228-8052 FAX: 407/228-8990 Manager, **Abarca, David**

Pasadena, CA, 478 E. Colorado Blvd., Pasadena, CA 91101 877/432-8802 or 626/796-5773 FAX: 626/796-0207 Manager, **Clark, Keith**

Philadelphia (King of Prussia), PA, Courtside Square, Bldg. #1, Suite 1100, 150 Allendale Rd., King of Prussia, PA 19406 800/593-9851 or 610/265-3341 FAX: 610/265-7638 Manager, **Bhajjan, Sarita**

Phoenix, AZ, 3425 W. Thunderbird Rd., Ste. 7, Phoenix, AZ 85053 800/617-4550 (Arizona/Nevada) or 602/789-0544 FAX: 602/789-0526 Manager, **Johnson, Gerald**

Pittsburgh (Mars), PA, 19015 Perry Hwy., Mars, PA 16046 800/835-9804 or 724/776-6150 FAX: 724/776-0076 Manager, **Kincaid, Bobi**

Raleigh, NC, North Market Sq., 1669 N. Market Dr., Raleigh, NC 27609 866/265-2665 or 919/872-8810 FAX: 919/876-8764 Manager, **Keen, Cindy**

Richmond, VA, 3700 W. End Dr., Richmond, VA 23294 877/260-0572 or 804/270-1070 FAX: 804/270-0987 Manager, **Thompson, Ellen**

Sacramento (Roseville), CA, Taylor Center, 2740 Marconi Ave., Sacramento, CA 95821 888/768-0142 or 916/485-4896 FAX: 916/485-5263 Manager, **Brockman, Don**

St. Louis (Ballwin), MO, 14560 Manchester Rd., Ballwin, MO 63011 877/837-8806 or 636/230-3336 FAX: 636/527-8488 Manager, **Duncan, Roger**

San Antonio, TX, 1742N. Loop, 1604 East @ Highway 281, Ste. 117, San Antonio, TX 78232 800/732-7881 or 210/525-9685 FAX: 210/490-4731 Manager, **Segundo, Vera**

Seattle (Kirkland), WA, 12703 NE 124th St., Kirkland, WA 98034 800/605-9403 or 425/820-1093 FAX: 425/820-9256 Manager, **Kersten, Lynne**

Syracuse, NY, 2620 Erie Blvd. E., Syracuse, NY 13224 800/615-7354 or 315/445-2161 FAX: 315/446-6812 Manager, **Hickok, Linda**

Teaneck, NJ, 1550 Teaneck Rd., Teaneck, NJ 07666 800/513-5189 or 201/837-0507 FAX: 201/837-1578 Manager, **Cooper, Loretta**

Tulsa, OK, Fontana Shopping Ctr., 4984 S. Memorial, Tulsa, OK 74145 877/281-5809 (Oklahoma Only) or 918/663-9885 FAX: 918/664-2437 Manager, **Green-Young, Brian**

Cokesbury Seminary Stores

Asbury Theological Seminary, 300 N. Lexington Ave., Wilmore, KY 40390 866/855-8252 or 859/858-4242 FAX: 859/858-8137 Manager, **Lindenberg, Jill**

Austin Presbyterian Theological Seminary, 100 E. 27th St., Austin, TX 78705-5797 512/476-9914 FAX: 512/476-6481 Assist. Manager, **Rice, Alisha**

Beeson Divinity School, Sanford University, 800 Lakeshore Dr., Birmingham, AL 35229-2235 205/726-2286 FAX: 205/726-2188 Supervisors, **Parks, John,** and **Nelson, Dave**

Candler School of Theology, Emory University, Emory University, Atlanta, GA 30322 404/727-6336 FAX: 404/727-6561 Assist. Manager, **Black, John**

Central Baptist Theological Seminary, 741 N. 31st St., Kansas City, KS 66102 913/371-2007 FAX: 913/371-2474 Supervisor, **Hugenot, Jerrod**

Duke Divinity School, Old Building, Durham, NC 27706 919/660-3417 FAX: 919/660-3490 Assist. Manager, **Bowie, Christine**

Garrett-Evangelical Theological Seminary, 2121 Sheridan Rd., Evanston, IL 60201 847/866-5204 FAX: 847/866-5205 Assist. Manager Supervisor, **Oladipo, Amos**

General Theological Seminary, 175 Ninth Ave., New York, NY 10011-4977 212/645-1984 FAX: 212/924-4869 Supervisor, **Deaton, Charlie**

Iliff School of Theology, 2201 S. University Blvd., Denver, CO 80210-4798 303/765-1445 FAX: 303/765-1439 Assist. Manager, **Kuemmerlin-McLean, Joanne**

Interdenominational Theological Center (Gammon), 653 Beckwith St. SW, Atlanta, GA 30314 404/525-1414 FAX: 404/524-1550 Store Supervisor, **Robinson, Charletta**

Lancaster Theological Seminary, 555 W. James St., Lancaster, PA 17603 717/393-1077 FAX: 717/393-2846 Supervisor, **Herman, Janice**

Methodist Theological School in Ohio, 3081 Columbus Pk., Delaware, OH 43015 740/362-3385 FAX: 740/362-3132 Supervisor, **Rainsberger, Ray**

Payne Theological Seminary, 1230 Wilberforce Clifton Rd., Wilberforce, OH 45384 937/376-2946 ext. 207 FAX: 937/376-3330 Sales Associates, **Taylor, Harry** and **Taylor, Wilma**

Perkins School of Theology, Southern Methodist University, Selecman Hall Annex, Dallas, TX 75275 214/768-3226 FAX: 214/891-1741 Assist. Manager, **Edwards, Jen**

Pittsburgh Theological Seminary, 616 N. Highland Ave., Pittsburgh, PA 15206 412/362-1691 FAX: 412/362-3726 Supervisor, **Eversmeyer, Janna**

St. Paul School of Theology, 5123 Truman Rd., Kansas City, MO 64127 816/483-2603 FAX: 816/241-9159 Supervisor, **Oyler, John**

Union, (Union Theological Seminary-Richmond, VA), 3406 Brook Rd., Richmond, VA 23227 804/353-6815 FAX: 804/353-9004 Assist. Manager, **Smith, Robin**

United Theological Seminary/Twin Cities, 3000 Fifth St. NW, New Brighton, MN 55112 888/421-4911 or 651/638-1960 FAX: 651/638-1924 Assist. Manager, **Okoneski, Katie**

United Theological Seminary, Bonebrake Hall, 1810 Harvard Blvd., Dayton, OH 45406 937/274-6194 FAX: 937/274-6253 Supervisor, **Hayes, Earl**

Vanderbilt University Divinity School, Rm. G 21A, Divinity School Bldg., 21st & Grand Ave., Nashville, TN 37240 615/322-7230 FAX: 615/343-3423 Assist. Manager, **Murdock, Andrea**

Virginia Theological Seminary, 3737 Seminary Rd., Alexandria, VA 22304 800/368-3756 or 703/370-6161 FAX: 703/370-1429 Manager, **Maddy, Brian**

Wesley Theological Seminary, 4500 Massachusetts Ave. NW, Washington, DC 20016 202/885-8681 FAX: 202/244-6260 Assist. Manager, **Cassedy, Karen**

Disciple Bible Study

201 Eighth Ave, S., POB 801, Nashville, TN 37202-9764 800/672-1789 or 615/749-6068 email: disciple@cokesbury.com

GENERAL COMMISSION ON ARCHIVES AND HISTORY

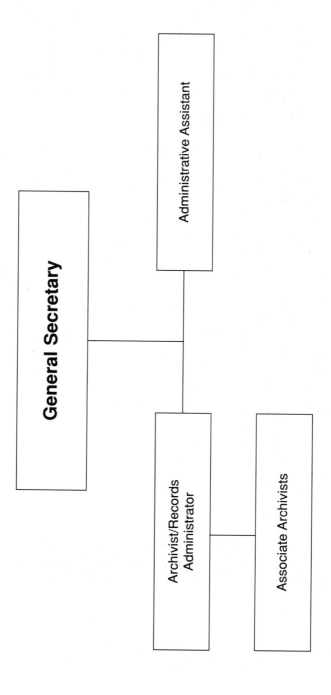

GENERAL COMMISSION ON ARCHIVES AND HISTORY
www.gcah.org

OFFICERS

President - **McCleskey, J. Lawrence**
Vice President - **Toquero, Solito Kuramin**
Secretary - **Thompson, Patricia J.**

MEMBERS

Bishops
McCleskey, J. Lawrence, 4908 Colonial Dr., Suite 108, Columbia, SC 29203 803/786-9486 FAX: 803/754-9327
Toquero, Solito Kuramin, 900 United Nations Ave., POB 756, Manila PHILIPPINES

Beal, Mauzel, 1811 Jefferson St., Conway, AR 72032 501/336-9321 FAX: 501/336-9001 email: beehill@cyberback.com
Dickerson, Dennis C., African Methodist Episcopal, POB 22031, Nashville, TN 37202 615/248-0905 FAX: 615/248-0901 email: WhhButler@cs.com
Getimane, Jose Mario, POB 41, Chicuque Rural Hospital, Maxixe, MOZAMBIQUE 011-258-23-30267 email: hrchicuque@teledata.mz
Hill, Lila, 5175 S. Howry Ln., Meridian, ID 83642-7043 208/362-5220 email: lila25@juno.com
King, William E., 169 Montrose Dr., Durham, NC 27705 919/403-1169 email: william.king@duke.edu
Lawton, Philip, POB 247, Felton, DE 19943 302/284-4186 email: philip.lawton@dol.net
Lee, Koonae Annie, East Meadow United Methodist Church, 470 East Meadow Ave., East Meadow, NY 11554
Lizcano, Ramiro H., 2535 W. New Hope Rd., Rogers, AR 72758 479/636-3325
McIntosh, Debra, 219 Hadden Circle, Brandon, MS 39042 601/974-1077
Mies, Emelie Sims, 2202 Clover Ln., Champaign, IL 61821 217/398-6013 email: emeliemies@netscape.net

Moss, Danny, 4815 South Harvard, Suite 260, Tulsa, OK 74135 918/742-7496

Pyatt, James L., 601 North Pink St., Cherryville, NC 28021 704/435-6732 FAX: 704/435-4468 email: pyatt@juno.com

Quick, William K., 2417 Perkins Rd., Durham, NC 27705 919/493-2967 email: wkquick@aol.com

Schuler, Ulrike, Pahlkestr. 46a, DE-42115 Wuppertal, GERMANY 202/711123 FAX: 202-2712337 email: schuler.stg@wtal.de

Swinson, Daniel L., Morrison UMC, 200 W. Lincolnway, Morrison, IL 61270 815/722-4030 FAX: 815/772-4039 email: swinson@essex1.com

Thompson, Patricia J., POB 538, Morrisville, VT 05661 802/888-2185 email: pajt8817@aol.com

Thrift, Nell, POB 3767, Lakeland, FL 33802 863/688-9276 FAX: 863/680-1912 email: Thriftmail@aol.com

Traster, Jean H., 2014 Iron Horse Ct., Arlington, TX 76017 817/468-8170 email: jeantraster@cs.com

Trigg, Donald, Sharon Center UMC, POB 239, Sharon Center, OH 44274 330/239-1616 FAX: 330/239-2636 email: DLT419@aol.com

Williams, Robert J., St. Andrews UMC, 327 Marlton Pike W., Cherry Hill, NJ 08002 856/429-4469 FAX: 856-427-0383 email: standrewsumc-ch@juno.com

Wimberly, Anne E. Streaty, Interdenominational Theological Center, 700 Martin Luther King Jr. Dr., SW, Atlanta, GA 30314 404/527-7739 FAX: 404/527-0901 email: awimberly@ite.edu

Yale, Stephen, Graduate Theological Union, 2400 Ridge Rd., Berkeley, CA 94709 650/201-7004 email: seyale@earthlink.net

STAFF
36 Madison Ave.,
POB 127
Madison, NJ 07940
973/408-3189 FAX: 973/408-3909
email: cyrigoyen@gcah.org
Web site: www.gcah.org

General Secretary - **Yrigoyen, Charles, Jr.**
Archivist/Records Administrator - **Patterson, L. Dale**
Administrative Assistant - **Merkel, Michelle K.**
Associate Archivist - **Shenise, Mark C.**
Associate Archivist - **Del Duca, Tracey M.**
Librarian - **Woodruff Tait, Jennifer**

GENERAL COMMISSION ON CHRISTIAN UNITY AND INTERRELIGIOUS CONCERNS

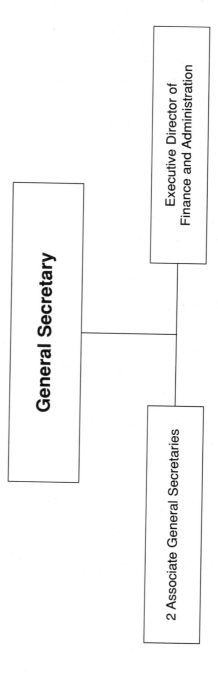

General Secretary

Executive Director of Finance and Administration

2 Associate General Secretaries

GENERAL COMMISSION ON CHRISTIAN UNITY AND INTERRELIGIOUS CONCERNS

www.gccuic-umc.org
email: info@gccuic-umc.org

OFFICERS

President: **Mutti, Albert Frederick**
Vice-President: **Readdean, Shirley**
Secretary: **Cruz, Dalila**

MEMBERS

Bishops

Klaiber, Walter, Wilhelm-Leuschner-Strasse 8, D-60329 Frankfurt, GERMANY 011-49-69-24-25-21-0 FAX: 011-49-69-24-25-21-29 email: emk.kirchenkanzlei@t-online.de

Mutti, Albert Frederick, 4201 SW 15th St., Topeka, KS 66604 785/272-0587 FAX: 785/272-9135 email: kansasbishop@kansaseast.org

Talbert, Melvin G., 108 Rausch Dr., Brentwood, TN 37027 615/309-8096 FAX: 615/661-8576 email: bishopmel@netzero.net

Weaver, Peter D., POB 820, Valley Forge, PA 19482 610/666-9090 FAX: 610/666-9181 email: bishop@epaumc.org

Directors

Aikman, Susanne, 3020 Lowell Blvd., Denver, CO 80211 303/477-8442 email: zsaikman@webtv.net

Bannister, Kathryn, POB 327, Bison, KS 67520 785/356-2067 FAX: 785/356-2581 email: kkbannister@hotmail.com

Barkat, Aslam, 479 Van Voorhis Rd., Morgantown, WV 26505 304/599-6306 FAX: 304/599-8388 email: info@suncrestumc.org

Black, Veena Srinivas, 1095 Apt. J, North Jamestown Rd., Decatur, GA 30033 404/636-2924 email: blackveena@hotmail.com

Brooks, Lonnie D., 8381 Pioneer Dr., Anchorage, AK 99504-4742 907/333-4529 FAX: 907/332-1400 email: lonnieb@acsalask.net

Bryant, Juanita, 3675 Runnymeade, Cleveland Heights, OH 44121 216/382-3559 FAX: 216/382-3516 email: JuanBr41aw@aol.com

Cruz, Dalila, 5622 Evers Rd., #4403, San Antonio, TX 78238 210/521-5540 email: dcruz16@satx.rr.com

Devadhar, Sudarshana, 3724 Dutchman Dr., Baldwinsville, NY 13027 315/635-4873 FAX: 315/635-5005 email: ontariodis@aol.com

Farmer, Penny Dollar, 315 Camp Don Lee Rd., Arapahoe, NC 28510 252/249-0697 FAX: 252/249-0497 email: penny$@donleecenter.org

Fields, James C., Jr., 167 Cord 33, Hanceville, AL 35077 334/242-8990 FAX: 334/242-3960 email: jfields@dir.state.al.us

Fitzner, Marcia E., POB 344, Willard, NM 87063 505/384-2495 FAX: 505/384-9528 email: mefitzner@worldnet.att.net

Glasco, Melvin, 7001 W. Parker Rd., #1227, Plano, TX 75093 972/306-4396 email: melvin_glasco@countrywide.com

Goto, Jennifer Irvine, 1798 Scenic Ave., #400, Berkeley, CA 94709 925/932-7474 email: jenlynnirvine@hotmail.com

Holtsclaw, Thomas G., 755 Brooks Dairy Rd., Roxboro, NC 27573 336/597-9194 email: shalom@esinc.net

Howard, Lula, 4009 Landside Dr., Louisville, KY 40220 502/499-7842 FAX: 502/493-4177 email: lulahoward@aol.com

Inman, Jack, 520 Virginia Dr., Winter Park, FL 32789 407/647-7585 email: Jabuin@aol.com

Jung, Hee-Soo, 1500 N. Casaloma Dr., Suite 305, Appleton, WI 54913-8220 920/991-0548 FAX: 920-991-0549 email: hsjungwisconsinumc.org

Klaiber, Walter, Wilhelm-Leuschner-Strasse 8, D-60329 Frankfurt, GERMANY email: emk.kirchenkanzlei@t-online.de

Lee, Yong, 2027 Polk Dr., Ames, IA 50010-4316 515/232-4053 FAX: 515-294-3072 email: yonglee@iastate.edu

Love, Janice, 419 Edisto Ave., Columbia, SC 29205 803/777-7363 FAX: 803-777-0213 email: love.jan@sc.edu

Marshall, Rachel, 913 Pawnee Drive, Elizabethtown, KY 42701 270/769-3331 270/765-2811 email: Rachel@memorial-umc.org

Matthews, Shelly, 943 Rutherford Rd., Greenville, SC 29609 864/294-3741 FAX: 864/294-2041 email: shelly.matthews@furman.edu

McReynolds, Russell F., 215 North Capitol Ave., Lansing, MI 48933 517/485-9477 email: mcreynoldsumc@voyager.net

Miller, Mark A., 1118 Gresham Rd., Plainfield, NJ 07062 908/226-1757 email: markandrew67@yahoo.com

Moore, Joy J., 204 N. Lexington Ave., Wilmore, KY 40390-1199 859/858-2000 FAX: 859/858-2274 email: joy_moore@asburyseminary.edu

Mulanax, Craig, 14350 West 116th St., #3321, Olathe, KS 66062 cell: 405/204-5856 email: pocoritt@aol.com

Mutti, Albert Frederick, 4201 SW 15th St., Topeka, KS 66604 785/272-0587 FAX: 785/272-9135 email: kansasbishop@kansaseast.org

Niesen, Marianne, 1603 Missoula Ave., Helena, MT 59601 406/442-5643 FAX: 406-449-6587 email: marianneum@aol.com

Nordby, Lars-Erik, Dr. Gattungsvei 9 N-1532, Moss, NORWAY
011-4722932822 FAX: 011-4723330921 email:
lars.erik.nordby@metodistkirken.no
Pope-Levison, Priscilla, School of Theology, Seattle Pacific Univ.,
3307 Third Ave. W., Seattle, WA 98119 206/281-2714
email: popep@spu.edu
Powell, Ida B., 3809 Manton Ln., Lynchburg, VA 24503-3017
804/384-1092 email: idapowell@juno.com
Readdean, Shirley, 2232 Turner Ave., Schenectady, NY 12306
518/372-7065 email: whirrly@earthlink.net
Simmons, Charles, 12955 Memorial Dr., Houston, TX 77079-7302
713/468-8356 FAX: 713 468-8429 email: chucksimmons@mdumc.org
Smith, Sandra Williams, 3459 FM 518 East, League City, TX 77573
281/334-1100 FAX: 281/538-1492 email: pastorsandy@hotmail.com
Stover, Gregory D., 4400 Reading Rd., #1, Cincinnati, OH 45229
513/421-2057 FAX: 513/421-2058 email: gstover@wocumc.org
Talbert, Melvin G., 108 Rausch Dr., Brentwood, TN 37027
615/309-8096 FAX: 615/661-8576 email: bishopmel@netzero.net
Topolewski, John L., 124 Sunset Ave., Vestal, NY 13850 607/687-2417
FAX: 607/687-2134 email: jtopolew@stny.rr.com
Warren, Hulen, 510 Avenue B, Bogalusa LA 70427 985/732-2568 FAX:
985/753-6999 email: pastor@auroraumc.nocoxmail.com
Weaver, Peter D., POB 820, Valley Forge, PA 19482 610/666-9090
FAX: 610/666-9181 email: bishop@epaumc.org
Williams, Jerry Ruth, 1967 Willow Lake Dr., Chesterfield,
MO 63017-7659 636/532-5934 FAX: 636/532-3462
email: micjerbob@aol.com

STAFF

475 Riverside Drive, Room 1300, New York, NY 10115
212/749-3553 FAX: 212/749-3556
Web site: www.gccuic-umc.org

Interim General Secretary: **Talbert, Melvin G.,**
email: mtalbert@gccuic-umc.org
Associate General Secretary: **Marshall, Anne,**
email: amarshall@gccuic-umc.org
Associate General Secretary: **Gamble, Betty,**
email: bgamble@gccuic-umc.org
Executive Director Finance & Administration: **Chapman, Clare J.,**
email: cchapman@gccuic-umc.org

GENERAL COMMISSION ON COMMUNICATION

www.umcom.org

OFFICERS

President: **Oden, William B.**
Vice President: **Novak, Margaret M.**
Chair, Personnel: **Shane, Mertice M.**
Chair, Finance: **Stansell, Elijah A., Jr.**
Chair, Evaluation and Legislative Committee: **Potter-Miller, Jaime**

MEMBERS

Bishops
Fisher, Violet L., 1010 East Ave., Rochester, NY 14607 716/271-3400
    FAX: 716/271-3404 email: nywestarea@aol.com
Oden, William B., POB 600127, Dallas, TX 75360-0127 214/522-6741
    FAX: 214/528-4435 email: DallasBishop@hpumc.org

North Central Jurisdiction

Henderson, Gary R., 23002 Lake Shore Blvd., Euclid, OH 44123-1325
    216/261-1688 FAX: 216/261-9735 email: twingrh@aol.com
Jadhav, Adam, c/o Mrs. Debbie Jadhav, 820 N. Brush College Rd.,
    Decatur, IL 62521 email: ajadhav@students.uiuc.edu
Ling, Stanley T., 32 Wesley Blvd., Worthington, OH 43085
    614/844-6200 800/437-0028 ext. 207 FAX: 614/781-2642
    email: sling@wocumc.org

Northeastern Jurisdiction

Bickerton, Thomas J., The Methodist Bldg., Room 111, 11th &
    Chapline Streets, Wheeling, WV 26003 304/232-5687 FAX: 304/232-
    7505 email: tjbick@aol.com
Potter-Miller, Jaime, 709 Cannall Dr., Somerset, PA 15501 814/243-
    4036 email: onlyme1118@aol.com
Shane, Mertice M., Koehler Fieldhouse, East Stroudsburg University,
    East Stroudsburg, PA 18301-2999 570/422-3067 FAX: 570/422-3665
    email: mshane@po-box.esu.edu

South Central Jurisdiction

Bailey, Charlene M., 15880 S. Blackfoot Ct., Olathe, KS 66062
    913/745-2217 email: lbailey1@myexcel.com
Boyd, C. Lane, 305 N. Baird, Midland, TX 79701 915/682-3701
    FAX: 915/682-3770 email: laneboyd@fumcmidland.org

Loy, O. Fred, POB 1546, Baton Rouge, LA 70821 225/346-0073
FAX: 225/346-3060 email: committeeof100@mindspring.com
Stansell, Elijah A., Jr., 5631 Evening Shore Dr., Houston, TX 77041
281/861-9000 email: eli@wt.net

Southeastern Jurisdiction

Bannister, Chase, 4608 Dolwick Dr., Durham, NC 27713 919/544-2356 email: chase.bannister@duke.edu
Brunk, Joe, POB 100, Booneville, KY 41314 606/593-6126
email: kybrunk@prtcnet.org
Hand, Dawn M., POB 18005, Charlotte, NC 28218 704/535-2260 ext. 122
FAX: 704/567-6117 email: dhand@wnccumc.org
Horton, Alvin J., 1100 Mount Pisgah Dr., Midlothian, VA 23113
804/794-5856 FAX: 804/379-3970 email: alhorton@cavtel.net

Western Jurisdiction

Robinson, Pat, POB 3172, Kenai, AK 99611-3172 907/283-2633
email: rbn@alaska.net

Central Conference

Mundeke, Djamba, 2867 Avenue Des Ecuries, Ngaliema, POB 4727,
Kinshasa II, DEM. REP. OF CONGO 011-243-993-6829 FAX: 011-243-880-3723 email: dmundeke@juno.com

Additional Members

Briddell, David W., 356 Murray Ave., Englewood, NJ 07631
201/567-5183 FAX: 201/567-7813 email: dbriddell@aol.com
Dunlap, Lee Ann, 13486 Kauffman Ave., Sterling, OH 44276
330/939-2401 FAX: 330/939-2401 email: preacher@neo.rr.com
Hygh, Larry, Jr., POB 6006, Pasadena, CA 91102-6006 626/568-7923
FAX: 626/796-7297 email: lhygh@cal-pac.org
Novak, Margaret M., POB 720, Chester, MT 59522 406/759-5538
FAX: 406/759-5892 email: banovak@ttc-cmc.net
Schwartz, Olivia L., 2705 Oxford Circle, Upper Marlboro, MD 20772
301/627-5649 email: ts1@prodigy.net
Zukemura, Leilani L. S., 20 S. Vineyard Blvd., Honolulu, HI 96813
808/536-1864 FAX: 808/531-7354 email: Leilani@hawaii.rr.com

STAFF
United Methodist Communications Headquarters
810 Twelfth Ave., South, Nashville, TN 37203-4744
615/742-5400 FAX: 615/742-5415
Web site: www.umcom.org

UM News Service Office—Washington
Contact Nashville office for new address and telephone number.

UM News Service Office—New York
Contact Nashville office for new address and telephone number.

General Secretary's Office (810 12th Ave., S.)

General Secretary: **Hollon, Larry,** 615/742-5410
email: lhollon@umcom.org

ADMINISTRATION MANAGEMENT TEAM
Deputy General Secretary for Administration/Treasurer, **Thiel, Sherri,** 615/742-5484 email: sthiel@umcom.org
Executive Assistant: **Saunders, Linda,** 615/742-5119
email: lsaunders@umcom.org

Facilities and Operations Team

Team Leader, **Loney, Carlton,** 615/742-5493
email: cloney@umcom.org
Director of Services: **Herity, Sheila,** 615/742-5402
email: sherity@umcom.org
Customer Service Center: Toll-free, 888/346-3862 (888-FINDUMC)
Maintenance: **Byrd, Jeff,** 615/742-5495

Financial Services Team

Team Leader: **Dawson, Tangi,** 615/742-5486
email: tdawson@umcom.org
Accounts Payable Staff Accountant: **Beck, Elaine,** 615/742-5480
email: ebeck@umcom.org
Accounts Receivable Staff Accountant: **Adams, JoAnne,** 615/742-5487
email: jadams@umcom.org

Technology Team

Technology Team Leader: **Smith, Chris,** 615/742-5114 email:
csmith@umcom.org

Database Administrator: **Fusco, John,** 615/742-5447
email: jfusco@umcom.org
Network Support Specialist: **West, Eric,** 615/742-5448
email: ewest@umcom.org
Applications Engineer: **Ridenour, Charlene,** 615/742-5134
email: cridenour@umcom.ogr

Human Resources Team

Team Leader: **Coleman, Newtonia Harris,** 615/742-5412
email: ncoleman@umcom.org
Human Resources Coordinator: **Allen, Helen,** 615/742-5137 email:
hallen@umcom.ogr
Manager, Payroll & Benefits: **Powers, Pat,** 615/742-5498
email: ppowers@umcom.org

PROGRAM MANAGEMENT TEAM

Communications Resourcing Team

Communications Resourcing Team, 888/278-4862 (888/CRT-4UMC)
(http://crt.umc.org)
Communications Resourcing Team Leader: **Nissen, Barbara,**
615/742-5139 email: bnissen@umcom.org
Director of Native People Communications: **Buckley, Ray,** 615/742-
5414 email: rbuckley@umcom.org
Resource Consultant: **Tucker-Shaw, Amelia,** 615/742-5134 email:
atucker-shaw@umcom.org
Resource Consultant: **Noble, Kathy,** 615/742-5441
email: knoble@umcom.ogr
Administrative Assistant: **Jarrett, Deborah,** 615/742-5481
FAX: 615/742-5485 email: djarrett@umcom.ogr

PUBLIC INFORMATION TEAM

Public Information Team Leader: **Drachler, Stephen,** 615/742-5411
email: sdrachler@umcom.org
Editor, **Willis, Nancye,** 615/742-5406 email: nwillis@umcom.org
Production/Administrative Assistant: **Price, Pam,** 615/742-5405
email: pprice@umcom.org

United Methodist News Service (including UMTV)

Director, **Underwood, Ginny,** 615/742-5124
email: gunderwood@umcom.org

Managing Editor, **Tanton, Tim,** 615/742-5473
email: ttanton@umcom.org
Nashville News Director: **Green, Linda,** 615/742-5475
email: lgreen@umcom.ogr
New York, NY News Director: **Bloom, Linda,** 212/870-3803 email:
lbloom@umcom.org
News Writer: **Gilbert, Kathy,** 615/742-5547 email:
kgilbert@umcom.org
Coordinating Producer, **Walsh, Fran,** 615/742-5458
email: fwalsh@umcom.org
Administrative Assistant: **Latham, Laura,** 615/742-5474
email: llatham@umcom.org

UMCom Productions Team

Team Leader, UMCom Productions: **Alexander, Leslie,** 615/742-5429
email: lalexander@umcom.org
Technical Manager: **Nelson, Larry,** 615/742-5459
email: lnelson@umcom.org

Igniting Ministry Team

Office, Toll-free: 877/281-6535 (www. igniting ministry.org)
Team Leader, Igniting Ministry: **Horswill-Johnston, Steve,** 615/742-
5128 email: im@umcom.org
Director of Matching Grants: **Vaughan, Jackie,** 615/742-5140
email: imgrants@umcom.org
Training Manager, **Reece, Emily,** 615/742-5134
email: ereece@umcom.org
Manager, Sales & Fulfillment: **Crawford, Susan,** 615/742-5418
email: scrawford@umcom.org

Connectional Giving Team

Team Leader, UMCom Connectional Giving: **McNish, Kent,** 615/742-
5142 email: kmcnish@umcom.org
Account Executive III: **Dunlap-Berg, Barbara,** 615/742-5489
email: bdunlap-berg@umcom.org
Account Executive II: **Hughes, Celinda,** 615/742-5109
email: chughes@umcom.org
Account Executive II: **Wood, Tracy,** 615/742-5117
email: twood@umcom.org
Director, Print Production and Distribution: **Cunningham, Elsie,**
615/742-5488 email: ecunningham@umcom.org

Product Marketing Team

Team Leader: **Niedringhaus, Charles,** 615/742-5101
  email: cniedringhaus@umcom.org
Igniting Ministry Product Manager, **LaFontaine, Leeticia,** 615/742-5408 email: llafontaine@umcom.org
Calendar and Publications Coordinator: **Carey, Lladale,** 615/742-5104
  email: lcarey@umcom.org
TechShop Coordinator: **Mcatee, Sean,** 615/742-5417
  email: smcatee@umcom.org
EcuFilm Coordinator: **Clark, Carol,** 615/742-5478
  email: cclark@umcom.org

Web Ministry Team

Team Leader: **Downey, Stephen,** 615/742-5434
  email: sdowney@umcom.org
Executive Producer, UMC.org: **Carlisle, Matt,** 615-742-5153
  email: mcarlisle@umcom.org
Internet Resource Consultant: **Russell, Chuck,** 615/742-5444
  email: crussell@umcom.org
Manager, Technical Systems Group: **Mai, Danny,** 615/742-5156
  email: dmai@umcom.org
Web Producer: **Denson, Lane,** 615/742-5764 email: ldenson@umcom.org
Web Programmer: **Ragland, Tom,** 615/742-3551 email: tragland@umcom.org
Internet Technical Support: **Mayfield, Shelia,** 615/742-5422
  email: smayfield@umcom.org
Production Assistant: **Cates, Jennifer,** 615/742-5147 email: jcates@umcom.org

Information Team

InfoServ

Director of InfoServ: **Holly, Mary Lynn,** 615/742-5424
  email: mholly@umcom.org

Publications

Publisher: **Hollon, Larry,** 615/742-5410 email: lhollon@umcom.org
Art Director: **Story, Suzanne,** 615/742-5131 email: sstory@umcom.org
Photographer: **DuBose, Mike,** 615/742-5150
  email: mdubose@umcom.org
Managing Editor, *Interpreter:* **Colvin, Gwen,** 615/742-5106
  email: gcolvin@umcom.org
Associate Editor, *Interpreter:* **Butler, Joey,** 615/742-5105
  email: jbutler@umcom.org

Director, Korean Language Resources, *United Methodists in Service*:
Cho, Sang Yean, 615/742-5118 email: scho@umcom.org
Director, Hispanic Resources, *el Interprete:* **Bachus, Amanda**, 615/742-5113 email: abachus@umcom.org

COMMISSION ON
THE GENERAL CONFERENCE

OFFICERS

Chairperson: **Perry, James M.,** 122 W. Franklin Ave., Room 400,
Minneapolis, MN 55404-2472 612/870-0058 FAX: 612-870-1260
email: jim.perry@mnumc.org

Vice Chairperson (Program): **Chalker, Kenneth W.,** First UMC, 3000
Euclid Ave., Cleveland, OH 44115 216/432-0150 FAX: 216/432-0134
email: kchalker@firstchurchclevland.com

Vice Chairperson (Facilities): **Foster, Nancy K.,** 4742 S. Irvington
Ave., Tulsa, OK 74135 918/663-0973 FAX: 918/663-1520
email: georgew11@mindspring.com

Secretary: **Extrum-Fernandez, Paul,** POB 980250, West Sacramento,
CA 95798-0250 916/374-1518 FAX: 916/372-5544
email:paulef@calnevumc.org

MEMBERS

Bauknight, Brian, Christ UMC, Bethel Park, 44 Highland Rd., Bethel
Park, PA 15102 412/835-6621 FAX: 412/835-9130
email: docbauk@aol.com

Chalker, Kenneth W., First UMC, 3000 Euclid Ave., Cleveland, OH
44115 216/432-0150 FAX: 216/432-0134 email:
kchalker@firstchurchclevland.com

Extrum-Fernandez, Paul, POB 980250, West Sacramento, CA 95798-
0250 916/374-1518 FAX: 916/372-5544
email: paulef@calnevumc.org

Foster, Nancy K., 4742 S. Irvington Ave., Tulsa, OK 74135 918/663-
0973 FAX: 918/663-1520 email: georgew11@mindspring.com

Gomez, Roberto L., El Mesias UMC, POB 4787, Mission,
TX 78573-4787 956/585-2334 FAX: 956/580-6727
email: RLGomez46@aol.com

Kohlepp, Glenn B., 204 Gregg Dr. Ext., Harmony, PA 16037
724/452-0589 FAX: 724/452-0299 email: gbkohlp@yahoo.com

Murphy-Geiss, Gail, 17984 E. Ida Ave., Centennial, CO 80015
719/389-6868 email: gmurphygei@aol.com

Parris, Shirley, 1136 Bergen St., Brooklyn, NY 11216-3302 718/771-
7771 FAX: 718/771-2763 email: shirparris@aol.com

Perry, James M., 122 W. Franklin Ave., Room 400, Minneapolis, MN
55404-2472 612/870-0058 FAX: 612/870-1260
email: jim.perry@mnumc.org

Siegrist, Roland, Figulystrasse, 32, A-4020 Linz, AUSTRIA 43-732-657137 FAX: 43-732-657138 email: ev@ernk.at

Stewart, Mollie M., POB 130, Valhermosa Springs, AL 35775 256/778-8357 FAX: 256/778-4188

Titus, Phylemon D., 15888 Archdale, Detroit, MI 48227 313/837-4070 FAX: 313/836-3411

Villalon, Marie-Sol, Old Dangay, Roxas, Oriental Mindoro, PHILIP-PINES 011/632-780-8874 FAX: 011-632-536-4806 email: msvillalon@yahoo. com

White, Denny, Jr., Western North Carolina Conference, 3400 Shamrock Dr.—28215, POB 18005, Charlotte, NC 28218-0005 704/535-2260 FAX 704/567-6117 email: dwhite@wnccumc.org

Williams, Aileen L., 985 11 1/4 Street SW, Rochester, MN 55902 507/285-9117 FAX: 507/285-3343 email: greenhs@aol.com

Wilson, David M., 3020 S. Harvey, Oklahoma City, OK 73109 405/632-2006 FAX: 405/632-0209 email: dwilson@oimc.org

EX-OFFICIO

Marshall, Carolyn M., General Conference Secretary, 204 N. Newlin St., Veedersburg, IN 47987-1358 317/636-3328 FAX: 317/636-0073 email: cmarshall@sprintmail.com

Lackore, Sandra Kelley, Treasurer, 1200 Davis St., Evanston, IL 60201-4193 847/425-6501 ext. 740 FAX: 847/425-6565 email: slackore@gcfa.org

Bowen, Gary K., Business Mgr., 1200 Davis St., Evanston, IL 60201-4193 847/425-6556 FAX: 847/425-6570 email: gbowen@gcfa.org

OBSERVER

Burton, Garlinda, United Methodist Communications, POB 320, Nashville, TN 37202 615/742-5102 FAX: 615/742-5460 email: gburton@umcom.umc.org

Cropsey, Marvin W., DCA Editor, UMPH, 201 8th Ave., South, Nashville, TN 37203 615/749-6292 FAX: 615/749-6512 email: mcropsey@umpublishing.org

Miller, Barbara Day, Music Director, Candler School of Theology, Atlanta, GA 30322 404/727-6153 FAX: 404/255-1460 email: bdaymil@emory.edu

Taylor, James, General Commission on Religion and Race, 100 Maryland Ave., NE, Suite 400, Washington D.C. 20002-5680 202/547-2271 ext. 17 email: jetshalom@worldnet.att.net

GENERAL COMMISSION ON RELIGION AND RACE

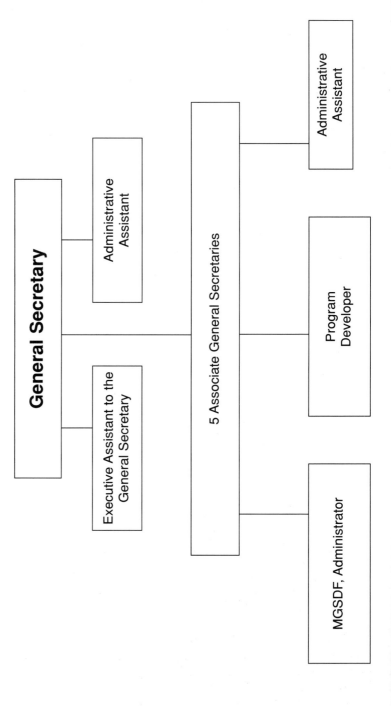

GENERAL COMMISSION ON RELIGION AND RACE
www.gcrr.org

OFFICERS

President: **Galván, Elias G.**
Vice President: **Whitfield, D. Max**
Secretary: **Woods, Vicki**

MEMBERS

Bishops
Galván, Elias G., 2112 Third Ave., Suite 301, Seattle, WA 98121-2333
Whitfield, D. Max, 7920 Mountain Road, N.E., Albuquerque, NM 87110-7805

Alexander, Anthony, Grace UMC, 216 State St., Harrisburg, PA 17104
Azhikakath, Dee Dee, 1431 W. Magee Road, Tucson, AZ 85704
Banks, David A., 625 Spottswood Dr., Sanford, NC 27330
Capen, Beth, 23 Rogers St., Kingston, NY 12401-6049
Carver, Philip, 2274 Holiday Rd., Coralville, IA 52241
Dang, Bau N., 5380 El Cajon Blvd., San Diego, CA 92115
Foote, Geneva, POB 243, Sapulpa, OK 74067
Grounds, Renee, 610 N. 3rd St., La Crescent, MN 55947
Hagiya, Grant, 109 Vista Del Parque, Redondo Beach, CA 90277
Hall, Senae, 1858 Lyons St., Shreveport, LA 71108
Handley, Jocelyn, 204 Williams St., Apt. 3, Ithaca, NY 14850
Holway, Dennis, 2372 Loussac Dr., Anchorage, AK 99517
Kelley-Sykes, Roslyn, 14316 Conway Meadows Court, E., #104
Kimball Casto, Jennifer, 25 West 5th Ave., Columbus, OH 43201
Lebrón, Germán, Apartado 8412, Ponce, Puerto Rico 00732-8412
Marcellus, Etta, 311 N. Washington Ave., Reidsville, NC 27320
Mexton, Gary G., Sr., N6206 County Rd., E., DePere, WI 54115
Minton, John D., Jr., 1703 Chestnut St., Bowling Green, KY 42101-3503
Moore-Colgan, Marion, 289 Main St., Poultney, VT 05764
Moyer, Bonda-Deere, P.O. Box 1399, Leslie, AR 72645-0389
Ormon, Jim, 418 South Main St., Petal, MS 39465

Park, HiRho, 7 Diamond Hill Court, Germantown, MD 20874
Pierre-Okerson, Judith, 7952 Plantation Blvd., Miramar, FL 33023
Quinones, Ivelisee,
Rodriguez, Samuel, 464 Bailey Ave., Ft. Worth, TX 76107
Romo, Minnie, 2115 W. Gramercy, San Antonio, TX 78201
Sablan, Franklin, Wilshire UMC, 711 South Plymouth Blvd., Los
    Angeles, CA 90005
Salley, James H., Africa University Development Office, 1001 19th
    Ave., S., Suite G-110, Nashville, TN 37202-0871
Seymour, James T., 139 N. State St., Dover, DE 19901
Stewart, Thomasina, POB 2313, Charleston, WV 25328
Tatem, Dorothy Watson, Office of Urban Ministries, Simpson House,
    2101 Belmont Ave., Philadelphia, PA 19131
Taufete'e, Faaagi, 2106 Palolo Ave., Honolulu, HI 96816
Thomas, Renita, 4188 Cedar Valley Lane, Conley, GA 30288
Thurman, Gary, Baker Memorial UMC, 345 Main St., East Aurora,
    NY 14052
Van Dussen, Greg, 8316 Park Rd., Batavia, NY 14020
Vazquez, Ilda, 709 S. Kansas, Weslaco, TX 78596
Ventura, Oscar, P.O. Box 7723, Grand Rapids, MI 49510
Williams, Jacob C., Jr., Trinity UMC, 404 North 6th St., LaFayette, IN
    47901
Woods, Vicki, 12 Thorndyke Rd., Worcester, MA 01606
Yeoh, Jenni M. L., 26205-119th Drive, SE, Kent, WA 98031

STAFF

100 Maryland Ave. NE, Ste. 400
Washington, DC 20002-5680
202/547-2271 FAX: 202/547-0358

General Secretary: **Jones, Chester R.**, ext. 20
Associate General Secretary: **Ware-Diaz, Suanne,** North Central
    Jurisdiction Liaison, ext. 13
Associate General Secretary: **Hawkins, Erin,** Southeastern
    Jurisdiction, ext. 19
Associate General Secretary: **Thomas-Sano, Kathleen,** Western
    Jurisdiction Liaison, ext. 14

Associate General Secretary: **Taylor, James,** Northeastern Jurisdiction Liaison, ext. 17

Associate General Secretary: **Pupo-Ortiz, Yolanda,** South Central Jurisdiction Liaison, ext. 15

Human Resource & Financial Services Manager: **Dixon, Kimberly,** ext. 11

Executive Assistant to General Secretary: **vacant,** ext. 18

Grants Administrator: **Bennett, Telina L.,** ext. 12

Administrative Assistant: **Green, Deborah,** ext. 21

Program Developer: **Tello, Michelle,** ext. 16

GENERAL COMMISSION ON THE STATUS AND ROLE OF WOMEN

General Secretary

Assistant to the General Secretariat in Program and Constituency Services

Assistant to the General Secretariat in Finance and Administration

Administrative Assistant

GENERAL COMMISSION ON THE STATUS AND ROLE OF WOMEN

www.gcsrw.org

OFFICERS

President: **Murphy-Geiss, Gail**
Vice President: **Arroyo, Rose**
Secretary: **Wilson, Bill H.**

Committee Chairpersons

Constituents, Advocacy, Resources & Education (CARE): **White, Mary**
Research & Monitoring: **Bond Hopson, Cynthia**

Administrative Committee Chairpersons

Nominations: **Arroyo, Rose**
Personnel: **Fitzsimmons, Charlotte**

MEMBERS

Bishops

Dabale, Done Peter, c/o General Board of Global Ministries, Attn: Rev. Zebediah Marewangepo, 475 Riverside Dr., Room 1307, New York, NY 10115 Address in Nigeria: UMCN Secretariat Mile Six, Jalingo-Numan Rd., POB 148, Jalingo Taraba State, NIGERIA 011-871-761-80665 Satellite phone: 011-871-761-80666 Satellite FAX: 011-871-761-808-666

Ough, Bruce R., 32 Wesley Blvd., Worthington, OH 43085-3585 614/844-6200 or 800/438-0028 FAX: 614/781-2625 email: bishop@wocumc.org

Aguirre, Sam, 2516 SW 124th St., Oklahoma City, OK 73170 405/954-0359 FAX 405/692-4271 email: shaguirre @ieee.org

Arroyo, Rose, 3535 N. Harlem, Chicago, IL 60634 773/534-4690 FAX: 773/794-3135 email: rosearroyo@yahoo.com

Attwood, Evelyn, POB 73, Babb, MT 59411 406/732-5556

Baker, Lynn R., 1229-4th St., Earle, AR 72331-1433 870/792-7314 email: lynn2david@prodigy.net

Briggs, Margie, 30911 S. Grant Rd., Creighton, MO 64739
816/421-3790 FAX: 816/421-3730
email: margie.briggs@broadwing.com

Collins, Janet H., 355 Lakeshore Dr., Lake Junaluska, NC 28745
828/456-6146 FAX: 828/456-4040

Crawford, Christine L., 1200 California NE, Albuquerque, NM 87110
505/262-0910 FAX: 505/242-6968
email: fortisesto@hotmail.com

Dauway, Lois M., 475 Riverside Dr., Rm. 1502, New York, NY 10115
212/870-3734 FAX: 212/870-3736 email: ldauway@gbgm-umc.org

Fitzsimmons, Charlotte, 4334 DeBellevue Dr., Baton Rouge,
LA 70809 225/924-6269 FAX: 225/928-9472
email: cfitzsimons@broadmoor-umc.org

Frantz, Steve, 72024 Fern Hill Rd., Ranier, OR 97048 503/777-7222
FAX: 503/777-7274 email: sfrantz@reed.edu

Frazier, Elizabeth, 306 White Oak Ct., Fayetteville, NC 28203
910/485-3043 FAX: 910/483-6290 email: EQFrazier@aol.com

Gates, Jim, 3618 Burch Mt. Rd., Wenatchee, WA 98801
509/662-8880 email: jrobinsgate@aol.com

Gregory, Guinevere P., 7920 Hamilton Ave., Pittsburgh, PA 15208
412/731-6155 email: sjbrown@ccac.edu

Guidry, Carolyn Tyler, 3527 Olympiad Dr., Los Angeles, CA 90043-
1124 323/737-8240 FAX: 323/737-7824 email: SHEDPE@aol.com

Hardeman, John C., 310 Colonial Dr., Florence, AL 35633
256/764-8888 email: hardemanj@yahoo.com

Harris, Sherman, 11508 Karen Dr., Potomac, MD 20854 301/299-2984
email: shermanharris@comcast.net

Hefley, Charles E., 4839 N. Parkway, Kokomo, IN 46901
765/452-3038 email: hefleyce@aol.com

Hopson, Cynthia Bond, 46 Ridgewood Cove, Jackson, TN 38305-1835
901/678-3095 FAX: 901/678-4287 email: cbhopson@memphis.edu

Kim, Haeran, 311 N. Fourth St., Dekalb, IL 60115 815/756-6301
email: haerankim@netzero.net

Martinez, Nanette H., 7182 W. 81st Ave., Arvada, CO 80003 720/888-
1586 FAX: 720/888-5218 email: nanette.martinez@level3.com

Minnix, Michael V., 550 Cleveland Ave., ChamburSburg, PA 17201
717/267-5629 FAX: 717/263-6792 email: dsmike@aol.com

Moseley, Annie F., 177 Daniels Dr., Madison Heights, VA 24572
434/845-4461 FAX: 434/845-6616 email: dandartcr@aol.com

Mull, Raquel, 2210 Silver SE Albuquerque, NM 87110 505/298-5138
email: nizhoni.1@email.com

Murillo, Sam, 118 Wheaton Hall Ln., Franklin, TN 37069
615/399-4860 FAX: 615/791-1337 email: smurtn@aol.com
Murphy-Geiss, Gail, 17984 E. Ida Ave., Centennial, CO 80015
303/400-6645 FAX: 303/722-0624 email: gmurphygei@aol.com
Oba, Gary, 440 Maxwell Rd., Eugene, OR 97404 541/689-3725
FAX: 541/689-4612 email: garyoba@aol.com
Penalva, David E., 410 N. Fenton Ave., Indianapolis, IN 46219
317/636-2819 FAX: 317/898-7865 email: Davicho@aol.com
Rice, Mattie Mae, 6412 Brentwood Rd., Little Rock, AR 72207
501/666-5937 email: Matti6412@aol.com
Santiago, Maria T., Honduras St. B-16, Oasis Gardens, Guaynabo,
Puerto Rico 00969 787/789-4678 email: arboles@whalemail.com
Simmons, Angelin Jones, 2661 Mullet Hall Rd., Johns Island, SC
29455 843/768-1080 email: ordist@umcsc.org
Soper, Brian, N4482 Wolff Rd., Cambridge, WI 53523 608/423-3336
FAX: 608/423-9851 email: GaySpaz@aol.com
Thai, Eva, 11331 Sharon St., Cerritos, CA 90703 562/640-3308
FAX: 562/424-8232 email: girlinatree@hotmail.com
Trevino-Teddlie, Jeannie, 5915 Bishop Blvd., POB 750133,
Dallas, TX 75275-0133 214/768-2768 FAX: 214/768-1042
email: jtrevted@mail.smu.edu
Turner, Molly C., POB 25068, Lansing, MI 48909 517/347-4030
FAX: 517/347-4003 email: mareaumc.@tir.com
Wall, Norma Jones, 6 Winding Way, West Orange, NY 07052
973/731-5402 email: NoWaJo@aol.com
White, Mary, 771 Conestoga Rd., Rosemont, PA 19011 215/236-0304
FAX: 215/256-8618 email: mwhite9891@aol.com
Wilson, Bill H., POB 516, Barboursville, WV 25504 304/736-9962
FAX: 304/736-1805 email: drbillwilson@aol.com
Wright, Betty S., 104 John St., Akron, NY 14001-1117 716/542-9760
FAX: 716/542-9760 email: ejswright@webtv.net

STAFF
1200 Davis St
Evanston, IL 60201
847/869-7330 or 800/523-8390 FAX: 847/869-1466
GCSRW@gcfa.org

Interim General Secretary

Burton, Garlinda, email: gburton@gcfa.org

Assistant to the General Secretariat in Program and Constituency
Services: **Coffing, Kim,** email: kcoffing@gcfa.org
Assistant to the General Secretariat in Finance and Administration:
Johnson, Elaine Moy, email: ejohnson@gcfa.org
Administrative Assistant: **Alonso, Ariel,** email: aalonso@gcfa.org

GENERAL COMMISSION ON UNITED METHODIST MEN

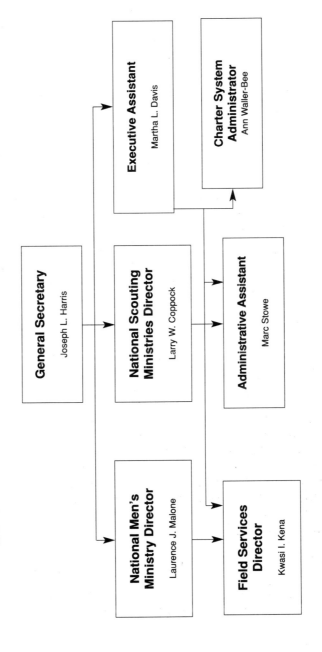

General Secretary

Joseph L. Harris

National Men's Ministry Director

Laurence J. Malone

Executive Assistant

Martha L. Davis

Charter System Administrator

Ann Waller-Bee

National Scouting Ministries Director

Larry W. Coppock

Administrative Assistant

Marc Stowe

Field Services Director

Kwasi I. Kena

GENERAL COMMISSION ON UNITED METHODIST MEN
www.gcumm.org

OFFICERS

President: **Lyght, Ernest S.**
Vice-President: **Powell, Robert**
Secretary: **Yannayon, Harold**
Treasurer: **King, Denver**
USA National President of UMM: **Hanke, Gilbert**
Central Conference President of UMM: **vacant**

MEMBERS

Bishops
Lyght, Ernest S., 20 Soundview Ave., White Plains, NY 10606
888/696-6922 FAX: 914/615-2246 email: bishopsga@aol.com
Watson, B. Michael, POB 13616, Macon, GA 31208 478/475-9286
FAX: 478/475-9248 email: bishopsga@aol.com

Batiste, Harold E., 709 Fawndale Ln., San Antonio, TX 78239-2633
210/654-6335 FAX: 210/654-4092 email: hebatistejr@aol.com
Beard, Samantha, POB 860084, Tuscaloosa, AL 35486 205/347-8273
email: rheabeard@aol.com
Burlew, John P., 4873 Candy Ln., Manlius, NY 13104 315/458-1211
FAX: 315/458-1220 email: jpburlew1@juno.com
Cabaniss, Ray W., 1320 Fairlawn Way, Golden Valley, MN 55416
763/377-6283
Chase, Bob, 401 Mulberry Grove Rd., Keyesport, IL 62253 618/749-
5745 email: rwchase@papadocs.com
Clark, Edward R., 1145 SW Cypress St., Apt. 7, McMinnville, OR
97128
503/472-3574 email: edmona@msn.com
Conklin, Faith J., 341 S. Kalmia St., Escondido, CA 92025
760/745-5100 FAX: 760/745-9338 email: revfaith@pacbell.net
Dowell, John, 1120 W. Kennedy Blvd., Tampa, FL 33606 813/251-
6458 FAX: 813/254-1984 email: jdowellumm@aol.com
England, Stan, 537 Shiloh Rd., Kennesaw, GA 30144 770/517-5480
FAX: 770/517-5480 email: stane@mindspring.com

Erskine, Rod, 21090 Maplewood Ave., Rocky River, OH 44116
440/331-4413 email: rode@stratos.net
Gilstrap, Walter, 254 Harland Rd. SW, Atlanta, GA 30311
404/691-4310 email: waltgilstrap36@yahoo.com
Gomez, Rudy, 2627 Pleasant Dr., Dallas, TX 75227 214/381-6869
Hall, Malcolm, 764 Bellmore Rd., North Bellmore, NY 11710-3727
516/296-5474 FAX: 516/296-6877 email: tmagic8006@aol.com
Hanke, Gilbert, 803 Wildwood, Nacogdoches, TX 75961 936/560-1618 FAX: 936/560-3554 email: ghanke@sfasu.edu
Henry, Dan, 227 Charlotte Ln., Bolingbrook, IL 60440-1371
800/216-1986 FAX: 630/972-1003 email: chenry241@attbi.com
Howard, Phillip G., 141 E. Ohio St., Indianapolis, IN 46204
317/263-9655 FAX: 317/263-9644 email: phoward@interdesign.com
Johnson, Norman, 668 Church St., NW, Atlanta, GA 30318
404/799-1653 FAX: 404/799-7097 email: nrjohnson66@aol.com
Jones, Chuck, 1143 Summer Lakes Dr., Orlando, FL 32835
407/522-4251 FAX: 407/522-2036 email: chuck330@bellsouth.net
King, Denver, 129 Rosefield St., Kingsport, TN 37660 423/246-7776
FAX: 423/246-7655
Kondo, Richard S., 1707 Park Ave., Alamogordo, NM 88310
505/437-4671 email: rskondo@zianet.com
Luhahi, Emile, 7 Ave Mfumu Saka, Righini Lemba, Kinshasa,
Democratic Republic of Congo 243/892-0005 FAX: 243/880-3723
email: emileluhahi@hotmail.com
Middleton King, Andrea, POB 65566, Washington, DC 20035-5566
301/972-5520 FAX: 410/309-9439 email: clergygirl@email.com
Powell, Robert, 110 Wentworth Dr., Dothan, AL 36305 334/793-1754
FAX: 334/678-1684 email: rpowell728@aol.com
Rios, Eliud, 6211 Thunder Dr., San Antonio, TX 78238 210/682-6093
FAX: 210/682-7060
Sarver, Ron, 305 Chastant Blvd., Lafayette, LA 70508 337/981-9401
FAX: 337/981-9404 email: ronummla@aol.com
Singleterry, Martha A., POB 894, Clovis, NM 88102-0894 505/769-1755 FAX: 505/769-2721 email: clovisdist@3lefties.com
Stewart, Carl, 300 Fannin St., Suite 2299, Shreveport, LA 71101
318/676-3765 FAX: 318/676-3768
email: carl_stewart@ca5.uscourts.gov
Taylor, Pete W., Jr., 7962 Sanford St., Oakland, CA 94605
510/638-7397 FAX: 510/633-0840 email: peteronnie@juno.com
Taylor, Victor, 9560 Drake Ave., Evanston, IL 60203 800/682-4335
FAX: 312/345-6056 email: taylor617@attbi.com

Waymire, Dale, POB 617, Madill, OK 73446 580/795-3327
FAX: 580/795-5331

Werft, Andrew E., 7964 W. Pershing Ave., Peoria, AZ 85381 623/878-3383

Westerfield-Tucker, Karen B., Duke University Divinity School,
Durham, NC 27708-0967 919/660-3468 FAX: 919/660-3473
email: ktucker@div.duke.edu

Yannayon, Harold, 2926 Homer Ave., Erie, PA 16506-2632 814/838-3119 FAX: 814/833-6757 email: haroldy@adelphia.net

STAFF

1001 19th Avenue South, Suite 170 (37212)
POB 340006
Nashville, TN 37203-0006
615/340-7145 FAX: 615/340-1770
Web site: gcumm.org

General Secretary: **Harris, Joseph L.,** 615/340-7136
email: jharris@gcumm.org
Executive Assistant: **Davis, Martha,** 615/340-7137
email: mdavis@gcumm.org
National Men's Ministry Director: **Malone, Lawrence J.,** 615/340-7147 email: lmalone@gcumm.org
National Civic Youth Ministry Director: **Coppock, Larry,**
615/340-7149 email: lcoppock@gcumm.org
Field Services Director: **Kena, Kwasi I.,** 615/340-7146 email:
kkena@gcumm.org

CONFERENCE OFFICES

Alabama-West Florida (SE)
532 E. Three Notch St., PO Drawer 700, Andalusia, AL 36420-0700
334/222-3127 or 334/222-3127 FAX: 334/222-0469
email: awfchq@aol.com Web site: www.awfumc.org

Alaska Missionary (W)
3402 Wesleyan Dr., Anchorage, AK 99508-4866 907/333-5050
FAX: 907/333-2304 email: umc@alaska.net Web site:
www.aphids.com/alaska/

Baltimore-Washington (NE)
9720 Patuxent Woods Dr., Suite 100, Columbia, MD 21046-1526
800/492-2525 FAX: 410/309-9430 email: dstewart@bwcumc.org
Web site: www.bwconf.org

California-Nevada (W)
(1276 Halyard Drive—95691), POB 980250, W. Sacramento,
CA 95798-0250 916/374-1500 FAX: 916/372-5544
email: genmail@calnevumc.org Web site: www.cnumc.org

California Pacific (W)
(110 S. Euclid Ave.—91101), POB 6006, Pasadena, CA 91102-6006
800/244-8622 FAX: 626/796-7297 email: mhuntington@cal-pac.org
Web site: www.cal-pac.org

Central Pennsylvania (NE)
303 Mulberry Dr., Mechanicsburg, PA 17050-2053 800/874-8474
FAX: 717/766-5976 email: cpc@cpcumc.org Web site:
www.cpcumc.org

Central Texas (SC)
464 Bailey, Ft. Worth, TX 76107-2153 800/460-8622 FAX: 817/338-
4541 email: doyle@ctcumc.org Web site: www.kansaseast.org

Dakotas (NC)
1331 W. University, POB 460, Mitchell, SD 57301-0460 605/996-6552
FAX: 605/996-1766 email: rcross@midco.net
Web site: www.dakotasumc.org

Desert Southwest (W)
1550 E. Meadowbrook Ave., Suite 200, Phoenix, AZ 85014-4040
800/229-8622 FAX: 602/266-5343 email: harold@desertsw.org
Web site: www.desertrsw.org

Detroit (NC)

1309 N. Ballenger Hwy, Suite 1, Flint, MI 48504 800/334-0544 ext. 330
FAX: 810/233-5700 email: office@umc-detconf.org
Web site: www.umc-detconf.org

East Ohio

POB 2800, 8800 Cleveland Ave., NW, North Canton, OH 44720-
0800 800/831-3972 FAX: 330/499-3279
email: paul.white@eocumc.com Web site: www.eocumc.com

Eastern Pennsylvania (NE)

(980 Madison & Monroe Blvd.—19403-2412) POB 820, Valley Forge,
PA 19482-0820 800/828-9093 FAX: 610/666-9093
email: epaumc@ptd.net Web site: www.epaumc.org

Florida (SE)

(1140 E. McDonald St.—33801), POB 3767, Lakeland, FL 33802-3767
800/282-8011 FAX: 863/680-1912 email: reception@flumc.org
Web site: www.flumc.org

Greater New Jersey (NE)

Cherry Hill Office: 1995 East Marlton Pike, Cherry Hill, NJ 08003-
1893 856/424-1700 FAX: 856/424-9282
email: confoff-ch@gnjumc.org Web site: www.gnjumc.org
Madison Office: 22 Madison St., Madison, NJ 07940 973/377-3800
FAX: 973/765-9868 email: Confoff-M@gnjumc.org
Web site: www.gnjumc.org

Holston (SE)

(9915 Kingston Pike, Suite C—37922-3367) POB 32929, Knoxville,
TN 37930-2939 865/690-4080 FAX: 865/690-7112 email:
AnneTravis@holston.org Web site: www.holstonconference.com

Illinois Great Rivers (NC)

2144 S. MacArthur Blvd., Suite 2B, Springfield, IL 62204-4500
217/747-0720 FAX: 217/744-2273 email: ThoHawkins@aol.com
Web site: www.igrac.com

Iowa (NC)

500 E. Court Ave., Suite C, Des Moines, IA 50309-1498 515/283-
1991 FAX: 515/283-0836 email: iaccom@iaumc.org
Web site: www.iaumc.org

Kansas East (SC)

4201-SW 15th St., POB 4187, Topeka, KS 66604-0187 785/272-9111
FAX: 785/272-9135 email: office@kansaseast.org Web site:
www.kansaseast.org

Kansas West (SC)
9440 E. Boston, Ste. 110, Wichita, KS 67207-3600 316/684-0266
FAX: 316/684-0044 email: Bsheldon@kswestumc.org Web site:
www.kswestumc.org

Kentucky (SE)
7400 Floydsburg Rd., Crestwood, KY 40014-8202 502/425-3884
FAX: 502/426-5181 email: rholladay@kyumc.org Web site:
www.kyumc.org

Little Rock (SC)
715 Center St., Ste. 202, Little Rock, AR 72201-4317 877/646-1816
FAX: 501/324-8018 email: tweir@arumc.org Web site:
www.arumc.org

Louisiana (SC)
527 North Blvd., Baton Rouge, LA 70802-5700 888/239-5286 FAX:
225/383-2652 email: laconfry@bellsouth.net Web site: www.la-
umc.org

Memphis (SE)
24 Corporate Blvd., Jackson, TN 38305-2395 731/664-8480
FAX: 731/660-5712 email: catfarmer@memphis-umc.org
Web site: www.memphis-umc.org

Minnesota (NC)
122 W. Franklin Ave., Rm. 400, Minneapolis, MN 55404-2472
612/870-0058 FAX: 612/870-1260 email: jim.perry@mnumc.org
Web site: www.mumac.org

Mississippi (SE)
(321 Mississippi St.—39201), POB 1147, Jackson, MS 39215-1147
601/354-0515 FAX: 601/948-5982 email: msumcom@mississippi-
umc.org Web site: www.mississippi-umc.org

Missouri East (SC)
4800 Santana Cir., Suite 200, Columbia, MO 65203-7138 877/736-
1806 FAX: 573-441/1780 email: erevelle@moareaumc.org
Web site: www.moumethodist.org

Missouri West (SC)
4800 Santana Cir., Suite 300, Columbia, MO 65203-7138 877/736-
1806 FAX: 573-441/1780 email: erevelle@moareaumc.org
Web site: www.moumethodist.org

Nebraska (SC)
2641 N. 49th St., Lincoln, NE 68504-2899 800/435-6107 FAX:
402/464-6203 email: cedwards@umcneb.org
Web site: www.umcneb.org

New England (NE)

(276 Essex St. 2nd Floor—01840-1516) POB 249, Lawrence, MA 01842-0449 978/682-8055 FAX: 978/682-8227
email: communicate@neumc.org Web site: www.neumc.org

New Mexico (SC)

7920 Mountain Rd. NE, Albuquerque, NM 87110-7805 800/678-8786 FAX: 505/265-6184 email: largedir@nmconfum.com
Web site: www.nmconfum.com

New York (NE)

20 Soundview Ave., White Plains, NY 10606-3302 888/696-6922 ext. 230 FAX: 914/684-6874 email: apearson@nyac.com
Web site: www.nyac.com

North Alabama (SE)

898 Arkadelphia Rd., Birmingham, AL 35204-3436 205/226-7950 FAX: 205/226-7975 email: mstewart@umcna.bsc.edu
Web site: www.umcna.bsc.edu

North Arkansas (SC)

715 Center St., Suite 202, Little Rock, AR 72201-4317 Toll Free: 877/646-1816 FAX: 501/324-8018 email: tweir@arumc.org
Web site: www.arumc.org

North Carolina (SE)

1307 Glenwood Ave., Suite 203, POB 10955, Raleigh, NC 27606-0955 800/849-4433 FAX: 919/834-7989 email: comments@nccumc.org
Web site: www.nccumc.org

North Central New York (NE)

8422 N. Main St., POB 1515, Cicero, NY 13039 315/699-8715 FAX: 315/699-8774 email: ncnyumc@aol.com Web site: www.ncnyumc.org

North Georgia (SE)

(4511 Jones Bridge Circle Northwest-30092-1406) POB 922997, Norcross, GA 30010-2997 678/533-1399 FAX: 678/533-1378
email: mbrantley@ngumc.org Web site: www.ngumc.org

North Indiana (NC)

POB 869 (1105 N. Western Ave.—46952-2501), Marion, IN 46952-0869 800/783-5138 FAX: 765/664-2307 email: ccom@nicumc.org
Web site: www.inareaumc.org

North Texas (SC)

POB 516069 (13959 Peyton Dr.-75240-3690), Dallas, TX 75251-6069 800/969-8201 972/490-3438 FAX: 972/490-7216
email: casad@ntcumc.org Web site: www.ntcume.org

Northern Illinois (NC)

8765 W. Higgins Rd., Suite 650, Chicago, IL 60631-4101 773/380-5060 FAX: 773/380-5067 email: ocarrasc@umcnic.org Web site: www.umcnic.org

Northwest Texas (SC)

1415 Avenue M, Lubbock, TX 79401-3939 806/762-0201 FAX: 806/762-0205 email: allsup@nwtxconf.org Web site: www.nwtxconf.org

Oklahoma (SC)

2420 N. Blackwelder Ave., Oklahoma City, OK 73106-1499 405/525-2252 FAX: 405/525-4164 email: david@okumc.org Web site: www.okumc.org

Oklahoma Indian Missionary (SC)

3020 S. Harvey St., Oklahoma City, OK 73109-6309 405/632-2006 FAX: 405/632-0209 email: dwoimc@aol.com Web site: www.gbgm-umc.org/oimc/

Oregon Idaho (W)

1505 SW 18th, Portland, OR 97201-2599 800/593-7539 FAX: 503/266-4158 email: steve@umoi.org Web site: www.umoi.org

Pacific Northwest (W)

2112 Third Ave., Suite 300, Seattle, WA 98121-2333 800/755-7710 FAX: 206/728-8442 email: elainejws@pnwumc.org Web site: www.pnwumc.org

Peninsula-Delaware (NE)

139 N. State St., Dover, DE 19901-3834 877/736-3351 FAX: 302/674-1573 email: jseymour@pen-del.org Web site: www.pen-del.org

Puerto Rico

POB 23339 UPR Station, San Juan, PR 00931-3339 787/765-3195 FAX: 787/751-3615 email: javera@coqui.net Web site: www.metodistapr.org

Red Bird Missionary (SE)

6 Queendale Center, Beverly, KY 40913 606/598-5915 FAX: 606/598-6405 email: Redbirdco@kih.net Web site: www.gbgm-umc.org/redbirdconference

Rio Grande (SC)

POB 781974 (16400 Huebner Rd.-78248), San Antonio, TX 78278-1974 210/408-4513 FAX: 210/408-4515 email: amariscal@umcswtx.org Web site: www.riogrande-umc.org

Rocky Mountain (W)

2200 S. University Blvd., Denver, CO 80210-4797 800/536-3736 FAX: 303/733-1730 email: gary@rmcumc.org Web site: www.rmcumc.org

South Carolina (SE)

4908 Colonial Dr., Columbia, SC 29203-6000 803/786-9486 FAX: 803/691-0220 email: cjohnson@umcsc.org Web site: www.umcsc.org

South Georgia (SE)

99 Arthur Moore Dr., POB 20408, St. Simons Island, GA 31522-0008 888/266-7642 FAX: 912/638-5258 email: brad@sgaumc.org Web site: www.sgaumc.com

South Indiana (NC)

POB 5008 (2427 E. Second St.-47401), Bloomington, IN 47407-5008 800/919-8160 FAX: 812/336-0216 email: info@sicumc.org Web site: www.umcnic.org

Southwest Texas (SC)

POB 781149 (16400 Huebner Rd.-79248), San Antonio, TX 78278-1149 888/349-4191 FAX: 210/408-4515 email: umcenter@umcswtx.org Web site: www.umcswtx.org

Tennessee (SE)

(1110 19th Ave. S.,—37212-2195) POB 120607, Nashville, TN 37212-0607 615/329-1177 FAX: 615/329-0884 email: ccom@tnumc.org Web site: tnumc.org

Texas (SC)

5215 Main, Houston, TX 77002-9792 713/521-9383 FAX: 713/521-4616 email: jwfoster@methodists.net Web site: www.methodists.net

Troy (NE)

396 Louden Rd., POB 560, Saratoga Springs, NY 12866-0560 800/684-9377 ext 117 FAX: 802/223-2232 email: info@troyac.org Web site: www.troyac.org

Virginia (SE)

(4016 W. Broad St.—23230-3916) POB 11367, Richmond, VA 23230-1367 800/768-6040 FAX: 804/359-5427 email: wasenawright@vaumc.org Web site: www.vaumc.org

West Michigan (NC)
(11 Fuller Ave. SE-49506) POB 6247, Grand Rapids, MI 49516-6247
888/217-1905 FAX: 616/459-0191 email: johnross@wmcumc.org
Web site: www.westmichiganconference.org

West Ohio (NC)
32 Wesley Blvd., Worthington, OH 43085-3585 800/437-0028
FAX: 614/781-2642 email: sling@wocumc.org
Web site: www.westohioumc.org

West Virginia (NE)
900 Washington St. E. (25301), POB 2313, Charleston, WV 25328-2313
800/788-3746 FAX: 304/344-2871 email: wvconfmin@aol.com
Web site: www.wvumc.org

Western New York (NE)
131 John Muir Dr., West Amherst, NY 14228 800/461-1174 FAX:
716/564-2365 email: wnyconf@aol.com
Web site: www.conferencenews.com/wnuconfumc/default.htm

Western North Carolina (SE)
(3400 Shamrock Dr.—28215) POB 18005, Charlotte, NC 28218-0005
800/562-7929 FAX: 704/567-6117 email: tsigmon@wnccumc.org
Web site: www.wnccumc.org

Western Pennsylvania (NE)
(1204 Freedom Rd.—16066-4999) POB 5002, Cranberry Township,
PA 16066-0002 800/886-3382 FAX: 724/776-1355
email: umcenter@umchurch.org Web site: www.umchurch.org

Wisconsin (NC)
750 Windsor St., Suite 202, POB 620, Sun Prairie, WI 53590-0620
888/240-7328 FAX: 608/837-8547 email: janefz@WisconsinUMC.org
Web site: www.wisconsinumc.org

Wyoming (NE)
(1700 Monroe St.—13760-5599), POB 58, Endicott, NY 13761-0058
607/757-0608 FAX: 607/757-0752
email: rmschlock@wyomingconference.org
Web site: www.wyomingconference.org

Yellowstone (W)
1601 Marketplace Dr., Suite 28, POB 183, Great Falls, MT 59404-
3489 800/808-0408 FAX: 406/727-2981 email: yacval@aol.com
Web site: www.gbgm-umc.org/yellowstone

JURISDICTIONAL OFFICERS

NCJ Secretary: **Stephenson, Janet,** 322 Hickory Dr., Ames IA 50014 515/292-2166 email: jdsteph@ames.net

NEJ Secretary: **Daugherty, Robert M.,** 1936 N. Eden Rd., Lancaster, PA 17601 717/299-2203 email: Rdaugherty@pptNet.com

SCJ Executive Director: **Matherson, Thalia F.,** Suite 240, 5646 Milton St., Dallas, TX 75206-3930 214/692-9081 FAX: 214/692-9083 email: scjumc@webaccess.net

SEJ Executive Director: **Carr, Jimmy L., Rev.,** 759 Lakeshore Dr., Lake Junaluska, NC 28745 888/525-3586 FAX: 828/456-4040 email: info@sejacumc.org Web site: www.sejac-umc.org

WJ Secretary: **Albright, Thomas H.,** 5600 64th St. NE, Marysville, WA 98270 360/659-8521 FAX: 360/658-9728 email: talright@msm.com

DIRECTORS OF ANNUAL CONFERENCE COUNCILS ON MINISTRIES

NORTH CENTRAL JURISDICTION

Dakotas Conference (Dakotas Area)
Cross, Randolph M., 1331 West University Ave., POB 460, Mitchell, SD 57301-0460

Detroit Conference (Michigan Area)
Huhtala, John C., Jr., 1309 N. Ballenger Hwy., Suite 1, Flint, MI 48504-7598

East Ohio Conference (Ohio East Area)
White, Paul R., 8800 Cleveland Ave., NW, POB 2800, North Canton, OH 44720-0800

Illinois Great Rivers Conference (Illinois Area)
Clark, Terry L., 2144 S. MacArthur Blvd., Suite 2B, Springfield, IL 62704-4500

Iowa Conference (Iowa Area)
Glenn, Twila M., 500 E. Court Ave., Suite. C, Des Moines, IA 50309-2019

Minnesota Conference (Minnesota Area)
Perry, James M., 122 W. Franklin Ave., Rm. 200, Minneapolis, MN 55404-2472

North Indiana Conference (Indiana Area)
Reynolds, Cynthia J., 1105 N. Western Ave., POB 869, Marion, IN 46952-0869

Northern Illinois Conference (Chicago Area)
Carrasco, Oscar N., 77 Washington St., Suite 1820, Chicago, IL 60602-3181

South Indiana Conference (Indiana Area)
Sharp, Robert T., (2427 E. 2nd St.—47401) POB 5008, Bloomington, IN 47407-5008

West Michigan Conference (Michigan Area)
Thompson, John Ross, (11 Fuller Ave. SE—49506), POB 6247, Grand Rapids, MI 49516-6247

West Ohio Conference (Ohio West Area)
Ling, Stanley T., 32 Wesley Blvd., Worthington, OH 43085-3585

Wisconsin Conference (Wisconsin Area)

Zekoff, Jane Follmer, (750 Windsor St., Suite 202), POB 620, Sun Prairie, WI 53590-0620

NORTHEASTERN JURISDICTION

Baltimore - Washington Conference (Washington Area)

Stewart, Donald S., Jr., 7178 Columbia Gateway Dr., Columbia, MD 21046-2132

Central Pennsylvania Conference (Harrisburg Area)

Salsgiver, Thomas L., (303 Mulberry Dr. - 10705), POB 2053, Mechanicsburg, PA 17055-2053

Eastern Pennsylvania Conference (Philadelphia Area)

Leister, Larry D., (980 Madison Ave., Norristown—19403) POB 820, Valley Forge, PA 19482-0820

Greater New Jersey Conference (New Jersey Area)

Sloane, Kenneth J., 1001 Wickapecko Dr., Ocean, NJ 07712-4733

New England Conference (Boston Area)

Stahl, Wanda J., (276 Essex St., 2nd Fl.-01840-1516), POB 249, Lawrence, MA 01842-0449

New York Conference (New York Area)

Pearson, Ann, 20 Soundview Ave., White Plains, NY 10606-3302

North Central New York Conference (New York West Area)

Mauser, Larry, (8422 N. Main St.), POB 1515, Cicero, NY 13039-1515

Peninsula-Delaware Conference (Philadelphia Area)

Seymour, James T., 139 N. State St., Dover, DE 19901-3834

Troy Conference (Albany Area)

Lemmel, Barbara A., POB 560, Saratoga Springs, NY 12866-0560

West Virginia Conference (West Virginia Area)

Flanagan, Randall F., (900 Washington St. E—25301), POB 2313, Charleston, WV 25328-2313

Western New York Conference (New York West Area)

Crispell, Gregory L., 131 John Muir Dr., West Amherst, NY 14228-1147

Western Pennsylvania Conference (Pittsburgh Area)
Homitsky, Larry P., (1204 Freedom Rd.), POB 5002, Cranberry Twp, PA 16066-0002

Wyoming Conference (Albany Area)
Johnson, Vicki A., (1700 Monroe St—13760-5512), POB 58, Endicott, NY 13761-0058

SOUTH CENTRAL JURISDICTION

Executive Director - **Matherson, Thalia F.,** 4849 Greenville Ave., Suite 1545, Dallas, TX 75206

Arkansas Conference (Arkansas Area)
Weir, Thomas E., 715 Center St., Suite 202, Little Rock, AR 72201-4317

Central Texas Conference (Fort Worth Area)
Allen, Doyle R., 464 Bailey Ave., Ft. Worth, TX 76107-2153

Kansas East Conference (Kansas Area)
Beach, Gary A., 4201 SW 15th St., POB 4187, Topeka, KS 66604-0187

Kansas West Conference (Kansas Area)
Fischer, Phil R., 9440 E. Boston St., Suite 110, Wichita, KS 67207-3600

Louisana Conference (Louisana Area)
Cottrill, Donald C., 527 North Blvd., Baton Rouge, LA 70802-5720

Missouri East Conference (Missouri Area)
Cox, Steve L., 4800 Santana Cir., Suite 300, Columbia, MO 65203-7138

Nebraska Conference (Nebraska Area)
Karges, Casey A., 2641 N. 49th St., POB 4553, Lincoln, NE 68504-0553

New Mexico Conference (Northwest Texas-New Mexico Area)
Large, James E., 7920 Mountain Rd. NE, Albuquerque, NM 87110-7805

North Texas Conference (Dallas Area)
Casad, Mary Brooke, (13959 Peyton Dr.—75240), POB 516069, Dallas, TX 75251-6069

Northwest Texas Conference (Northwest Texas-New Mexico Area)

Allsup, C. Eddie, 1415 Avenue M, Lubbock, TX 79401-3939

Oklahoma Conference (Oklahoma Area)

Severe, David L., 1501 NW 24th St., Oklahoma City, OK 73106-3635

Oklahoma Indian Missionary Conference (Oklahoma Area)

Wilson, David M., 3020 S. Harvey St., Oklahoma City, OK 73109-6309

Rio Grande Conference (San Antonio Area)

Mariscal, Arturo, (16400 Huebner Rd.—78248), POB 781974, San Antonio, TX 78278-1974

Southwest Texas Conference (San Antonio Area)

Frederick, Austin K., Jr., (16400 Huebner Rd.—78248), POB 781149, San Antonio, TX 78278-1149

Texas Conference (Houston Area)

Foster, James William, 5215 Main St., Houston, TX 77002-9752

SOUTHEASTERN JURISDICTION

Executive Director of SEJ, Carr, Jimmy L., 400 N. Lakeshore Dr., POB 67, Lake Junaluska, NC 28745-0067

Alabama-West Florida Conference (Alabama-West Florida Area)

Stinson, Mary E., POB 700, Andalusia, AL 36420-0700

Florida Conference (Florida Area)

Burkholder, Anne L., (1140 E. McDonald St.—33801), POB 3767, Lakeland, FL 33802-3767

Holston Conference (Holston Area)

Travis, Ann S., POB 32939, Knoxville, TN 37930-2939

Kentucky Conference (Louisville Area)

Holladay, K. Richard, 7400 Floydsburg Rd., Crestwood, KY 40014-82021

Memphis Conference (Nashville Area)

Hopson, Roger A., 24 Corporate Blvd., Jackson, TN 38305-2315

Mississippi Conference (Mississippi Area)
Moore, John C., (321 Mississippi St.–39201), POB 1147, Jackson, MS 39215-1147

North Alabama Conference (Birmingham Area)
Cohen, Dale R., 898 Arkadelphia Rd., Birmingham, AL 35204-3436

North Carolina Conference (Raleigh Area)
Smith, Charles M., 1307 Glenwood Ave., Rm 203, POB 10955, Raleigh, NC 27605-0955

North Georgia Conference (North Georgia Area)
Brantley, D. McArthur, (4511 Jones Bridge Cir. N.W. 30092) POB 922997, Atlanta, GA 30010-2997

Red Bird Missionary Conference (Louisville Area)
Wiertzema, Ruth Ann, 6 Queendale Center, Beverly, KY 40913-9601

South Carolina Conference (Columbia Area)
Johnson, Charles L., Sr., 4908 Colonial Dr., Suite 101, Columbia, SC 29203-6000

South Georgia Conference (South Georgia Area)
Brady, Remer L., III, (99 Arthur Moore Dr.), POB 20408, St. Simons Island, GA 31522-0008

Tennessee Conference (Nashville Area)
Ganues, Randall C., 1110 19th Ave. S., POB 120607, Nashville, TN 37212-0607

Virginia Conference (Richmond Area)
Garrett, Susan S., (10330 Staples Mill Rd.), POB 1719, Glenn Allen, VA 23060-0659

Western North Carolina Conference (Charlotte Area)
Sigmon, Thomas R., (3400 Shamrock, Dr.—28215), POB 18005, Charlotte, NC 28218-0005

WESTERN JURISDICTION

Alaska Missionary Conference (Portland Area)
Holway, Dennis, 3402 Wesleyan Dr., Anchorage, AK 95508-4866

California-Nevada Conference (San Francisco Area)
Wiberg, Linda D., (1276 Halyard Dr.—95691), POB 980250, West Sacramento, CA 95798-0250

California-Pacific Conference (Los Angeles Area)
Huntington, Marilynn M., (110 S. Euclid Ave. - 91101), POB 6006, Pasadena, CA 91102-6006

Desert Southwest Conference (Phoenix Area)
Morley, Daniel R., 2540 W. Baseline Rd., Mesa, AZ 85202-5403

Oregon-Idaho Conference (Portland Area)
Harkness, R. Scott, 1505 SW 18th Ave., Portland, OR 97201-2599

Pacific Northwest Conference (Seattle Area)
Stanovsky, Elaine J., 2112 3rd Ave., Suite 300, Seattle, WA 98121-2394

Rocky Mountain Conference (Denver Area)
Hodges, Ronald R., 2200 S. University Blvd., Denver, CO 80210-4708

Yellowstone Conference (Denver Area)
Novak, Margaret M., PO Box 720, Chester, MT 59522-0720

IGLESIA METODISTA AUTONOMA AFILIADA DE PUERTO RICO

Ortiz, Victor, UPR Station, POB 23339, San Juan, PUERTO RICO 00931-3339

ASSOCIATION OF ANNUAL CONFERENCE LAY LEADERS

OFFICERS

President: **Holt, Gloria E.,** 6740 Clear Creek Cir., Trussville, AL 35173
205/661-9292 FAX: 205/856-8788 email: Gholt@umcna.bsc.edu
Vice-President: **Gleaton, Tommy,** POB 6283, Denver, CO 80206
303/756-1588 FAX 603/907-0752 email: Tgle105463@aol.com
Secretary: **Webster, Darlene,** 12062 Jeffrey Lane, Princess Anne, MD
21853-2128 410/651-1788 email: Dwebstercll@aol.com
Treasurer: **Krost, Mike,** 15914 N. Brougham Dr., Chillicothe, IL 61523
H: 309/274-6625 O: 309/274-4775 FAX: 309/274-4976
email: Mkrost@mtco.com
Past President: **Archibald, Julius A., Jr.,** 90 Park Ave, Plattsburgh, NY 12901
518/561-4395 FAX: 518/561-6455 email:
Julius.Archibald@plattsburgh.edu

Jurisdictional Chairpersons

NORTH CENTRAL JURISDICTION

Shaw, James C., 5229 Leone Pl., Indianapolis, IN 46226-1751 317/547-6982 FAX: 317/547-8626 email: Jcshaw@iquest.net

NORTHEASTERN JURISDICTION

Wigal, Betty L., Rt. 1, Box 242E., Parkersburg, WV 26101
304/464-4230 email: Bettywigal@aol.com

SOUTH CENTRAL JURISDICTION

Young, Carl W., 417 Kenswick Ct., Edmond, OK 405/340-9200
FAX: 405/340-9233 email: carl.w.young@worldnet.att.net

SOUTHEASTERN JURISDICTION

Minton, John D., Jr., 1703 Chestnut St., Bowling Green, KY 42101-3503
592/746-7408 FAX: 502/796-6015 email: j-minton@msn.com

WESTERN JURISDICTION

Walker, Beverly J., 1266 S. W. fouth Street, Gresham, OR 97080
503/665-9747

NORTH CENTRAL JURISDICTION

Dakotas
Wagner, Ray, POB 156, Rogers, ND 58479 701/646-6510
email: rwagnd@hotmail.com

Detroit
Cook, Shirley, 806 Olive Rd., Oxford, MI 48371 248/628-4432

East Ohio
Payne, W. Richard, 16857 Sycamore Rd., Mt. Vernon, OH 43050
740/397-0570

Illinois Great Rivers
Krost, Mike, 15914 N. Brougham Dr., Chillicothe, IL 61523
309/676-2121 ext. 364 FAX: 309/637-5437 email: mkrost@mtco.com

Iowa
Bell, Dennis, 1016 Ridge Rd., Denison, IA 51442 712/263-3157
email: dgbell@frontiernet.net

Minnesota
Dahlberg, Mary Jo, 38336 Casselberry Dr., North Branch, MN
55056 661/674-2718 email: mjdahlberg@aol.com

North Indiana
Dwiggins, Jack W., 10837 S. Springboro Rd., Brookston, IN 47923
765/563-3409 email: dwigginsj@aol.com

Northern Illinois
Curless, Roger L., 441 Feathercock Dr., Aurora, IL 60506-5208
630/571-8681 FAX: 630/571-3760
email: Roger.curless@cendantmobility.com

South Indiana
Shaw, James C., 5229 Leone Pl., Indianapolis, IN 46226-1751
317/574-6982 email: jcshaw@iquest.com

West Michigan
Bobier, Cris, 1001 Dakin St., Lansing, MI 48912-1911 517/485-3459
FAX: 517/485-4130 email: Crisppumc@aol.com

West Ohio

Oglesby, Mildred, 2444 Madison Rd. #307, Cincinnati, OH 45208
513/871-0593 FAX: 513/533-3431 email: Meoglesby@aol.com

Wisconsin

Graeber, Sheri, 3159 Omro Rd., Oshkosh, WI 54904 920/236-2709
email: slgraeber@wisconsinumc.org
Oren, Andrew (Associate), 3156 S. Kinnickinnic Ave., Milwaukee,
WI 53207 414/744-4306 email: Ajoren@ticon.net

NORTHEASTERN JURISDICTION

Baltimore-Washington

Williams, Calvin, 15801 Good Hope Rd., Silver Spring,
MD 20905-4037 800/492-2525 FAX: 410/309-9430
email: Caldot53@aol.com

Central Pennsylvania

Gordon, Joan, POB 254, Lamar, PA 16848 570/726-3215
email: Jgordon@cub.kcnet.org
Hart, Vance (Associate), RD 1, Box 84, Williamsburg, PA 16693
email: Acclcpc@csrlink.net

Eastern Pennsylvania

Thompson, Lenora, 45 East City Line Ave. #422, Bala Cynwyd, PA
19004 H: 215/878-0408 O: 215/473-8219
email: Lenorathompson@hotmail.com

Greater New Jersey

Ace, Connie, POB 393, Whitehouse, NJ 08888 908/534-6023
FAX: 908/534-4547 email: cace@eclipse.net
Brown, Jay, 1145 S. Beecham Rd., Williamstown, NJ 08094
856/216-8003 FAX: 856/728-1054 email: usn65@aol.com

New England

Mackenzie, MaryAnne, 4 Grand St., Somersworth, NH 03878
603/692-7465 email: Mack@ttic.net
Flananary, Fay (Associate), 217 Lloyd Ave., Belchertown, MA 01007
413/323-8669 email: Flana3@msn.com

New York

Hunsinger, Robert G., 63 Pickerel Rd., Monroe, NY 10950
845/783-1932 FAX: 201/935-7508 email: rhunsing@frontier.net.net

North Central New York

Bassett, Sharon, 8428 Brewerton Rd., Cicero, NY 13039
315/699-0008 FAX: 315/699-0008 (call before sending)
email: bassetts1@cs.com

Peninsula-Delaware
Webster, Darlene, 12062 Jeffrey Ln., Princess Anne, MD 21853-2128
410/651-1788 email: dwebstercll@aol.com

Troy
Archibald, Julius A., Jr., 90 Park Ave., Plattsburgh, NY 12901
518/564-3252 FAX: 518/564-3152
email: Julius.archibald@plattsburgh.edu

West Virginia
Wigal, Betty L., Rt. 1, Box 242E, Parkersburg, WV 26101
304/464-4230 email: bettywigal@aol.com

Western New York
Richardson, Gerald, 1217 Delaware Ave., #904, Buffalo, NY 14209
716/885-0701 FAX: 716/887-3365 or 3355 email:
Geraldrichardson@oasas.state.ny.us

Western Pennsylvania
Denardo, Nancy, 400 Dersam St., McKeesport, PA 15133
412/664-4815 FAX: 412/233-9005 email: ndenrn@aol.com

Wyoming
Hamill, Raymond L., RR 3, Box 1357, Honesdale, PA 18431
717/253-5229 FAX: 717/253-2025 email: hamill@epix.net

SOUTH CENTRAL JURISDICTION

Central Texas
Dodd, Bliss, 829 Timberhill Dr., Hurst, TX 76053 817/531-4963
FAX: 817/531-4814 email: bdodd829@aol.com

Kansas East
Fox, Dale, 1701 Ash, Ottawa, KS 66067 785/242-6874
email: Ddfox@weblink2000.net

Kansas West
Brewster, Dixie, 1668 W. 140th Ave., Milton, KS 67106
316/478-2828 email: Brewsters@havilandtelco.com

Louisiana
Randolph, Ned, 1808 White St., Alexandria, LA 71301 318/449-
3732

Missouri East
Williams, Jerry Ruth, 1967 Willow Lake Dr., Chesterfield,
MO 63017-7659 636/532-5934 FAX: 636/532-3462
email: Micjerbob@aol.com

Missouri West
Edmondson, Kelly, 1239 Cheatham Ct., Warrensburg, MO 64093
660/543-4674 email: Kellyedmondson@hotmail.com

Nebraska
Schwaninger, Lavina, 28400 SW 14, Martel, NE 68404
402/787-2265 email: Llschwan@alltell.net

New Mexico
Wood, William H. (Bill), 10268 Saigon, El Paso, TX 79925 915/598-8845 FAX: 915/584-9515 email: BBWD@aol.com

North Arkansas
Whitaker, Asa, 160 Ottinger St., Batesville, AR 72501 870/793-3007
FAX: 870/793-9398 email: asa@ipa.net

North Texas
Talbert, Tom, 6217 Kovarik, Wichita Falls, TX 76310 940/766-3551
FAX: 940/696-0968 email: talbsac@wf.net

Northwest Texas
Blair, Jackie, 1707 Hillcrest Dr., Canyon, TX 79015 806/655-9551
email: jblair@nts-online.net

Oklahoma Indian Missionary
Foote, Geneva, POB 243, Sapulpa, OK 74067 918/321-3109
email: bfoote1930@earthlink.net

Oklahoma
Young, Carl W., 417 Kenswick Ct., Edmond, OK 73034
405/340-9200 FAX: 405/340-9233 email: Carl.w.young@worldnet.att.net

Rio Grande
Escareño, Della, 551 Gettysburg Dr., San Antonio, TX 78228-2059
210/732-3123 email: descareno529@aol.com

Southwest Texas
Loeb, Carol, 4610 Lomond, Corpus Christi, TX 78413 361/850-9099
email: hloeb18537@aol.com

Texas
Dillard, Melvin, 2656 S. Loop West Suite 585, Houston, TX 77054
H: 713/667-6900 O: 713/669-9313 FAX: 713/669-9367
email: mdassociates@argolink.net

SOUTHEASTERN JURISDICTION

Alabama-West Florida
Dunaway, Roy S., Jr., 35 Melanie Ln., Eufaula, AL 36027
334/687-9617 email: Rdunaway@ionet.net

Florida
Sessums, T. Terrell, 5020 Bayshore Blvd., Tampa, FL 33611
813/224-9000 email: terrell.sessums@ssnlaw.com

Holston
Lockaby, Bob, 7514 Island Manor Dr., Harrison, TN 37341
423/756-5171 FAX: 423/266-1605 email: Rlockaby@gplt.com

Kentucky
Minton, John D., Jr., 1703 Chestnut St., Bowling Green, KY 42101-3503
502/746-7408 FAX: 502/796-6015 email: Jno1703@aol.com

Memphis
Archer, Anita Kay, 262 Old Humboldt Rd., Jackson TN 38305
901/668-4002 FAX: 901/422-4004 email:Akarcher@aeneas.net

Mississippi
Scott, William D., III, 566 N. Swaney Rd., Holly Springs,
MS 38635-1208 601/232-5338 FAX: 601/232-7300
email: chscott@olemiss.edu

North Alabama
Holt, Gloria E., 6740 Clear Creek Cir., Trussville, AL 35173
205/661-9292 FAX: 205/856-8788 email: Gholt@umcna.bsc.edu

North Carolina
Rouse, Jeanne, POB 52547, Durham, NC 27717-2547 919/489-4834
email: jrrouse@ipass.net

North Georgia
Whittemore, Joe M., POB 770, Hartwell, GA 30643 706/376-3168
FAX: 706/376-5945 email: wscpas@hartcom.net

Red Bird Missionary
Sizemore, Joyce, Box 24, Queendale Ctr., Beverly, KY 40913
606/598-8228 email: coach6227@yahoo.com

South Carolina
Rogerson, Carolyne G., 2925 Mayer St., Georgetown, SC 29440
803/546-2383 FAX: 803/527-2293 email: Carolynerogerson@aol.com

South Georgia
Black, Charlene R., POB 242, Young Harris, GA 30582
706/379-4311 ext. 5115 email: cblack@gsvms2.cc.gasou.edu

Tennessee
Alexander, Betty Masters, 147 Allen Dr., Hendersonville, TN 37075
615/822-4932 FAX: 615/824-8784 email: Alexbetebn@msn.com

Virginia
Hardman, Ronald L., 11179 Eagle Watch, Smithfield, VA 23430-5731 757/357-0169 FAX: 757/357-4549

Western North Carolina
Young, Jack, 1008 Westwood Ave., High Point, NC 27262-3738 336/889-3336 FAX: 336/884-1313 email: cyoung6054@aol.com

WESTERN JURISDICTION

Alaska Missionary
Smalley, Susan, 105 Linwood, Kenai, AK 99611 907/283-7469 FAX: 907/283-6029 email: hsmalley@alaska.net

California-Nevada
Taylor, Pete W., Jr., 7962 Sanford St., Oakland, CA 94605 510/638-7397

California-Pacific
Dixon, Gaunnie Hardin, 3603 Dunn Dr., #202, Los Angeles, CA 90034 310/558-9900 FAX: 310/559-6764 email: gaunnie@cs.com

Desert-Southwest
Charlton, Susan, 6230 E. Exeter Blvd., Scottsdale, AZ 85251 480/949-5919 email: susiecharlton@aol.com

Oregon-Idaho
Walker, Beverly J., 1266 SW Fourth St., Gresham, OR 97080-6820 503/665-9747 FAX: 503/655-5709 email: beverly@pdxlive.com

Pacific Northwest
Bratt, Gene, (Associate), 24208 102nd Pl., W., Edmonds, WA 98020 206/546-4316

Russell, Jim, (Associate), 19425 NE 181 St., Woodinville, WA 98072 425/788-9124 email: Jimrussell@juno.com

Rocky Mountain
Gleaton, Tommy, POB 6283, Denver, CO 80206 303/756-1588 FAX: 603/907-0752 email: Tgle105463@aol.com

Yellowstone
Doyle, Lin, Box 8, Hyattville, WY 82428 307/469-2253 FAX: 307/469-2245 email: ldoyle@tctwest.net

SECRETARIES OF THE ANNUAL CONFERENCES

NORTH CENTRAL JURISDICTION

Dakotas Conference (Dakotas Area)
Ellingson, Mark S., 2102 2nd Ave., NE, Reynolds, ND 58275-9494
Detroit Conference (Michigan Area)
Schramm, Linda A., 244 S. Elk, Sandusky, MI 48471-1358
East Ohio Conference (Ohio East Area)
Henderson, Gary R., 23002 Lake Shore Blvd., Euclid, OH, 44123-1325
Illinois Great Rivers Conference (Illinois Area)
Shelquist, Charles G., 408 E. Lincoln Ave., Onarga, IL 60955-1315
Iowa Conference (Iowa Area)
Ney, Sue, 506 S. Portland St., Bancroft, IA 50517-8004
Minnesota Conference (Minnesota Area)
Blaisdell, Linda, 122 W. Franklin Ave., Rm. 400, Minneapolis, MN 55404-2472
North Indiana Conference (Indiana Area)
Butler, James D., 114 N. Ironwood Dr., South Bend, IN 46615-2516
Northern Illinois Conference (Chicago Area)
McCabe, Harriet H., 9 W. Bailey Rd., Naperville, IL 60565-2359
South Indiana Conference (Indiana Area)
Hurley, Curtis N., POB 84, Bedford, IN 47421-0084
West Michigan Conference (Michigan Area)
Johnson, William C., 2244 Porter St., SW, Wyoming, MI 49509-2222
West Ohio Conference (West Ohio Area)
Wilson, L. Cean, 32 Wesley Blvd., Worthington, OH 43085-3585
Wisconsin Conference (Wisconsin Area)
Myers, Kevin Rice, (750 Windsor St., Ste. 202), POB 620, Sun Prairie, WI 53590-0620

NORTHEASTERN JURISDICTION

Baltimore-Washington Conference (Washington Area)
Harrell, Stanley G., 5604 Chesterfield Dr., Temple Hills, MD 20748-4044

Central Pennsylvania Conference (Harrisburg Area)
Sowers, Shirley J., 2430 Bradford Dr., York, PA 17402-3643

Eastern Pennsylvania Conference (Philadelphia Area)
Wood, Dorothy S., 95 2nd Ave., Phoenixville, PA 19460-3659

Greater New Jersey Conference (New Jersey Area)
Harriott, Michael M., 11 Madison Ave., Montclair, NJ 07042-4418

New England Conference (Boston Area)
Blackadar, John M., (276 Essex St., 4th floor—01840-1516) POB 249, Lawrence, MA 01842-0449

New York Conference (New York Area)
Curry, Leo W., 2543 Marion Ave., Bronx, NY 10458-4703

North Central New York Conference (New York West Area)
Austin, Dale E., POB 301, Freeville, NY 13068-0301

Peninsula-Delaware Conference (Philadelphia Area)
Etter, Boyd B., POB 522, North East, MD 21901-0522

Troy Conference (Albany Area)
Shanklin, Thomas L., POB 362, 17 Nichols Rd., Lempster, NH 03605-0362

West Virginia Conference (West Virginia Area)
Kenaston, Judith M., POB 2313, Charleston, WV 25328-2313

Western New York Conference (New York West Area)
Richardson, Mary E., POB 884, Adams Basin, NY 14410-0884

Western Pennsylvania Conference (Pittsburgh Area)
Wilson, John R., 118 Charles St., Dorseyville, PA 15238-1008

Wyoming Conference (Albany Area)
Brauer, Virginia, RR 2, Box 245, Mehoopany, PA 18629-9662

SOUTH CENTRAL JURISDICTION

Arkansas Conference (Arkansas Area)
Crossman, Robert O., 1075 Hogan Ln., Conway, AR 72034-8126

Central Texas Conference (Forth Worth Area)
McClure, Charles L., 464 Bailey Ave., Fort Worth, TX 76107-2124 (Also Conference Treasurer)

Kansas East Conference (Kansas Area)
Robertson, Karen, (201 SW 15th St.), POB 4187, Topeka, KS 66604

Kansas West Conference (Kansas Area)
McMillan, Anita, POB 295, Clearwater, KS 67026-0295

Louisiana Conference (Louisiana Area)
Rhoads, Carl E., III, 527 North Blvd., Baton Rouge, LA 70802-5720

Missouri Conference (Missouri Area)
Dace, Jimmie R., 5567 Highway 54, Osage Beach, MO 65065-3027
Turnbough, Mark, 1001 Sunset Ave., Liberty, MO 64068-2015

Nebraska Conference (Nebraska Area)
Ford, Ralph H., 614 N. Hastings, Hastings, NE 68901-5114

New Mexico Conference (Northwest Texas-New Mexico Area)
Shoemaker, Terry, POB 1638, Albuquerque, NM 87103-1638

North Texas Conference (Dallas Area)
Bearden, Leighton H., POB 447, Rowlett, TX 75030-0447

Northwest Texas Conference (Northwest Texas-New Mexico Area)
Gregory, C. Marvin, POB 500, Tahoka, TX 79373-0500

Oklahoma Conference (Oklahoma Area)
Rettig, Charles R., 7903 E. 15th St., Tulsa, OK 74112-7052

Oklahoma Indian Missionary Conference (Oklahoma Area)
Fitzpatrick, Diana, 3609 Midland Dr., Norman, OK 73072-5141

Rio Grande Conference (San Antonio Area)
Briones, Francisco J., 403 McNeel Rd., San Antonio, TX 78228-2541

Southwest Texas Conference (San Antonio Area)
Seilheimer, David A., (16400 Huebner Rd.—78248) POB 781149, San Antonio, TX 78278-1149 (Also Conference Statistician & Treasurer)

Texas Conference (Houston Area)
Megill, Gregory A., POB 1385, Crosby TX 77532-1385

SOUTHEASTERN JURISDICTION

Alabama-West Florida Conference (Alabama-West Florida Area)
Epler, Neil C., 5200 Perin Rd., Mobile, AL 36693-3157

Florida Conference (Florida Area)
Arnett, Carmen S., 1801 12th Ave. S., Lake Worth, FL 33461-5799

Holston Conference (Holston Area)
Humphreys, Dennie D., POB 32939, Knoxville, TN 37930-2939

Kentucky Conference (Louisville Area)
Bowdan, Melvin R. (Mel), Jr., 2236 Clear Creek Rd., Nicholasville, KY 40356-8757

Memphis Conference (Nashville Area)
Fesmire, C. Wayne, 78 Sunhaven Dr., Jackson, TN 38305-2005

Mississippi Conference (Mississippi Area)
Beam, Jerry B., 563 E. Main St., Philadelphia, MS 39350-2429

North Alabama Conference (Birmingham Area)
Lacey, Mark S., 6690 Cahaba Valley Rd., Birmingham, AL 35242-2825

North Carolina Conference (Raleigh Area)
Bryan, James L., POB 10955 (1307 Glenwood Ave.), Raleigh, NC 27605-0955

North Georgia Conference (Atlanta Area)
Weber, Donn Ann, 2650 N. Druid Hills NE, Atlanta, GA 30329-3551

Red Bird Missionary Conference (Louisville Area)
Warden, David C., 2993 Beach Creek Rd., Manchester, KY 40962-6107

South Carolina Conference (Columbia Area)
Gramling, Dr. Roger M., POB 21305, Columbia, SC 29221-1305

South Georgia Conference (South Georgia Area)
Brady, Remer L. "Brad", III, POB 20408, St. Simons Island, GA 31522-0008

Tennessee Conference (Nashville Area)
Unruh, Von W., 368 N. Main St., Kingston Springs, TN 37082-9031

Virginia Conference (Richmond Area)
Blinn, Robert C., POB 1081, Collinsville, VA 24078

Western North Carolina Conference (Charlotte Area)
White, Charles D., Jr., (3400 Shamrock Dr.-28215) POB 18005, Charlotte, NC 28218-0005

WESTERN JURISDICTION

Alaska Missionary Conference (Portland Area)
Wingfield, Brenda K., 3402 Wesleyan Dr., Anchorage, AK 99508-4866

California-Nevada Conference (San Francisco Area)
Pearson, Virginia M., 625 Randolph St., Napa, CA 94559-2914

California-Pacific Conference (Los Angeles Area)
Hwang, Keith Andrew, (110 S. Euclid Ave.—91101) POB 6006, Pasadena, CA 91102-6006

Desert Southwest Conference (Phoenix Area)
Long, Rebecca Oakes, 655 N. Craycroft, Tucson, AZ 85711-1482

Oregon-Idaho Conference (Portland Area)
Burtner, Robert W., 1582 Willagillespie Rd., Eugene, OR 97401-7824

Pacific Northwest Conference (Seattle Area)
Stanton, Wesley E., 5634 S. Park Ave., Tacoma, WA 98408-5634

Rocky Mountain Conference (Denver Area)
Tarman, Carolyn, 701 43rd Ave., Greeley, CO 80634-1404

Yellowstone Conference (Denver Area)
DeBree, Susan K., 132 N. Adams Ave., Buffalo, WY 82834-1707

IGLESIA METODISTA AUTONOMA AFILIADA DE PUERTO RICO

Gabriel, Lizette, UPR Station, POB 23339, San Juan, PUERTO RICO 00931-3339

TREASURERS OF THE ANNUAL CONFERENCES

NORTH CENTRAL JURISDICTION

Dakotas Conference (Dakotas Area)
Armstrong, Donald, 1331 W. University Ave., POB 460, Mitchell, SD 57301-0460 605/996-6552 FAX: 605/996-1766
email:don.armstrong@dakotasumc.org

Detroit Conference (Michigan Area)
Morford, Anna May, 1309 N. Ballenger Hwy, Suite 1, Flint, MI 48504-7919 810/233-5500 FAX: 810/233-5700
email: morfordct@aol.com

East Ohio Conference (Ohio East Area)
Vargo, Jessica H., 8800 Cleveland Ave. NW, POB 2800, North Canton, OH 44720-0800 330/499-3272 FAX: 330/499-3279
email: vargoj@eoumc.com

Illinois Great Rivers Conference (Illinois Area)
Barton, Brenda L., (1211 N. Park St. - 61701), POB 515, Bloomington, IL 61702-0515 309/828-5092 ext. 204
FAX: 309/829-8369 (Also Conference Statistician)
email: brendabarton1@aol.com

Iowa Conference (Iowa Area)
Smith, Charles W., 500 E. Court Ave., Ste. C, Des Moines, IA 50309-2019 515/283-1996 FAX: 515/288-1906
email: chuck.smith@iaumc.org (Also Conference Statistician)

Minnesota Conference (Minnesota Area)
Carroll, Barbara, 122 W. Franklin Ave., Suite 400, Minneapolis, MN 55404-2472 612/870-0058 ext. 235 FAX: 612/870-1260
email: barbara.carroll@mnumc.org

North Indiana Conference (Indiana Area)
Williams, H. Brent, 1105 N. Western Ave., POB 869, Marion, IN 46952-0869 765/664-5138 FAX: 765/664-2307
email: brent@nicumc.org (Also Conference Statistician)

Northern Illinois Conference (Chicago Area)
Chafin, Lonnie, 77 W. Washington St., Suite 1820, Chicago, IL 60602-3181 312/346-9766 ext. 122 FAX: 312/346-9730
email: lchafin@umcnic.org

South Indiana Conference (Indiana Area)

Wilson, Brent L., POB 5008 (2427 E. Second St.-47401),
Bloomington, IN 47407-5008 812/336-0186 FAX: 812/336-0216
email: bwilson@sicumc.org

West Michigan Conference (Michigan Area)

Tumonong, Prospero I., (11 Fuller Ave., SE-49506), POB 6247,
Grand Rapids, MI 49516-6247 616/459-4503 ext. 341
FAX: 616/459-0191 email: treas@wmcumc.org

West Ohio Conference (Ohio West Area)

Sutton, R. Stanley, 32 Wesley Blvd., Worthington, OH 43085-3585
614/844-6200 FAX: 614/781-2642 email: ssutton@wocumc.org

Wisconsin Conference (Wisconsin Area)

King, Lisa M., (750 Windsor St.), POB 620, Sun Prairie,
WI 53590-0620 608/837-7320 ext. 221 FAX: 608/825-8287
email: lisaking@wisconsinumc.org

NORTHEASTERN JURISDICTION

Baltimore-Washington Conference (Washington Area)

c/o Conference Treasurer, 7178 Columbia Gateway Dr., Columbia,
MD 21046-2132 410/309-3400 ext. 460 FAX: 410/309-9436
(Also Conference Statistician)

Central Pennsylvania Conference (Harrisburg Area)

Haverstock, Zedna M., (303 Mulberry Dr.—17050-3141) POB 2053,
Mechanicsburg, PA 17055-2053 717/766-5275 FAX: 717/766-5976
email: zedna@cpcumc.org (Also Conference Statistician)

Eastern Pennsylvania Conference (Philadelphia Area)

Kumar, A. Moses R., (980 Madison Ave., Norristown—19403)
POB 820, Valley Forge, PA 19482-0820 610/666-9090 ext. 209
FAX: 610/666-9093 email: moses@epaumc.org

Greater New Jersey Conference (New Jersey Area)

Scheer, Dennis H., 1001 Wickapeko Dr., Ocean, NJ 07712-4733
732/359-1030 FAX: 732/359-1039 email: treasurer@gnjumc.org

New England Conference (Boston Area)

Carnahan, Charles R., (276 Essex St., 4th floor—01840-1516), POB
249, Lawrence, MA 01842-0449 978/682-8055 ext. 12 FAX: 978/682-
8227 email: Ccarnahan@neumc.org

New York Conference (New York Area)
Swiggett, Ernest L., 20 Soundview Ave., White Plains, NY 10606-3302 914/615-2212 FAX: 914/615-2243 email: eswiggett@nyac.com (Also Conference Statistician)

North Central New York Conference (New York West Area)
Mauser, Larry, 8422 N. Main St., POB 1515, Cicero, NY 13039-1515 315/699-8715 ext. 319 FAX: 315/699-8774 email: ncnylarry@aol.com (Also Conference Statistician)

Peninsula-Delaware Conference (Philadelphia Area)
Westbrook, William E., Jr., 139 N. State St., Dover, DE 19901-3834 302/674-2626 FAX: 302/674-2729 email: westbrook@pen-del.org

Troy Conference (Albany Area)
Doherty, Joseph J., POB 560, Saratoga Springs, NY 12866-0560 518/584-8214 FAX: 518/584-8378 email: jdoherty@troyac.org

West Virginia Conference (West Virginia Area)
Berner, James M., (900 Washington St.—25301), POB 2469, Charleston, WV 25329-2469 304/344-8331 FAX: 304/344-9584 email: tresrr@aol.com (Also Conference Statistician)

Western New York Conference (New York West Area)
Gasiewicz, Barbara, 131 John Muir Dr., West Amherst, NY 14228-1147 716/564-2316 FAX: 716/564-2365 email: barbg@conference-news.com (Also Conference Statistician)

Western Pennsylvania Conference (Pittsburgh Area)
Mitchell, Douglas D., 1204 Freedom Rd., POB 5002, Cranberry Twp., PA 16066-1902 724/776-2300 ext. 240 FAX: 724/776-1355 email: ummoney@umchurch.org

Wyoming Conference (Albany Area)
Schmitt, Don, (1700 Monroe St.-13760), POB 58, Endicott, NY 13761-0058 607/757-0608 FAX: 607/757-0752 email: dschmitt@wyomingconference.org

SOUTH CENTRAL JURISDICTION

Arkansas Conference (Arkansas Area)
Eason, Joe D., (715 Center St., Suite 202—72201), POB 2941, Little Rock, AR 72203-2941 501/324-8000 FAX: 501/324-8018 email: jeason@arumc.org (Also Statistician)

Central Texas Conference (Fort Worth Area)
McClure, Charles L., 464 Bailey Ave., Fort Worth, TX 76107-2124 817/877-5222 FAX: 817/338-4541 email: charles@ctcumc.org (Also Conference Secretary)

Kansas East Conference (Kansas Area)
Henson, Paul W., 4201 SW 15th St., POB 4187, Topeka, KS 66604-0187 785/272-9111 FAX: 785/272-9135
email: phenson@kansaseast.org (Also Conference Statistician)

Kansas West Conference (Kansas Area)
Maltbie, Debbie, 9440 E. Boston St., Suite 110, Wichita, KS 67207-3600 316/684-0266 FAX: 316/684-0044
email: dmaltbie@kswestumc.org (Also Conference Statistician)

Louisiana Conference (Louisiana Area)
Rhoads, Carl E., III, 527 North Blvd., Baton Rouge, LA 70802-5720 225/346-1646 FAX: 225/383-2652 email: crhoads@bellsouth.net
(Also Conference Statistician & Secretary)

Missouri East Conference (Missouri Area)
Wilbur, Reuben L., 4800 Santana Cir., Suite 500, Columbia, MO 65203-7138 573/441-1770 FAX: 573/441-1780
email: wilbur@ecunetumc.org (Also Conference Statistician)

Nebraska Conference (Nebraska Area)
Winkelmann, Jeri, 2641 N. 49th St., POB 4553, Lincoln, NE 68504-0553 402/464-5994 FAX: 402/464-6203 email: jwink@umcneb.org

New Mexico Conference (Northwest Texas-New Mexico Area)
Kinane, Daniel M., 7920 Mountain Rd. NE, Albuquerque, NM 87110-7805 505/255-8786 FAX: 505/265-6184
email: nmtreas@nmconfum.com (Also Conference Statistician)

North Texas Conference (Dallas Area)
Guier, L. Marvin, III, (13959 Peyton Dr.-75240), POB 516069, Dallas, TX 75251-6069 972/490-3438 FAX: 972/490-8524
email: guier@ntcumc.org (Also Conference Statistician)

Northwest Texas Conference (Northwest Texas-New Mexico Area)
Pittman, Mark, 1415 Avenue M, Lubbock, TX 79401-3939 806/762-0201 ext. 12 FAX: 806/762-0205 email: pittman@nwtxconf.org

Oklahoma Conference (Oklahoma Area)
McNaught, JoAnn, 1501 NW 24th St., Oklahoma City, OK 73106-3635 405/530-2067 FAX: 405/524-0750
email: jmcnaught@okumc.org (Also Conference Secretary)

Oklahoma Indian Missionary Conference (Oklahoma Area)
Galyon, Dennis, 3020 S. Harvey St., Oklahoma City, OK 73109-6309

405/632-2006 FAX: 405/632-0209 email: dgalyon@engelbach-roberts.com (Also Conference Statistician)

Rio Grande Conference (San Antonio Area)
Trafton, Marge, (1315 E. Main #110—78332), POB 3478, Alice, TX 78333-3478 361/668-6715 FAX: 361/668-9919 email: rgctreas@awesomenet.net

Southwest Texas Conference (San Antonio Area)
Seilheimer, David A., (16400 Huebner Rd.-78248), POB 781149, San Antonio, TX 78278-1149 210/408-4500 FAX: 210/408-4536 email: daseilh@umcswtx.org (Also Conference Secretary & Statistician)

Texas Conference (Houston Area)
Hayes, Robert E., Jr., 5215 Main St., Houston, TX 77002-9792 713/521-9383 FAX: 713/521-3724 email: hayes@methodists.net

SOUTHEASTERN JURISDICTION

Alabama-West Florida Conference (Alabama-West Florida Area)
Dunnewind, Frank S., (532 E. Three Notch St.) P.O. Drawer 700, Andalusia, AL 36420-0700 334/222-3127 ext. 111 FAX: 334/222-0469 email: fdunne@alaweb.com (Also Conference Statistician)

Florida Conference (Florida Area)
Casey-Rutland, Ransom, (1140 E. McDonald St.—33801), POB 3767, Lakeland, FL 33802-3767 863/688-5563 ext. 113
FAX: 863/688-4595 email: rcasey-rutland@flumc.org (Also Conference Statistician)

Holston Conference (Holston Area)
McDonald, Clyde H., (9915 Kingston Pike—37922), POB 32939, Knoxville, TN 37930-2939 865/690-4080 FAX: 865/690-3162 email: clydemcdonald@holston.org

Kentucky Conference (Louisville Area)
Watts, Michael B., 7400 Floydsburg Rd., Crestwood, KY 40014 502/425-3884 FAX: 502/426-5181
email: mwatts@kyumc.org (Also Conference Statistician)

Memphis Conference (Nashville Area)
Finger, James M., 24 Corporate Blvd., Jackson, TN 38305-2315

731/664-5540 FAX: 731/660-2085 email: james380@usit.net (Also Conference Statistician)

Mississippi Conference (Mississippi Area)
Stotts, David, (321 E. Mississippi—39201), POB 1201, Jackson, MS 39215-1201 601/354-0515 FAX: 601/948-5983
email: treasurer@mississippi-umc.org

North Alabama Conference (Birmingham Area)
Selman, Scott Y., 898 Arkadelphia Rd., Birmingham, AL 35204-3436 205/226-7989 FAX: 205/226-7975
email: sselman@umcna.bsc.edu

North Carolina Conference (Raleigh Area)
Strother, Sharon E., (1307 Glenwood Ave.), POB 10955, Raleigh, NC 27605-0955 919/832-9560 FAX: 919/834-7989
email: sestrother@nccumc.org

North Georgia Conference (North Georgia Area)
Cox, Keith M., (4511 Jones Bridge Cir. NW, 30092-1406), POB 922977, Norcross, GA 30010-2997 678/533-1392 FAX: 678/533-1397
email: treasurer@ngumc.org

Red Bird Missionary Conference (Louisville Area)
Fowler, Judith, 6 Queendale Center, Beverly, KY 40913-9601 606/598-5915 FAX: 606/598-6405
email: treasurer@redbirdconference.org

South Carolina Conference (Columbia Area)
Buie, Becky L., (4908 Colonial Dr. - 29203), POB 3787, Columbia, SC 29230-3787 803/735-8790 FAX: 803/691-0700
email: bbuie@umcsc.org (Also Conference Statistician)

South Georgia Conference (South Georgia Area)
Hagan, Miriam C., (777 Mulberry St., Suite B—31201), POB 52101, Macon, GA 31208-4013 478/738-0048 FAX: 478/738-9768
email: miriam@sgaumc.org

Tennessee Conference (Nashville Area)
Little, R. Terry, Jr., 1110- 19th Ave. S., POB 120607, Nashville, TN 37212-0607 615/327-1162 FAX: 615/327-1169
email: tlittle@tnconfoas.org (Also Conference Statistician)

Virginia Conference (Richmond Area)
Branscome, James L., (10330 Staples Mill Rd.—23060), POB 1719,

Glen Allen, VA 23219-1719 804/521-1105 FAX: 804/521-1172
email: JimBranscome@vaumc.org (Also Conference Statistician)
Western North Carolina Conference (Charlotte Area)
Wyman, William C., Jr., (3400 Shamrock Dr.—28215), POB 18005,
Charlotte, NC 28218-0005 704/535-2260 FAX: 704/537-7710
email: bwyman@wnccumc.org

WESTERN JURISDICTION

Alaska Missionary Conference (Portland Area)
Bickman, Susan M., 3402 Wesleyan Dr., Anchorage, AK 99508-4866
907/333-5050 FAX: 907/333-2304 email: umc@gci.net
California-Nevada Conference (San Francisco Area)
Knudsen, J. Diane, (1276 Halyard Dr.—95691), POB 980250, West
Sacramento, CA 95798-0250 916/374-1520 FAX: 916/372-5544
email: dianek@calnevumc.org
California-Pacific Conference (Los Angeles Area)
Gara, Dan J., (110 S. Euclid Ave.—91101), POB 6006, Pasadena, CA
91102-6006 626/568-7300 FAX: 626/796-7297
email: dgara@cal-pac.org
Desert Southwest Conference (Phoenix Area)
Huffman, Joel, 1550 E. Meadowbrook Ave., Suite 200, Phoenix, AZ
85014-4040 602/266-6956 ext. 205 FAX: 602/266-2196
email: joel@desertsw.org (Also Conference Statistician)
Oregon-Idaho Conference (Portland Area)
Meyers, Robert C., 1505 SW 18th Ave., Portland, OR 97201-2599
503/226-7931 press 22 FAX: 503/226-4158 email: bob@umoi.org
Pacific Northwest Conference (Seattle Area)
Parrish, Craig A., 2112 3rd Ave., Suite 300, Seattle, WA 98121-2333
206/728-7462 FAX: 206/728-8442 email: cparrish@pnwumc.org
Rocky Mountain Conference (Denver Area)
O'Neill, Dan, 2200 S. University Blvd., Denver, CO 80210-4708
303/733-3736 ext. 205 FAX: 303/733-1730 email: dan@rmcumc.com
(Also Conference Statistician)

Yellowstone Conference (Denver Area)

Saas, Anita, 1220 Avenue C, Billings, MT 59102 406/256-1385 ext. 3002 FAX: 406/256-4948 email: yacanita@aol.com

IGLESIA METODISTA AUTONOMA AFILIADA DE PUERTO RICO

Borreo, Agustin, U.P.R. Station, Apartado 23339, San Juan, PUERTO RICO 00931-3339 787/765-3195 FAX: 787/751-3615

UNITED METHODIST INFORMATION TECHNOLOGY ASSOCIATION

Alabama-West Florida Conference
Dunnewind, Frank S., POB 700, Andalusia, AL 36420 888/873-3127
or 334/222-3127 FAX: 334/222-0469 email: fdunne@awfumc.org
Arkansas Area
Burris, Todd, POB 2941, Little Rock, AR 72201 501/324-8004 FAX:
501/324-8043 email: tburris@arumc.org
Baltimore-Washington Conference
Knight, Martha, 7178 Columbia Gateway, Columbia,
MD 21046-1526 410/309-3466 FAX: 410/309-9436
email: mknight@bwcumc.org
Central Texas Conference
Cullen, Bobby, 464 Bailey Ave., Ft. Worth, TX 76107-2153
817/877-5222 FAX: 817/338-4541 email: bobby@ctcumc.org
Dakotas Conference
Armstrong, Donald, POB 460, 1331 W. University Ave., Mitchell,
SD 57301-0460 605/996-6552 FAX: 605/996-1766
email: don.armstron@dakotasumc.org
Desert Southwest Conference
Heston, Betty, 1550 E. Meadowbrook Ave., Suite 200, Phoeniz,
AZ 85014-4040 602/266-6956 800/229-8622 FAX: 602/266-5343
email: betty@desertsw.org
Detroit Conference
Morford, Anna May, 1309 N. Ballinger, Suite 1, Flint, MI 48504
810/233-5500 or 800/334-0544 email: morfordct@aol.com
Eastern Pennsylvania Conference
Whittaker, Larry, POB 820, Valley Forge, PA 19482 610/666-9090
FAX: 610/666-9093 email: larry@epaumc.org
East Ohio Conference
Peek, Charles, 8800 Cleveland Ave., North Canton, OH 44720
330/499-3972 ext. 123 800/831-3972 FAX: 330/499-3279
email: admin@eocumc.com
Florida Conference
Casey-Rutland, Ransom, POB 3767, Lakeland, FL 33802-3767
863/688-5563 FAX: 863/680-1912 email: rcasey-rutland@flumc.org
Holston Conference
McDonald, Clyde, POB 2506, Johnson City, TN 37605 423/928-2156
FAX: 423/928-8807 email: clydemcdonald@holston.org

Illinois Great Rivers Conference
Barton, Brenda L., POB 515, Bloomington, IL 61702-0515
309/828-5092 FAX: 309/829-4820 email: brendabarton1@aol.com
Iowa Conference
Minshall, Roland, 500 Court Ave., Suite C, Des Moines, IA 50309-
2019 515/283-1991 FAX: 515/288-1906
email: roland.minshall@iaumc.org
Kansas East Conference
Henson, Paul W., POB 4187, Topeka, KS 66604 785/272-9111
FAX: 785/272-9135 email: phenson@kansaseast.org
Kansas West Conference
Maltbie, Debbie, 9440 E. Boston, Suite 110, Wichita, KS 67207-3600
316/684-0266 FAX: 316/684-0044 email: dmaltbie@kswestumc.org
Kentucky Conference
Watts, Michael B., 7400 Floydsburg Rd., Crestwood, KY 40014
502/425-3884 FAX: 502/426-5181 email: mwatts@kyumc.org
Minnesota Conference
Walsh, Patrick, 122 W. Franklin Ave., Room 400, Minneapolis,
MN 55404-5472 612/870-0058 FAX: 612/870-1260
email: patwalsh@mnumc.org
Missouri Area Conference
Wilbur, Reuben L., 4800 Santa Circle, Suite 500, Columbia, MO 65203
573/441-1770 FAX: 573/441-1780
email: rwilbuur@moumethodist.org
New England Conference
Field, Scott, POB 249, Lawrence, MA 01842-0449 978/682-8055 FAX:
978/682-8227 email: sfield@neumc.org
New Mexico Conference
Kinane, Daniel M., 7920 Mountain Rd., NE, Albuquerque, NM 87110
505/299-6375 or 800/678-8786 FAX: 505/265-6184
email: nmtreas@nmconfum.com
New York Conference
Dickson, Everett, 20 Soundview Ave., White Plains, NY 10606 914/997-
1750 FAX: 914/684-6874 email: edickson@nyac.com
North Alabama Conference
Williams, Warren, 898 Arkadelphia Rd., Birmingham, AL 35204-3436
205/226-7966 FAX: 205/226-7975 email: wwilliams@umcna.bsc.org
North Carolina Conference
Ward, Douglas, 1307 Glenwood Ave., Raleigh, NC 27605 909/832-
9560 email: dward@nccumc.org
North Central New York Conference

Stevens, Shirley, POB 1515, Cicero, NY 13039 315/699-8715
  FAX: 315/699-8774 email: ncnyshirl@aol.com
North Georgia Conference
Murphy-McCarthy, Michael, PO Box 922997, Norcross, GA 30010
  404/659-0002 ext. 3237 FAX: 404/592-1141
  email: michael@ngumc.org
North Indiana Conference
Lehrian, Tim, POB 869, Marion, IN 46952 765/664-5138 800/783-5138
  FAX: 765/664-2307 email: tim.lehrian@nicumc.org
North Texas Conference
Guier, L. Marvin, III, POB 516069, Dallas, TX 75251 972/490-5505
  FAX: 972-490-8524 email: guier@ntcumc.org
Northern Illinois Conference
Sims, Jerry, 140 DesPlaines Ave., Forest Park, IL 60130 312/346-9766
  email: jsims@umcnic.org
Northwest Texas Conference
Prumer, Rosemary, 1415 Ave. M, Lubbock, TX 79401 806/762-0201
  FAX: 806/762-0205 email: rprumer@nwtxconf.org
Oklahoma Conference
McKnaught, Joann, 1501 NW 24th St., Oklahoma City, OK 73106
  405/530-2066 FAX: 405/525-4164 email: jmcnaught@okumc.org
Oregon-Idaho Conference
Sittser, Sandra, 1505 SW 18th Ave., Portland, OR 97201-2599
  503/226-7931 or 800/593-7539 FAX: 503/226-4158
  email: sandra@umoi.org
Pacific Northwest Conference
Galvin, Bruce, 2112 Third Ave., Suite 300, Seattle, WA 98121
  206/728-7462 FAX: 206/728-8442 email: pnwumctrea@msn.com
Peninsula/Delaware Conference
Westbrook, William E., Jr., 139 N. State St., Dover, DE 19901
  302/674-2626 FAX: 302/674-1573 email: wwestbrook@pen-del.org
Rocky Mountain Conference
Wright, Lorrie, 2200 S. University Blvd., Denver, CO 80210-4797
  303/733-3736 FAX: 303/733-1730 email: lorrie@rmcumc.com
South Carolina Conference
Buie, Becky L., POB 3778, Columbia, SC 29230 803/735-8790
  FAX: 803/691-0700 email: bbuie@umcsc.org
South Georgia Conference
Hagan, Miriam C., POB 52101, Macon, GA 31208-4013 912/738-0048
  or 800/535-4224 FAX: 912/738-9768 email: miriam@sgaumc.org
South Indiana Conference

Wilson, Brent L., POB 5008, Bloomington, IN 47407-5008
812/336-0186 FAX: 812/336-0216 email: bwilson@sicumc.org
Tennessee Conference
Freeman, William, POB 120607, 1110 19th Ave., S., Nashville, TN
37212 615/327-1162 FAX: 615/327-1169
email: wfreeman@tnumc.org
Texas Conference
McKay, David, 5215 Main St., Houston, TX 77002-9792 713/521-9383
FAX: 713/521-3724 email: david.mckay@txcumc.org
West Michigan Conference
Moore, Frederick, POB 6247, Grand Rapids, MI 49516-6247 616/459-
4503 FAX: 616/459-0191 email: fmoore@wmcumc.org
West Ohio Conference
Fritz, Sheri, 32 Wesley Blvd., Worthington, OH 43085-3585 614/844-
6200 ext. 211 FAX: 614/781-2642 email: sfritz@wocumc.org
West Virginia Conference
Berner, James M., POB 2469, Charleston, WV 25329 304/344-8331
FAX: 304/344-8338 email: tresrr@aol.com
Western New York Conference
Gasiewicz, Barbara, 131 John Muir Dr., Amherst, NY 14228
716/564-2316 FAX: 716/564-2365
email: barbg@conferencenews.com
Western Pennsylvania Conference
Mitchell, Douglas D., 1204 Freedom Rd., Cranberry Twp., PA 16066-
4914 800/536-9245 FAX: 724/776-1355
email: ummoney@umchurch.org

AGENCIES

General Board of Discipleship
Johnson, Robert, 1908 Grand Ave., Nashville, TN 37212
email: bjohnson@gbod.org
General Board of Pensions & Health Benefits
Maggi, Sharon, 1201 Davis St., Evanston, IL 60201 email:
sharon_magi@gbop.org
General Council on Finance and Administration
McGorry, Peter, 1200 Davis St., Evanston, IL 60201 507/263-7331
FAX: 507/263-7929 email: pmcgorry@gcfa.org
**General Commission on Christian Unity and Interreligious
Concerns**

Chapman, Clare J., 475 Riverside Dr., Room 1300, New York,
NY 10115-0111 212/749-3553 FAX: 212/749-3556
email: cchapman@gccuic-umc.org

United Methodist Communications

Smith, Chris, POB 320, Nashville, TN 37202 615/742-5114
FAX: 615/742-5469 email: csmith@umcom-umc.org

UNITED METHODIST FOUNDATION DIRECTORS

The National Association of United Methodist Foundations
  Harris, Jack D., Executive Secretary, 2230 Linden Ct., Wichita, KS
  67207 316 / 686-1390 FAX: (316) 686-1390 email: umfes@aol.com
ALABAMA
Alabama-West Florida United Methodist Foundation
  Turner, Terri H., POB 8066, Dothan, AL 36304 334 / 793-6820
  FAX: 334/794-6480 email: alwflumf@centurytel.net
North Alabama United Methodist Foundation, Inc.
  Carlton, Charles B., 898 Arkadelphia Road, Birmingham, AL
  35204-5011 205 / 226-7980 or 800 / 239-7950 FAX: 205 / 226-7995
  email: umcfoundation@aol.com
ALASKA
Alaska United Methodist Foundation
  Lindsay, Rev. Gregory, 1127 Timerline Ct., POB 33491, Juneau, AK
  99803 907 / 364-2215 email: dahltandg@gci.net
ARIZONA
Desert Southwest United Methodist Foundation
  Brown, Dr. Richard M., Ed.D, CFRE, 1550 E. Meadowbrook, Suite
  200 Phoenix, AZ 85014-4040 602 / 266-6956 Ext. 203 FAX: 602 /
  266-2196 email: dsumf@earthlink.net
ARKANSAS
United Methodist Foundation of Arkansas
  Argue, James B. Jr., 5300 Evergreen Drive, Little Rock, AR 72205-
  1814 501 / 664-8632 FAX: 501 / 664-6792 email: jargue@umfa.org
CALIFORNIA
California/Nevada Conference Claimants' Endowment Board
  Resch, John P. Jr., 37 W. Yokuts, Suite A-3, Stockton, CA 95207 209/
  472-7288 FAX: 209 / 472-7071
California-Nevada United Methodist Foundation
  Parsons, Rev. Dr. Mark, 1276 Halyard Drive, West Sacramento, CA
  95691 916 / 374-1579 or 888 / 789-7374 FAX: 916 / 372-7716
  email: califnvumf@aol.com
California-Pacific United Methodist Foundation, Inc.
  Berentsen, Jan C., 110 South Euclid Avenue, POB 6006, Pasadena,
  CA 91102-6006 626/568-7347 or 800/244-UMCC FAX: 626/405-9208
  email: jan@cpumf.org

COLORADO
Rocky Mountain Conference United Methodist Foundation, Inc.
Bierbach, Marilyn M., POB 100339, Denver, CO 80250-0339
303/778-6370 FAX: 303/777-6292 email: umfinc@qwest.net

FLORIDA
The Florida United Methodist Foundation, Inc.
Marston, Rev. Thomas W., POB 3767, Lakeland, FL 33802-3767
863/ 688-5563 Ext. 106 or 800/282-8011 Ext.106 FAX: 863/682-6936
email: Tmarston@fumf.org

GEORGIA
North Georgia United Methodist Foundation, Inc.
Fletcher, Rev. Robert R., 15 Technology Parkway, South Norcross,
GA 30092 770/449-6726 FAX: 770/449-6680 email: ngumf@aol.com
South Georgia United Methodist Foundation, Inc.
Carroll, Rev. John B., POB 52101, Macon, GA 31208-4013 478/738-
0048 or 800/535-4224 FAX: 478/738-9768 email: sgumf@sgumfoun-
dation.org

ILLINOIS
**The United Methodist Foundation of the Illinois Great Rivers
Annual Conference, Inc.**
Frost, Rev. Ted, CFRE, POB 5509, Springfield, IL 62705-5509
217/726-5402 FAX: 217/726-5404 email: igracumf@worldnet.att.net
United Methodist Foundation (Northern Illinois Conference, Inc.)
Nicol, Rev. Harry, 77 West Washington Street, Suite 1820 Chicago,
IL 60602 312/346-9766 Ext. 103 FAX: 312/346-9730
email: hnicol@umcnic.org

INDIANA
Indiana Area Foundation of the United sMethodist Church
Fields, Clyde D., 1100 W. 42nd Street, Suite 210, Indianapolis, IN
46208-3302 317/924-1321 FAX: 317/924-4859
email: Cfields@INAREAumc.Org
North Indiana United Methodist Foundation, Inc.
Ruckman, Royce L., 1001 N. Western Avenue, Suite D, Marion, IN
46952 765/664-2327 or 800/783-5138 FAX: 765/664-259
email: foundation@niumc.org
South Indiana Foundation of the United Methodist Church, Inc.
Lang, Rev. Marie E., 4000 E. Southport Road, Suite 250,
Indianapolis, IN 46237-3229 317/788-7879 or 877/391-8811
FAX: 317/788-0089 email: marie@sifumci.org

IOWA
Iowa United Methodist Foundation
Harner, David P., 500 E. Court Avenue, Suite C, Des Moines, IA

50309 515/283-1991 FAX: 515/288-1906
email: david.harner@iaumc.org

KANSAS

Kansas Area United Methodist Foundation
  Childs, Steven P., 100 E. 1st, POB 605, Hutchinson, KS 67504-0605
  620/664-9623 or 888/453-8405 FAX: 620/662-8597
  email: foundation@kaumf.org

KENTUCKY

The Kentucky United Methodist Foundation, Inc.
  Squires, Billy L., 1312 E. Broadway, Suite A, Campbellsville, KY
  42718 270/789-1452 or 888/841-7935 FAX: 270/789-4954
  email: kumf@kih.net

LOUISIANA

United Methodist Foundation of Louisiana
  Reeves, Dr. Michael, 8337 Jefferson, Baton Rouge, LA 70809
  225/346-1535 or 800/256-9317 FAX: 225/343-0756 email:
  umfla@aol.com

MARYLAND

**United Methodist Foundation of the Baltimore-Washington
Conference, Inc.**
  Leckrone, Rev. Terry L., 9720 Patuxent Woods Drive, Suite 100,
  Columbia, MD 21046-1526 410/309-3485 or 800/492-2525 Ext. 485
  FAX: 410/309-9434 email: tleckrone@bwcumc.org

MICHIGAN

Detroit Annual Conference United Methodist Foundation
  Fike, John G., 17117 W. Nine Mile Road, Suite 1545, Southfield, MI
  48075 248/557-1144 or 888/356-6202 FAX: 248/559-6605
  email: johnfike@msn.com

United Methodist Foundation of the West Michigan Conference
  Barrett, Rev. Wayne C., POB 6247, Grand Rapids, MI 49516-6247
  616/459-4503 FAX: 616/459-0191 email: WCBUMF@aol.com

MINNESOTA

Minnesota United Methodist Foundation, Inc.
  Day, Darleen, 122 W. Franklin Avenue, Minneapolis, MN 55404
  612/870-0058 Ext. 248 FAX: 952/844-6099 email: dmeyer@cbbur-
  net.com

MISSISSIPPI

Mississippi United Methodist Foundation, Inc.
  Mitchell, Rev. T. Jerry, POB 1986, Jackson, MS 39215-1986 601/948-
  8845 FAX: 601/360-0843 email: jmitchell@ms-umf.org

MISSOURI
Missouri United Methodist Foundation, Inc.
Atkins, David P., 111 South 9th Street, Suite 230, POB 1076, Columbia, MO 65205-1076 573/875-4168 or 800/332-8238 FAX: 573/875-4595 email: foundation@mumf.org

MONTANA
Yellowstone United Methodist Foundation
Mullette-Bauer, Rev. Bill, POB 6853, Helena, MT 59604 406/442-6501 email: ycfoundation@aol.com

NEBRASKA
The Nebraska United Methodist Foundation
Heller, James W., 2641 No. 49th, POB 4553, Lincoln, NE 68504-0553 402/464-5994 or 800/435-6107 FAX: 402/464-6203 email: jheller@umcneb.org

NEW ENGLAND
Preachers' Aid Society of New England
Gallen, Thomas J., POB 3386, Plymouth, MA 02361-3386 508/830-9500 FAX: 508/830-9582 email: PAS18@msn.com
United Methodist Foundation of New England
Tan, Rev. Wee-Li, 10 Bricketts Mill Road, Suite 5, POB 370, Hampstead, NH 03841-0370 603/329-4444 or 800/595-4347 FAX: 603/329-4430 email: info@umfne.org

NEW JERSEY
United Methodist Foundation of Greater New Jersey
Harris, Barbara L., 34 Bissell Road, Lebanon, NJ 08833-4424 908/236-6501 email: bharris@gnjumc.org
Centenary Fund and Preacher's Aid Society of Northern New Jersey Annual Conference
Duncan, Rev. Robert J., Jr., 22 Madison Avenue, Madison, NJ 07940-2099 570/775-0461 Fax: 570/775-0484 email: rjdjrda@yahoo.com

NEW MEXICO
New Mexico Conference Methodist Foundation, Inc.
Coon, Rev. Sanford D., 7920 Mountain Road NE, Albuquerque, NM 87110 505/255-8786 or 800/678-8786 FAX: 505/265-6184 email: nmcmfi@aol.com

NEW YORK/CONNECTICUT
New York - Connecticut Foundation of the United Methodist Church, Inc.
Rarich, Dr. Jeffrey L., 20 Soundview Avenue, White Plains, NY 10606 914/997-1570, Ext. 238 or 888/696-6922, Ext. 238 FAX: 914/615-2247 email: foundation@nyctfoundation.org

United Methodist Church Foundation, Inc. (New York West Area)
  Salyer, Ronald W., POB 1515, Cicero, NY 13039-1515 607/868-5016
  FAX: 607/868-5016 email: ron8022@yahoo.com_

NORTH CAROLINA

United Methodist Foundation, Inc.
  James, I. Lynn, CFRE, POB 10955, 1307 Glenwood Avenue,
  Raleigh, NC 27605 919/836-0029 or 800/555-4718 FAX: 919/836-
  0092 email: ijames@nccumc.org

United Methodist Foundation of Western North Carolina, Inc.
  Snipes, Rev. David A., 3400 Shamrock Drive, POB 18005,
  Charlotte, NC 28218 704/535-2260 or 800/562-7929 FAX: 704/567-
  1130 email: dsnipes@wnccumc.org

NORTH DAKOTA/SOUTH DAKOTA

Dakotas United Methodist Foundation
  Blumer, Dr. Bruce L., POB 460, Mitchell, SD 57301-0460 605/996-6552
  or 800/224-6552 FAX: 605/996-1766 email:
  bblumer@DakotasUMF.org

OHIO

Ohio East Area United Methodist Foundation
  Sadler, Maggie C., 8800 Cleveland Avenue, NW, North Canton,
  OH 44720 330/499-3972, Ext. 138 or 800/831-3972 FAX: 330/498-
  5099 email: maggie@eocumc.com

Council on Development (West Ohio)
  Traucht, Gregory K., 32 Wesley Boulevard, Worthington, OH 43085
  614/844-6200 or 800/437-0028 FAX: 614/781-2642 email:
  gtraucht@wocumc.org

OKLAHOMA

The Oklahoma United Methodist Foundation, Inc.
  Crooch, Dr. John, 4201 Classen Blvd., Oklahoma City, OK 73118-
  2400 405/525-6863 FAX: 405/521-1429 email: www.okumf.org

OREGON/IDAHO

United Methodist Foundation
  Bolin, Karen, 1505 SW 18th Avenue, Portland, OR 97201 503/226-
  7931 FAX: 503/262-4158 email: kbolin@acsip.com

PENNSYLVANIA

**The United Methodist Stewardship Foundation of Central
Pennsylvania**
  Fuller, Rev. Gerald W., 303 Mulberry Drive, Suite 300,
  Mechanicsburg, PA 17050-3141 717/766-7343 or 800/272-0113 Fax:
  717/766-1673 email: sfcpa@netrax.net

United Methodist Foundation of Western Pennsylvania

Leasure, Rev. Frederick H., CFRE, 223 Fourth Avenue, Suite 707, Pittsburgh, PA 15222 412/232-0650 FAX: 412/232-0675 email: adminast@UMFoundation.org

Eastern Pennsylvania-Peninsula United Methodist Foundation, Inc.
Hawkins, Kathleen V., POB 820, Valley Forge, PA 19482-0820 610/666-9090 FAX: 610/666-9093 email: kathleen@epaumc.org

SOUTH CAROLINA
The South Carolina United Methodist Foundation, Inc.
Gramling, Dr. Roger M., POB 5087, Columbia, SC 29250-5087 803/771-9125 FAX: 803/771-9135 email: scumf@bellsouth.net

TENNESSEE
The Holston Conference of the United Methodist Church Foundation, Inc.
Redding, Roger, POB 32939, Knoxville, TN 37930-2939 865/690-4080 FAX: 865/690-3162 email: RogerRedding@Holston.org

Nashville Area United Methodist Foundation
Templeton, Rev. Edd, 520 Commerce Street, Suite 203, Nashville, TN 37203-3714 615/259-2008 FAX: 615/259-2082 email: etempleton@nashaumf.org

TEXAS
United Methodist Foundation of the Texas Annual Conference
Taylor, Rev. Charles J., 5215 Main Street, Houston, TX 77002 713/521-9383 or 800/521-9617 email: umfoundation-tac.com

Texas Methodist Foundation
Locke, Thomas R., 11709 Boulder Lane, Suite 100, Austin, TX 78726-1808 512/331-9971 or 800/933-5502 FAX: 512/331-0670 email: tlocke@tmf-fdn.org

Central Texas Methodist Foundation
Sprayberry-Hall, Patricia, 3214 West 4th Street, Ft. Worth, TX 76107 817/332-1394 or 800/333-4096 FAX: 817/332-2369 email: pat@ctmf.org

VIRGINIA
The United Methodist Foundation of the Virginia Conference, Inc.
Bergdoll, James R., 10330 Staples Mill Road, POB 1717 Glen Allen, VA 23060 804/521-1172, Ext. 120 or 800/768-6040 FAX: 804/521-1174 email: foundation@vaumc.org

WASHINGTON
United Methodist Foundation of the Northwest
Wilson, Thomas B., POB 656, Cashmere, WA 98815 509/782-2954 or 800/488-4179 FAX: 509/782-3104 email: umfnw@nwi.net

WEST VIRGINIA
United Methodist Foundation of West Virginia, Inc.
Peters, Rev. David R., 900 Washington Street, East, Room 203, POB 3811, Charleston, WV 25338-3811 304/342-2113 or 800/788-3746, Ext. 45 FAX: 304/342-2632 email: info@umfwv.org
WISCONSIN
Wisconsin United Methodist Foundation, Inc.
Helwig, Rev. William F., POB 620, Sun Prairie, WI 53590-0620 608/837-9582 or 888/903-9863 FAX: 608/837-2492 email: wumf@wumf.org

OTHER MEMBERS
Foundation for Evangelism
Ervin, Paul R. Jr., POB 985, Lake Junaluska, NC 28745-0985 828/456-4312 or 800/737-8333 FAX: 828/456-4313 email: paulervin@prodigy.net
General Board of Global Ministries
Carter, William T., 475 Riverside Drive, Room 1316, New York, NY 10115 212/870-3600 FAX: 212/870-3938 email: wcarter@gbgm-umc.org
Bibbee, Barbara J., 6779 Engle Road, Suite J, Middleburg Heights, OH 44130-7926 440/816-1270 FAX: 440/816-1269 email: bbibbee@gbgm-umc.orgs
General Council on Finance and Administration
Allen, James R., 1000 17th Avenue, Nashville, TN 37212 615/329-3393, Ext. 17 FAX: 615/329-3394
Harris Methodist Health Foundation
Carter, Tim, 1301 Pennsylvania Avenue, 9th Floor, Fort Worth, TX 76104 817/878-5240 FAX: 817/878-5110 email: timcarter@TexasHealth.org
Hennepin Avenue United Methodist Church
Rev. Boatman, Lawrence M., 511 Groveland, Minneapolis, MN 55403 612/871-5303 FAX: 612/871-4684 email: pbarrett@visi.com
Holston United Methodist Home for Children
Masker, Arthur S., POB 188, Greeneville, TN 37744-0188 423/638-4171 FAX: 423/638-7171 email: artmasker@holstonhome.org
Methodist Health Care System
Henderson, M. James, 6565 Fannin, MS D200, Houston, TX 77030 713/479-4260 FAX: 713/479-4263
Oklahoma Indian Missionary Conference
Galyon, Dennis, 3020 S. Harvey Street, Oklahoma City, OK 73109 405/632-2006 FAX: 405/632-0209

Planned Giving Resource Center/General Board of Discipleship
Joiner, Rev. Donald W., POB 340003, Nashville, TN 37203-0003 615 340-7080 FAX: 615/340-7183 email: djoiner@gbod.org
SEJ Administrative Council
Hanna, Rev. Jim, POB 67, Lake Junaluska, NC 28745 888/290-7492 FAX: 704 456-4040 email: jahnnah@sejac-umc.org
St. Paul's Methodist Foundation of Houston
Ragsdale, Susie, 5501 S. Main, Houston, TX 77004 713/528-0527 FAX: 713/528-7748 email: sragsdale@stpaulshouston.org
United Methodist Church Foundation, Inc
Bonner, Byrd, 1200 Davis Street, Evanston, IL 60201 847/420-1796 FAX: 847/425-6566 email: bbonner@umcfoundation.org
United Methodist Development Fund
Dixon, Sam W., Jr., 475 Riverside Drive, Suite 1519, New York, NY 10115 212/870-3856 or 800/862-8633 FAX: 212/870-3895 email: sdixon@gbgm-umc.org
United Methodist Higher Education Foundation
Miller, George M., POB 340005, Main, Houston, TX 77004 713/528-0527 FAX: 713/528-7748 email: gmiller@gbhem.org
United Methodist Homes of New Jersay
Cooling, Rev. David A., POB 1166, Naptune, NJ 07754-1166 732/922-9800 or 800/352-6521 FAX: 732/922-9807 email: dcooli@umh-nj.org
United Methodist Men Foundation
Coppock, Larry, POB 340006-0006, nashville, TN 37212 615/340-7145 FAX: 615/340-1770 email: lcoppock@gcumm.org

SECRETARIES OF THE ANNUAL CONFERENCES IN THE CENTRAL CONFERENCES

Austria Provisional
  Nausner, Wilfried, Wielandgasse 10, A-8010 Graz, AUSTRIA
Bicol Philippines Provisional
  Lucena, Raquel, St Luke UMC, 2450 Vinzons Avenue, Daet, 4600 Camarines Norte, PHILIPPINES
Bulacan Philippines
  Parcasio, Roberto, Jesus the Savior UMC, Mt Carmel Subdivision, Iba, 3020 Meycauayan, Bulacan, PHILIPPINES
Bulgaria Provisional
  Altunjan, Samuel, PO Box 464, BG - 9300 Dobritsch, BULGARIA
Central Congo
  Albert, Telunga Talusungu & Redmond, Ehata Shutsha, B.P. 4727 Kin 2, DEMOCRATIC REPUBLIC OF CONGO
Central Luzon Philippines
  Melchor, Pablito, The United Methodist Church, Paniqui, Tarlac, PHILIPPINES
Central Russia Annual Conference
  Garbuzova, Ludmila, U1 Yasenevaya 19-3-221, Moscow, RUSSIAN FEDERATION
Czech and Slovak Republics
  Lehock, Vladimír, 28. pluku 15, CZ-101 00 Praha 10 Vr_ovice, CZECH REPUBLIC
Denmark
  Mogens Hansen, Frederikshalsgade 7, DK-8200, Crhus, SWEDEN
East Africa
  Bonaventure, Ndorimana, PO Box 97, Gitega, REPUBLIC OF BURUNDI
East Congo
  Luhata, Okoko Richard, United Methodist Church, B.P. 226 Kindu (Maniema), DEMOCRATIC REPUBLIC OF CONGO
East Germany
  Fischer, Gottfried, Hhhndorfer Strasse 22, D-01157 Dresden, GERMANY
East Mindanao Philippines Provisional
  Cardinez, Bernardo, First United Methodist Church, 416 Vinzon St., Bo. Obrero, 8000 Davao City, PHILIPPINES

Eastern Angola
Estonia
   Pajusoo, Toomas, Apteegi 3, EE0001 Tallinn, ESTONIA
Eastern Russia-Kazakhstan Annual Conference Provisional
   Tsoy, Svetlana, U1 Pervostroitelyei 15-342, 681000 Komsomolsk-na-Amure, RUSSIAN FEDERATION
Finland-Finnish Provisional
   Sahlin, Tuula, Vinddraget 15B, S-802 77, Gävle, SWEDEN
Finland-Swedish Provisional
   Växby, Kaija-Riikka, Apollogatan 5 B 33, FIN-00100, Helsingfors, FINLAND
Hungary Provisional
   Szabo, Andor, BezerJdj u.2/c, H-7200 Dombóvár, HUNGARY
Liberia
   Quire, Jr., Rev. Samuel J., Liberia Annual Conference, United Methodist Church, Box 10-1010, 1000 Monrovia, 10 LIBERIA
Lukoji
   Yav, Mufind, Paroisse DE Mwajinga-Mission, B.P. 5, Sandoa, DEMOCRATIC REPUBLIC OF CONGO
Middle Philippines
   Tangunan, Leoncio, c/o Mariano T. Badua, North Nueva Ecija District, Blk. 10, Lot, Cecilla Village, 3100 Cabanatuan City, PHILIPPINES
Mindanao Philippines
   Ramos, Rev. Amelia G. Rizal, Avenue, 9407, Kabacan, Cotabato, PHILIPPINES
Mozambique
   Chaúque, Manuel Fabiao, Rua Fraincisco Barreto #229,C. P. 2640, Maputo, MOZAMBIQUE
Nigeria
   Dandazo, John B., UMCN, PO Box 155, Jalingo, Taraba State, NIGERIA
North Central Philippines
   Pascasio, Arnulfo, The United Methodist Church, Echague, Isbela, PHILIPPINES
North German
   Hanf, Armin, Friedrich-Engels-Strasse 24, D-34117 Kassel, GERMANY
North Katanga
   Monga, Kalamba Ka Banze, PO Box 11237, Chingola, ZAMBIA

North Mindanoa Philippines

Northeast Philippines
Madelar, Nieves, Aldersgate College, 3709 Solano, Nueva Vizcaya, PHILIPPINES

Northern Philippines
Crismo, Phoebe, Blk. 27, Lot. 29 Palmera Northland, City 2, San Jose, Del Monte, Bulacan, PHILIPPINES

North - West Katanga
Kasweka, Tanga, Eglise Methodiste - Unie, B.P. 76, Musumba, DEMOCRATIC REPUBLIC OF CONGO

North West Russia Annual Conference Provisional
Matveyeva, Tatyana, 40 Korpus 1, apt. 200, Veliki Novgorod, RUSSIAN FEDERATION

Northwest Mindanao Philippines
Hechanova, Sharon Paz C., c/o 0073 Cipriano Lu St., New Frontier Court, Brgy. Santiago, Tibanga, 9200 Iligan City, PHILIPPINES

Northwest Philippines
Torio, Fe M., The United Methodist Church, Galimuyod, Ilocos Sur, PHILIPPINES

Norway
Pedersen, Kjell R., Frostvedtn. 62, N-3259 Larvik, NORWAY

Oriental and Equator Congo
Lunula, Emongo & Onandju, Daniel Oyowe, B.P. 4727 Kin 2, DEMOCRATIC REPUBLIC OF CONGO

Palawan Philippines Provisional
Manglicmot, Rey

Pamapango
Layug, Victor, Crispulo M. Icban Memorial, San Juan, Apalit, 2016 Pampanga, PHILIPPINES

Pangasinan Philippines
Cruz, Dadice, Lingayen Christian Center, Lingayen, Pangasinan, PHILIPPINES

Philippines
Estrella, Ruby-Nell M., UMC Headquarters, 3rd Fl, Room 308, 900 U.N.Avenue, Ermita, Manila 1000, PHILIPPINES

Philippines Annual Conference East
Mabuti, Zosimo T. ,The United Methodist Church, Quezon Avenue, Angono, Rizal, PHILIPPINES 1930

Poland
Kleszczynski, Adam, Narutowicza 40/19, PL-90-135 Lodz, POLAND

Sierra Leone
Jarrett, Joseph A. M., c/o UMC House, PO Box 523, 31 Lightfoot Boston St, Freetown, Sierra Leone, WEST AFRICA

South Congo
Mpundu, Kapungwe, Paroisse Zion-Kenia, B.P 522 LUBUMBASHI
South Germany
  Rothfuss, Helmut, Gerhart-Hauptmann-Strasse 35, D-70734, Fellbach, GERMANY
Southwest Germany
  Schreiber, Gerhard, Agnesienberg 2a, D-55545, Bad Kreuznach, GERMANY
South - West Katanga
  Kanyangare, Chamusa, Eglise Methodiste - Unie, Pariosse Galilaya, B.P. 450, Likasi/ville, Provine du Katanga, DEMOCRATIC REPUBLIC OF CONGO
Southern Russia-Ukraine-Moldova Annual Conference Provisional
  Pererva, Galina, U1 Shishkova 61-147, Voronezh, RUSSIAN FEDERATION
Southwest Philippines Provisional
  Domingo, Igmidio, c/o The United Methodist Church, Roxas, Oriental Mindoro, PHILIPPINES
Sweden
  Englund, Alf, Bistingsmåla 1231, S-383 91 Mönsterås, SWEDEN
Switzerland/France
  Humbel, Thomas, Rinistrasse 5, CH-8712 Stäfa, SWITZERLAND
Tanganyika/Tanzania
  Moma, Lusarga Kitenge, PO Box 11237, Chingola, ZAMBIA
Visayas Philippines
  Maregmen, Rev. Maximo, 14-a Lopez Extention, Labangon, Cebu City, PHILIPPINES
West Congo
  W'Olenga, Lokaso Olongo & Otshudi, Loma, B.P. 4727, Kinshasa II, DEMOCRATIC REPUBLIC OF CONGO
West Middle Philippines
  Violenta, Jr., Victor, Trinity UMC, Calaguiman, Samal, Bataan, 2113 PHILIPPINES
Western Angola
  Guimarães, Ambrósio Francisco P., Rua Nossa Senhora da Muxima n° 12, PO Box 68, Luanda, ANGOLA
Yugoslavia - Macedonia Provisional
  Virag-Palik, Marija L., Musickog 7, YU-21000, NOVI SAD
East Zimbabwe
  Nhiwatiwa, E.K., Africa University, Box 1320 Mutare, ZIMBABWE
West Zimbabwe

CONFERENCE COMMUNICATIONS DIRECTORS/COORDINATORS

Alabama-West Florida Conference
vacant, 532 East Three Notch St., Andalusia, AL 36420 334/222-3127
 FAX: 334/222-0469
Alaska Missionary Conference
McCurdy, Randall, 1801 O'Malley Rd., Anchorage, AK 99516
 907/344-3025 FAX: 907/334-4322 email: randysjumc.gci.net
Baltimore-Washington Conference
Alsgaard, Erik and **Coleman, John,** 9720 Patuxent Woods Dr., Suite
 100, Columbia, MD 24106 800/492-2525 FAX: 410/309-9794
 email: connection@bwcumc.org Web site: www.bwconf.org
California-Nevada Conference
Jones, Jeneane, POB 980250, West Sacramento, CA 95798-0250
 916/374-1584 FAX: 916/372-5544 email: jeneane@calnevumc.org
California-Pacific Conference
Hygh, Larry, Jr., POB 6006 (110 S. Euclid Ave.), Pasadena, CA 91102-91101
 626/568-7329 FAX: 626/796-7297 email: lhygh@cal-pac.org
 Web site: www.cal-pac.org
Central Pennsylvania Conference
Wolgemuth, Jerry, 900 S. Arlington Ave., Rm. 112, Harrisburg,
 PA 17109 717/766-7441 email: jerry@cpcumc.org
Central Texas Conference
Stephens, Carolyn, 464 Bailey, Ft. Worth, TX 76107 800/460-8622
 FAX: 817/338-4541 email: carumc@aol.com
 Web site: www.ctxumc.org
Dakotas Conference
Fisher, Donna, 12311 Whitetail Rd., Deadwood, SD 57732-7301
 605/355-9532 FAX: 605/996-1766 email: dfisher@rapidnet.com
 Web site: www.DakotasUMC.org
Desert Southwest Conference
Athey, Wally, 1550 E. Meadowbrook Ave., Suite 200, Phoenix, AZ
 85014-4040 800/229-8622 FAX: 602/266-5343 or 266-2196
 email: wally@desertsw.org Web site: www.desertsw.org
Detroit Conference
Huhtala, John C., Jr., (contact), 1309 N. Ballenger Hwy. #1, Flint, MI
 48504-7519 810/233-5500, ext. 330 FAX: 810/233-5700 email: jhuhta-
 la@umc-detconf.org Web site: www.umc-detconf.org

East Ohio Conference
Panovec, Kay, POB 2800 (8800 Cleveland Ave., NW), North Canton,
OH 44720 800/831-3972 FAX: 330/499-3279
email: kay@eocumc.com Web site: www.eocumc.com
Eastern Pennsylvania Conference
Naber, Suzanne M. Keenan, POB 820, Valley Forge, PA 19482-0820
610/666-9090 ext. 227 FAX: 610/436-6887
email: communications@epaumc.org
Web site: www.epaumc.org
Florida Conference
Parham, Elizabeth, 2113 E. South St., Suite 19, Orlando, FL 32803-6502
407/897-1134 FAX: 407/896-7779 email: tparham@flumc.org
Web site: www.flumc.org
Wacht, Michael, 2113 E. South St., Suite 19, Orlando, FL 32803-6502
407/897-1134 FAX: 407/896-7779 email: mwacht@flumc.org
Web site: www.flumc.org
Holston Conference
Slimp, Kevin, POB 32939, Knoxville, TN 37930-2939 865/690-4080
FAX: 865/690-3162 email: kevinslimp@holston.org
Web site: www.holston.org
Illinois Great Rivers Conference
Meister, Susan J., 2144 MacArthur Blvd., Suite 2B, Springfield,
IL 62704-4500 217/747-0720 FAX: 217/722-1873
email: SusanJoyMeister@aol.com Web site: www.igrac.org
Indiana Area
DeMichele, Lynn, 1100 W. 42nd St., Suite 210, Indianapolis, IN 46208
317/924-1321 FAX: 317/924-4859 email: ldemichele@inareaumc.org
Web site: http://inarea.umc.org
Iowa Conference
Harris, Kristin Knudson, 500 E. Court Ave., Suite C, Des Moines, IA
50309 515/283-1996, ext. 106 FAX: 515/283-0836
email: KKHarris@iaumc.org Web site: www.iaumc.org
Kansas East Conference
Beach, Gary A. (contact), POB 4187 (4201 S.W. 15th St.), Topeka,
KS 66604-0187 785/272-9111 FAX: 785/272-9135
email: gbeach@kansaseast.org Web site: www.kansaseast.org
Kansas West Conference
Diehl, Lisa Elliott, 9440 E. Boston, Suite 110, Wichita, KS 67207-3600
316/684-0266 FAX: 316/684-0044 email: ldiehl@kswestumc.org Web
site: www.kswestumc.org
Kentucky Conference
Peters, Rhoda A., 7400 Floydsburg Rd., Crestwood, KY 40014
502/425-3884 FAX: 502/426-5181 email: rpeters@kyumc.org
Web site: www.gbgm-umc.org/kyconf

Little Rock and North Arkansas Conferences (Arkansas Area)
Reeder, Billy, 715 Center St., Room 204, Little Rock, AR 77201-4317
  501/324-8031 FAX: 501/324-8018 email: reeder@arume.org
  Web site: www.arumc.org
Louisiana Conference
Backstrom, Betty, 527 North Blvd., Baton Rouge, LA 70802-5700
  225/346-1646 FAX: 225/383-2652 email: lanow@bellsouth.net
  Web site: www.la-umc.org
Memphis Conference
Farmer, Cathy, 24 Corporate Blvd., Jackson, TN 38305 731/664-8480
  FAX: 731/660-5712 email: catfarmer@memphis-umc.org
  Web site: http://memphis-umc.org
Minnesota Conference
Rebeck, Victoria, 122 W. Franklin Ave., Suite 400, Minneapolis,
  MN 55404-2472 612/870-0058 ext. 232 FAX: 612/870-1260
  email: victoria.rebeck@mnumc.org
  Web site: www.mumac.org
Mississippi Conference
Green, Gwen, POB 1093 (321 Mississippi St.—39201), Jackson,
  MS 39215-1147 601/354-0515 FAX: 601/948-5982
  email: gwen@mississippi-umc.org
  Web site: www. mississippi-umc.org
Missouri West/East Conferences (Missouri Area)
Gordy-Panhorst, Karen, 4800 Santana, Suite 300, Columbia,
  MO 65203 573/441-1770 573/441-1780
  email: kgordy-panhorst@moarea.umc.org
  Web site: www.moarea.umc.org
Nebraska Conference
Edwards, Cheryl, POB 4553 (2641 N. 49th St.), Lincoln, NE 68504
  800/435-6107 FAX: 402/464-6203 email: cedwards@umcneb.org
  Web site: www.umcneb.org
New England Conference
Hickcox, Michael, United Methodist Center, POB 249 (276 Essex
  St.—01842), Lawrence, MA 01842-0449 978/682-7676
  FAX: 978/682-7677 email: communicate@neumc.org
  Web site: www.neumc.org
New Mexico Area
McAchran, Julianne, 7920 Mountain Rd., N.E., Albuquerque, NM
  87110-7805 505/255-8786 FAX: 505/265-6174 email:
  nmumrumc@nmconfum.com Web site: www.nmconfum.com
New York Conference
Collier, Don, 20 Soundview Ave., White Plains, NY 10606 914/997-
  1570, ext. 219 FAX: 914/615-2244 Website: www.nyac.com/

North Alabama Conference
Clifton, Danette, 898 Arkadelphia Rd., Birmingham, AL 35204-3436
205/226-7972 FAX: 205/226-7975 email: dclifton@umcna.bsc.edu
Web site: http://umcna.bsc.edu

North Central New York
Fulmer, Sharon, 314 2nd St., Liverpool, NY 13088 315/461-9270
FAX: 315/461-0106 email: srfulmer@aol.com
Web site: www.ncnyumc.org

North Carolina Conference
Norton, Bill, POB 10955 (1307 Glenwood Ave.), Raleigh, NC 27605
800/849-4433 ext. 263 FAX: 919/834-7989
email: bnorton@nccumc.org Web site: http://nccumc.org

North Georgia Conference
McDaniel, Timothy J., 1159 Ralph McGill Blvd., Suite 106, Atlanta,
GA 30308 404/659-0002 ext. 3210 FAX: 404/577-6857
email: timmcdaniel@mindspring.com
Nugent, Mark, 1159 Ralph McGill Blvd., Suite 106, Atlanta, GA 30308
404/659-0002 ext 3238 FAX: 404/592-1141
email: mnugent@ngumc.org

North Indiana Conference
Shrock, Paula, 8420 E. 100 North, Greentown, IN 46936 765/628-2524
email: beshrock@netusa1.net
Web site: http://members.aol.com/hoosierum/index.htm

North Texas Conference
LaBarr, Joan G., POB 516069 (13959 Peyton Dr.—75240), Dallas,
TX 75251-6069 972/490-3438 FAX: 972/490-7216
email: labarr@ntcumc.org Web site: www.ntcumc.org

Northern Illinois Conference
Rhodes, Linda S., One North LaSalle St., Suite 2151, Chicago,
IL 60540 312/541-1602 FAX: 312/541-1604
email: lrhodes@umcnic.org Web site: www.umcnic.org

Northwest Texas Conference
Interim: **Willis, Joanna,** 1415 Avenue M, Lubbock, TX 79401
806/762-0201 FAX: 806/762-0205 email: jwillis@nwtxconf.org Web
site: www.nwtxconf.org

Oklahoma Conference
Bowdon, Boyce A., 2420 N. Blackwelder, Oklahoma City, OK 73106-
1410 405/525-2252 ext. 209 FAX: 405/525-4164
email: bbowdon@okumc.org Web site: www.okumc.org

Oklahoma Indian Missionary Conference
Wilson, David M., 3020 S. Harvey, Oklahoma City, OK 73109
405/632-2006 FAX: 405/632-0209 email: dwoimc@aol.com
Web site: www.gbgm-umc.org/oimc

Oregon-Idaho Conference
Sullivan, Linda, 1505 SW 18th Ave., Portland, OR 97201
  503/226-7391 FAX: 503/226-4158 email: Linda@umoi.org
Pacific Northwest Conference
Stanovsky, Elaine J. (contact), 2112 Third Ave., Room 300, Seattle,
  WA 98121-2333 206/728-7462 ext. 218 FAX: 206/728-8442
  Web site: www.gbgm-umc.org/conferences/pacificnw/
Peninsula-Delaware Conference
Ward, Tommy, 139 N. State St., Dover, DE 19901 302/674-2626 ext. 24
  FAX: 302/674-1573 email: tward@pen-del.org
  Web site: www.pen.del.org
Red Bird Missionary Conference
Wiertzema, Ruth Ann, 6 Queendale Center, Beverly, KY 40913
  606/598-5915 FAX: 606/598-6405 email: redbirdco@kih.net
  Web site: http://gbgm-umc.org/redbirdconference
Rio Grande Conference
Mariscal, Arturo, POB 781974, San Antonio, TX 78278 210/408-4512
  FAX: 210/408-4515 email: amariscal@umcswtx.org
  Web site: www.riogrande-umc.org
Rocky Mountain and Yellowstone Conferences
Keene, Gary M., 2200 University Blvd., Denver, CO 80210-4797
  303/733-3736 ext. 304 FAX: 303/733-1730 email: gary@rmcumc.com
  Web site: www.rmcumc.org
South Carolina Conference
Shearin, Victoria (contact), 4908 Colonial Dr., Suite 101, Columbia,
  SC 29203-0000 803/735-8792 FAX: 803/691-0220 email:
  vshearin@umcsc.org Web site: www.umcsc.org
South Georgia Conference
Haggerty, Kelly, POB 20408 (99 Arthur J. Moore Blvd.), St. Simons
  Island, GA 31522 912/638-8626 FAX: 912/638-5258 email:
  kelly@sgaumc.com Web site: www.sgaumc.org
Southwest Texas Conference
Cannon, Douglas, POB 781149 (16400 Huebner Rd.—78248), San
  Antonio, TX 78278-1149 888/349-4191 FAX: 210/408-4515
  email: dcannon@umcswtx.org Web site: www.umcswtx.org
Tennessee Conference
Brummitt, Juanita, 1110 19th Ave., S., POB 120607, Nashville,
  TN 37212-0607 615/329-1177 FAX: 615/329-0884
  email: jbrummitt@tnumc.org Web site: http://tnumc.org
Texas Conference
McKay, David, 5215 Main St., Houston, TX 77002-9792 713/521-9383
  ext. 334 FAX: 713/521-3724 email: dwmckay@methodists.net
  Web site: www.methodists.net

Troy Conference
Nye, Holly, POB 560, 396 Louden Rd., Saratoga Springs, NY 12866
518/584-8214 ext. 114 FAX: 518/584-8378 email: hollyn@troyac.org
Web site: www.gbgm-umc.org/troyconference
Virginia Conference
Zoellner, Kimberly (editor), POB 11367 (4016 Broad St.), Richmond,
VA 2323-01367 804/359-9451 FAX: 804/359-5904
email: KimZoellner@vaumc.org Web site: www.vaumc.org
West Michigan Conference
Thompson, John Ross (contact person), 11 Fuller Ave. S.E., Grand
Rapids, MI 49516-6247 616/459-4503, ext. 321 FAX: 616/459-0191
West Ohio Conference
Slack, R. Thomas, 32 Wesley Blvd., Worthington, OH 43085-3505
800/437-0028 FAX: 614/781-2642 email: tslack@wocumc.org
Web site: www.westohioumc.org
West Virginia Conference
Burger, Thomas, POB 2313 (900 Washington St., E.—25301),
Charleston, WV 25328 800/788-3746 FAX: 304/344-8338
email: umethwv@aol.com Web site: http://wvumc.org
Western New York Conference
Kasperek, Marilyn, 8499 Main St., Buffalo, NY 14221 716/564-2316
FAX: 716/564-2365 email: Mjkasperek@aol.com
Web site: http://wnyconfumc.org/
Western North Carolina Conference
Hand, Dawn M., POB 18005 (3400 Shamrock Dr.), Charlotte, NC
28218 704/535-2260 ext. 122 FAX: 704/567-6117
email: dhand@wnccumc.org Web site: http://wnccumc.org
Western Pennsylvania Conference
Rehn, Mark, POB 5002 (1204 Freedom Rd.), Cranberry Township,
PA 16066-4914 724/776-2300 FAX: 724/776-1355
email: umlink@umchurch.org Web site: www.umchurch.org
Wisconsin Conference
D'Alessio, Thomas, POB 620 (750 Windsor St.), Sun Prairie,
WI 53590-0620 608/837-7328 FAX: 608/837-8547
email: dalessio@WisconsinUMC.org
Web site: www.wisconsinumc.org
Wyoming Conference
Perry, Donald, POB 58 (1700 Monroe St.—13760), Endicott,
NY 13761-0058 607/757-0608 FAX: 607/757-0752
email: dperry@wyomingconference.org
Web site: www.wyomingconference.org

UNITED METHODIST NEWS SERVICE OFFICES

Nashville, Tennessee

POB 320, Nashville, TN 37202,
615/742-5470 FAX: 615/742-5469
email: newsdesk@umcom.org
Web site: http://umns.umc.org
News Service Director — **Underwood, Ginny,** 615/742-5124
   email: gunderwood@umcom.org
News Writer, Nashville — **Green, Linda,** 615/742-5475
   email: lgreen@umcom.org
Managing Editor: **Tanton, Tim,** 615/742-5473
   email: ttanton@umcom.org
Administrative Assistant: **Latham, Laura,** 615/742-5474
   email: llatham@umcom.org
News Writer: **Gilbert, Kathy,** 615/742-5471
   email: kgilbert@umcom.org
Walsh, Fran, Coordinating Producer, 615/742-5438 email:
   fwalsh@umcom.org

New York, NY

475 Riverside Dr., Suite 1948, New York, NY 10115 212/870-3803
FAX: 212/870-2171
News Director — **Bloom, Linda,** email: lbloom@umcom.org

UNITED METHODIST CHURCHWIDE PUBLICATIONS

ADULT BIBLE STUDIES (quarterly)
Editor — **Moore, Eleanor**
POB 801, Nashville, TN 37202 615/749-6467
ALIVE NOW! (bimonthly-devotional)
Editor — **Tidwell, Melissa**
1908 Grand Ave., Nashville, TN 37202 615/340-7216
APUNTES (quarterly)
Editor — **Pedraja, Luis**
Memphis Theological Seminary, 168 E. Parkway, S., Memphis, TN 38104 901/458-8232, ext. 116
CHRISTIAN SOCIAL ACTION (bi-monthly-social justice)
Editor — **Hakola, Gretchen**
100 Maryland Ave. NE, Washington, DC 20002 202/488-5631
email: ghakola@umc-gbcs.org FAX: 202/488-1617
Web site: www.umc-gbcs.org/gbcs005.htm
CIRCUIT RIDER (bimonthly)
Managing Editor — **Reddig, Jill S.**
POB 801, Nashville, TN 37202 615/749-6334
FAX: 615/749-6061 email: jreddig@umpublishing.org
Web site: www.cokesbury.com
DAILY BIBLE STUDY (quarterly)
Editor — **Moore, Eleanor**
POB 801, Nashville, TN 37202 615/749-6467
EL APOSENTO ALTO (quarterly-devotional)
Editor — **Gaud, Carmen M.**
1908 Grand Ave., Nashville, TN 37202 615/340-7246
EL INTÉRPRETE (6 times per year)
Contact: **Bachus, Amanda**
POB 801, Nashville, TN 37202 615/742-5115 FAX: 615/742-5460
email: abachus@umcom.org
INTERPRETER (8 issues per year)
Interim Editor — **Colvin, Gwen**
POB 320, 810 12th Ave. South, Nashville, TN 37202 615/742-5102
FAX: 615/742-5460 email: gcolvin@umcom.umc.org
Web site: www.interpretermagazine.org

THE FLYER (quarterly newsletter-status and role of women)
Editor — **Roth, Bonny S.**
1200 Davis St., Evanston, IL 60201 847/869-7330 FAX: 847/869-1466
LEADER IN THE CHURCH SCHOOL TODAY (quarterly)
Editor — **Kidd, Ron**
POB 801, Nashville, TN 37202 615/749-6921 FAX: 615/749-6512
MATURE YEARS (quarterly)
Editor — **Cropsey, Marvin W.**
POB 801, Nashville, TN 27202 615/749-6292
MEMBER NEWS (weekly)
Editor — **Terr, Nancy**
601 W. Riverview Ave., Dayton, OH 45406 937/227-9494
MENSNEWS (bi-monthly)
Editor — **Malone, Lawrence J.**
POB 860, Nashville, TN 37702-0860 615/340-7147
FAX: 615/340-1770
METHODIST HISTORY (quarterly)
Editor — **Yrigoyen, Charles, Jr.**
POB 127 Madison, NJ 07940 973/408-3189 FAX: 973/408-3909
email: cyrigoyen@gcah.org Web site: www.gcah.org
NEWSCOPE (weekly-newsletter)
Editor — Schleicher, Andrew
POB 801, Nashville, TN 37202 615/749-6320 FAX: 615/749-6512
email: aschleicher@umpublishing.org Web site:
www.umpublishing.org
NEW WORLD OUTLOOK (bimonthly-missions)
Editor — **House, Christie R.**
475 Riverside Dr., Rm. 1476, New York, NY 10115 212/870-3765
FAX: 212/870-3654 email: chouse@gbgm-umc.org
Web site: http://gbgm-umc.org/nwo
ORIENTATION (annually-college)
Editor — **Hiers, Terri J.**
POB 871, Nashville, TN 37202 615/340-7383
POCKETS (monthly-children)
Editor — **Knight, Janet R.**
1908 Grand Ave., Nashville, TN 37202 615/340-7238
QUARTERLY REVIEW (quarterly-scholarly)
Editor — **Pieterse, Hendrik R.**
POB 871, Nashville, TN 37202 615/340-7334 FAX: 615/340-7048

RESPONSE (monthly-women's missions)
Editor — **Jones, Dana**
475 Riverside Dr., Rm. 1501, New York, NY 10115 212/870-3755
FAX: 212/870-3736 email: djones@gbgm-umc.org
Web site: http://gbgm-umc.org/response

UMMen: Uniting Men and Meaning (Quarterly)
Editor — **Malone, Lawrence J.**
POB 860, Nashville, TN 37202-0860 615/340-7147
FAX: 615/340-1770

THE UNITED METHODIST REPORTER (weekly newspaper)
Editor — **Patterson, Ron**
Managing Editor: **Astle, Cynthia,** POB 660275, Dallas, TX 75266
800/947-0207 FAX: 214/630-0079
email: united-methodist-reporter@compuserve.com
Web site: www.umr.org

UNITED METHODIST IN SERVICE (6 times per year)
Editor — **Cho, Sang Yean, Rev.**
POB 320, Nashville, TN 37202 615/742-5118 FAX: 615/742-5460
email: cho@umcom.umc.org

UNITED METHODIST RURAL FELLOWSHIP BULLETIN (quarterly)
Editor — **Kail, Edward A., Rev.**
309 First Ave., N., Humboldt, IA 50548 515/332-1773
email: eandmkail@hotmail.com

THE UPPER ROOM (monthly-daily devotions)
Editor — **Redding, Mary Lou**
1908 Grand Ave., POB 189, Nashville, TN 37202 615/340-7237

WEAVINGS (bi-monthly-spiritual life)
Editor — **Mogabgab, John S.**
1908 Grand Ave., Nashville, TN 37202 615/340-7249

WORLD PARISH (World Methodist Council News)
Editor — **Freeman, George H.**
POB 518, Lake Junaluska, NC 28745 704/456-9432
FAX: 704/456-9433 email: georgefreeman@mindspring.com

WORSHIP ARTS (bimonthly-worship, music, arts - formerly **NEWS NOTES**)
Editor — **Wiltse, David**
POB 6247, Grand Rapids, MI 49516-6247 616/459-4503
FAX: 616/459-0191 email: graphics@iserv.net
Web site: www.fummawa.org

RELIGION NEWS SERVICE

RELIGION NEWS SERVICE (MONDAY, WEDNESDAY, FRIDAY)

Editor, Director — **Anderson, David E.**
1101 Connecticut Ave. NE, Suite 350, Washington, DC 20036
202/463-8777 FAX: 202/463-0033

ANNUAL CONFERENCE AND AREA PUBLICATIONS

*Designates conference editions of *THE UNITED METHODIST REPORTER,* produced in Dallas.
Designates conference editions of the biweekly **UNITED METHODIST REVIEW, produced in Dallas.
***Designates conference editions of *THE MONTHLY UNITED METHODIST RECORD,* produced in Dallas.

NORTH CENTRAL JURISDICTION

CHICAGO AREA
Northern Illinois Conference
NORTHERN ILLINOIS CONFERENCE UNITED METHODIST REPORTER (weekly)
Editor — **Rhodes, Linda S.**
One North LaSalle St., Suite 2151, Chicago, IL 60602 312/541-1602
FAX: 312/541-1604 email: lrhodes@umcnic.org
Web site: www.gbgm-umc.org/nillconf/

DAKOTAS AREA

Dakotas Conference
THE DAKOTAS CONNECTION (quarterly)
MONDAYS@DAKOTASUMC.ORG (weekly)
Editor — **Fisher, Donna,** 12311 Whitetail Rd., Deadwood, SD 57732
605/996-6552 FAX: 605/996-1766 email: dfisher@rapidnet.com
Web site: www.dakotasumc.org

ILLINOIS AREA

Illinois Great River Conference
THE CURRENT (bi-weekly)
Editor — **Meister, Susan,** 2144 MacArthur Blvd., Suite 2B,
  Springfield, IL 62704-4500 217/747-0720 FAX: 217/722-1873
  email: igracthecurrent@aol.com Web site: www.igrac.org

INDIANA AREA

North and South Indiana Conferences
HOOSIER UNITED METHODIST NEWS (monthly)
Editor — **vacant**
1100 W. 42nd St., Suite 210, Indianapolis, IN 46208 317/924-1321 ext.
  18 FAX: 317/924-4859 Web site: www.inareaumc.org

IOWA AREA

Iowa Conference
CONNECT (biweekly, electronically)
GRACE UPON GRACE (quarterly)
Editor — **Harris, Kristin Knudson**
500 E. Court Ave., Suite C, Des Moines, IA 50309 515/283-1996 ext.
  106 FAX: 515/283-8672 email: KKHarris@iaumc.org
  Web site: www.iaumc.org

MICHIGAN AREA

Detroit and West Michigan Conferences
MICHIGAN CHRISTIAN ADVOCATE (bi-weekly)
Editor — **Whiting, Ann**
316 Springbrook Ave., Adrian, MI 49221 517/265-2075
  FAX: 517/263-7422 email: MIAdvocate@aol.com
  Web site: www.westmichiganconference.org/

MINNESOTA AREA

Minnesota Conference
THE MINNESOTA CONNECT (bimonthly)
Editor — **Brands, Sandra**
122 W. Franklin Ave., Room 400, Minneapolis, MN 55404-2472
  612/230-6139 ext. 232 FAX: 612/870-1260
  email: sandra.brands@mnumc.org Web site: www.mumac.org

OHIO AREA

East Ohio Conference
EAST OHIO TODAY (biweekly)
Editor — **Panovec, Kay**
POB 2800 (8800 Cleveland Ave., N.W.), North Canton, OH 44720
330/499-3972 ext. 118 FAX: 330/499-3279
email: kay@eocumc.com Web site: www.eocumc.com

West Ohio Conference
WEST OHIO NEWS/UNITED METHODIST REVIEW (19 per year)
Editor — **Slack, R. Thomas**
32 Wesley Blvd., Worthington, OH 43085-3585 800/437-0028
FAX: 614/781-2642 email: tslack@wocumc.org
Web site: www.westohioumc.org

WISCONSIN AREA

Wisconsin Conference
WINDOW (monthly)
Editor — **D'Alessio, Thomas**
POB 620 (750 Windsor St.), Sun Prairie, WI 53590-0620 608/837-7328
FAX: 608/837-8547 email: dalessio@WisconsinUMC.org
Web site: www.wisconsinumc.org

NORTHEASTERN JURISDICTION

ALBANY AREA

Troy Conference
***THE CONNECTION UM RECORD* (monthly)
Editor — **Nye, Holly**
POB 560 (396 Louden Rd.), Saratoga Springs, NY 12866 518/584-8214
ext. 114 FAX: 518/584-8378 email: h_nye@juno.com
Web site: www.troyac.org

Wyoming Conference
***THE VOICE/UM REVIEW* (biweekly)
Editor — **Perry, Donald**
POB 58 (1700 Monroe St.—13760), Endicott, NY 13761-0058 607/757-
0608 FAX: 607/757-0752 email: dperry@wyomingconference.org
Web site: www.wyomingconference.org

BOSTON AREA

New England Conference
(every 3 weeks)
CROSSCURRENTS
Editor — **Sulesky, Cynthia**
UM Center, POB 249 (276 Essex St.), Lawrence, MA 01842
    978/682-8055 FAX: 978/682-8227 email: CrossCurrents@neumc.org
    Web site: www.neumc.org

HARRISBURG AREA

Central Pennsylvania Conference
THE LINK (11 per year)
Editor — **Wolgemuth, Gerald**
303 Mulberry Dr., Mechanicsburg, PA 17050-2053 717/766-7441
    717/766-5976 FAX: 717/766-5976 email: jerry@cpcumc.org
    Web site: www.cpcumc.org/link/index.html

NEW JERSEY AREA

Greater New Jersey Conference
UNITED METHODIST RELAY (monthly)
Editor — **VanCleef, Robin E.**
POB 333 (1 Mayflower Ct.), Whiting, NJ 08759 732/350-6444
    FAX: 732/849-0409 email: UMRelay@aol.com
    Web site: www.gnjumc.org

NEW YORK AREA

New York Conference
***THE VISION** (biweekly)
Editor — **Collier, Dan**
20 Soundview Ave., White Plains, NY 10606 614/997-1570 888/686-
    6922 FAX: 914/615-2244 email: TheVISION@nyac.com
    Web site: http://nyac.com

NEW YORK WEST AREA

North Central New York Conference
****NORTH CENTRAL NEW YORK CONNECTIONS* (monthly)
Editor — **Fulmer, Sharon**
POB 1515, Cicero, NY 13039 315/699-8715 ext. 318
    FAX: 315/699-8774 email: srfulmer@aol.com
    Web site: www.ncnyumc.org

Western New York Conference
***UNITED METHODIST RECORD** (monthly)
Editor — **Kasperek, Marilyn**
131 John Muir Dr., West Amherst, NY 14228 716/564-2316
FAX: 716/564-2365 email: Mjkasperek@aol.com Web site:
http://conferencenews.com/wnyconfumc

PENNSYLVANIA AREA

Eastern Pennsylvania Conference
NEWSpirit (monthly)
Editor—**Beiderman, Don**
POB 820, Valley Forge, PA 19482-0820 800/828-9093 ext. 227 610/666-
9090 ext. 227 FAX: 610/666-9093
email: newspirited@aol.com Web site: http://epaumc.org

Peninsula-Delaware Conference
***THE COMMUNICATOR/UM REVIEW** (biweekly)
Editor — **Ward, Tammy**
139 N. State St., Dover, DE 19901 302/674-2626 ext. 24 FAX: 302/674-
1573 email: tward@pen-del.org Web site: http://pen-del.org

PITTSBURGH AREA

Western Pennsylvania Conference
***INTERLINK** (biweekly)
Editor — **Rehn, Mark**
1204 Freedom Rd., POB 5002, Cranberry Township, PA 16066-4914
724/776-2300 FAX: 724/776-1355 email: umlink@umchurch.org
Web site: www.wpaumc.org

WASHINGTON AREA

Baltimore-Washington Conference
UNITED METHODIST CONNECTION (bi-monthly)
Editor — **Alsgaard, Erik**
9720 Patuxent Woods Dr., Suite 100, Columbia, MD 21046
800/492-2525 ext. 420 or 410/309-3425 FAX: 410/309-9794
email: ealsgaard@bwcumc.org Web site: www.bwconf.org

WEST VIRGINIA AREA

West Virginia Conference
WEST VIRGINIA UNITED METHODIST (10 per year)
Editor — **Burger, Thomas**
POB 2313 (900 Washington St., E.), Charleston, WV 25328 (25301)

800/788-3746 FAX: 304/344-2871 email: umethwv@aol.com
Web site: www.wvumc.org

SOUTH CENTRAL JURISDICTION

ARKANSAS AREA

Little Rock and North Arkansas Conferences
ARKANSAS UNITED METHODIST (biweekly)
Editor — **Dennis, Jane**
715 Center St., Rm. 204, Little Rock, AR 72201-1317 501/324-8031
    FAX: 501/324-8018 email: jdennis@arumc.org
    Web site: www.arumc.org

DALLAS AREA

North Texas Conference
*NORTH TEXAS UNITED METHODIST REPORTER (weekly)
Editor — **Robertson, Robert L. (Bob)**
POB 516069 (13959 Peyton Dr.—75240), Dallas, TX 75251-6069
    972/490-3438 FAX: 972/490-7216 email: labarr@ntcumc@airmail.net
    Web site: www.ntcumc.org

FORT WORTH AREA

Central Texas Conference
*CENTRAL LINK (monthly)
Editor — **Stephens, Carolyn**
464 Baily, Fort Worth, TX 76107 800/460-8622 FAX: 817/338-4541
    email: carumc@aol.com Web site: www.ctxumc.org

HOUSTON AREA

Texas Conference
*CROSS CONNECTIONS UM REPORTER (weekly)
Editor — **Benson, Nicole**
5215 Main St., Houston, TX 77002-9792 713/521-9383
    FAX: 713/521-3724 email: nbenson@methodists.net
    Web site: www.txcumc.org

KANSAS AREA

Kansas East Conference
CONNECTION (10 per year)
Editor — **Robertson, Karen**
POB 4187 (4201 SW 15th St.—66604), Topeka, KS 66604-0187
785/272-9111 FAX: 785-272-9135 email: krobertson@kansaseast.org
Web site: www.kansaseast.org

Kansas West Conference
*KANSAS WEST CONNECTION (monthly)
Editor — **Diehl, Lisa Elliott**
9440 E. Boston, Suite 110, Wichita, KS 67207-3600 316/684-0266
FAX: 316/684-0044 email: ldiehl@kswestumc.org
Web site: http://kswestumc.org/comm/connection.htm

LOUISIANA AREA

Louisiana Conference
LOUISIANA NOW! (biweekly)
Editor — **Backstrom, Betty**
527 North Blvd., Baton Rouge, LA 70802-5700 225/346-1646 ext. 227
FAX: 225/383-2652 email: lanow@bellsouth.net
Web site: www.la-umc.org

MISSOURI AREA

Missouri East and West Conferences
**MISSOURI REVIEW (bi-weekly)
BRIDGES (quarterly)
Editor — **Koenig, Fred**
2 East Ridgley, Columbia, MO 65203 573/256-7211
email: fkoenig@moareaumc.org Web site: www.moumethodist.org

NEBRASKA AREA

Nebraska Conference
NEBRASKA MESSENGER (8 per year)
Editor —
POB 4553 (2641 N. 49th St.—68504), Lincoln, NE 68504 800/435-6107
FAX: 402/464-6203 Web site: www.umcneb.org

NORTHWEST TEXAS—NEW MEXICO AREA

New Mexico Conference

NEW MEXICO UM REPORTER (weekly)
Editor — **McAchran, Julianne**
7920 Mountain Rd. NE, Albuquerque, NM 87110-7805 505/255-8786
   or 800/678-8786 FAX: 505/265-6184
   email: nmumrumc@nmconfum.com
   Web site: www.nmconfum.com

Northwest Texas Conference
NORTHWEST TEXAS UM REVIEW (biweekly)
Editor — **Willis, Joanna**
1415 Avenue M, Lubbock, TX 79401 806/762-0201 FAX: 806/762-0205
   email: jwillis@nwtxconf.org Web site: www.nwtxconf.org

OKLAHOMA AREA

Oklahoma Conference
**THE OKLAHOMA CONTACT/UM REVIEW* (bi-weekly)
Editor — **Bowdon, Boyce A.**
2420 N. Blackwelder, Oklahoma City, OK 73106-1410 405/525-2252,
   ext. 209 FAX: 405/525-4164 email: Bbowdon@okumc.org
   Web site: www.okumc.org

Oklahoma Indian Missionary Conference
ADVOCATE (bi-monthly)
Editor — **Wilson, David M.**
3020 S. Harvey, Oklahoma City, OK 73109 405/632-2006
   FAX: 405/632-0209 email: dwilson@oimc.org
   Web site: www.gbgm-umc.org/oimc

SAN ANTONIO AREA

Rio Grande Conference
***RIO GRANDE EDITION UM RECORD (SPANISH)* (monthly)
Editor — **Mariscal, Arturo**
POB 781974 (164400 Huebner Rd.—78248), San Antonio, TX 78278
   210/408-4513 FAX: 210/408-4515 email: amariscal@umcswtx.org

Southwest Texas Conference
UNITED METHODIST WITNESS (biweekly)
Editor — **Cannon, Douglas**
POB 781149 (16400 Huebner Rd.), San Antonio, TX 78278-1149
   888/349-4191 FAX: 210/408-4515 email: dcannon@umcswtx.org
   Web site: www.umcswtx.org

SOUTHEASTERN JURISDICTION

ALABAMA-WEST FLORIDA AREA

Alabama-West Florida Conference
ALABAMA-WEST FLORIDA ADVOCATE (quarterly)
AWF TODAY - (newsletter 8/issues)
Editor — **Earnest, Meredyth**
1500 E. Fairview Ave., Montgomery, AL 36106 334/834-3424
  FAX: 334/834-3879 email: meredyth@awfumc.org

ATLANTA AND SOUTH GEORGIA AREAS

North and South Georgia Conferences
WESLEYAN CHRISTIAN ADVOCATE (bi-weekly)
Editor — **Smith, Alice**
POB 427 (5312 W. Mountain St.—30083), Stone Mountain, GA 30086
  770/465-1685 FAX: 770/465-0685 email: alice@wcadvocate.org
  Web site: www.wcadvocate.org

BIRMINGHAM AREA

North Alabama Conference
THE VOICE (monthly)
Editor: **Clifton, Danette**
898 Arkadelphia Rd., Birmingham, AL 35204-3436 205/226-7972
  FAX: 205/226-7941 email: dclifton@umcna.bsc.edu
  Web site: http://umcna.bsc.edu

CHARLOTTE AND RALEIGH AREA

Western North Carolina and North Carolina Conferences
NORTH CAROLINA CHRISTIAN ADVOCATE (bi-weekly)
Editor — **Rippin, Kevin**
POB 508, Greensboro, NC 27402-0508 336/272-1196
  FAX: 336/271-6634 email: rippink@gborocollege.edu
  Web site: www.ncadvocate.org

COLUMBIA AREA

South Carolina Conference
THE ADVOCATE (monthly)
Editor — **Burgdorf, Karl "Davie"**
4908 Colonial Dr., Suite 207, Columbia, SC 29203-6070 803/786-9486

FAX: 803/735-8168 email: burgdorf@umcsc.org
Web site: www.sadvocate-online.org

FLORIDA AREA

Florida Conference
FLORIDA UNITED METHODIST REVIEW (bi-weekly)
Editor — **Parham, Elizabeth (Tita)**
2113 East South St., Suite 19, Orlando, FL 32803-6502 407/897-1134
    FAX: 407/896-7779 email: tparham@flumc.org
    Web site: www.flumc.org

HOLSTON AREA

Holston Conference
THE CALL/UNITED METHODIST REVIEW (bi-weekly)
Editor — **Bender, Annette**
POB 32939, Knoxville, TN 37930-2939 865/690-4080
    FAX: 865/690-3162 email: annettebender@holston.org
    the call@holston.org Web site: www.holston.org

LOUISVILLE AREA

Kentucky Conference
NETNEWS (monthly)
Editor: **Peters, Rhoda A.**
7400 Floydsburg Rd., Crestwood, KY 40014 502/425-3884
    FAX: 502/426-5181 email: kyumc.org@aye.net
    Web site: www.kyumc.org

Red Bird Missionary Conference
THE CARDINAL (quarterly)
Editor: **Wiertzema, Ruth Ann**
6 Queendale Center, Beverly, KY 40913 606/598-5915
    FAX: 606/598-6405 email: redbirdco@kih.net
    Web site: www.gbgm-umc.org/redbirdconference/

MISSISSIPPI AREA

Mississippi Conference
MISSISSIPPI UNITED METHODIST ADVOCATE (bi-weekly)
Editor — **Woodrick, Woody**
POB 1093, Jackson, MS 39215-1093 601/354-0515 FAX: 601/948-5983

email: advocate@mississippi-umc.org
Web site: www.mississippi-umc.org

NASHVILLE AREA

Memphis Conference
*THE MEMPHIS CONFERENCE UNITED METHODIST
REPORTER* (weekly)
Editor — **Farmer, Cathy**
24 Corporate Blvd., Jackson, TN 38305 731/664-8480
  FAX: 731/660-5712 email: catfarmer@memphis-umc.org
  Web site: http://memphis-umc.org

Tennessee Conference
TENNESSEE CONFERENCE UNITED METHODIST REPORTER
(weekly)
Interim Editor — **Nankervis, Tom**
POB 120607 (1110 19th Ave., S.), Nashville, TN 37212 615/329-1177
  FAX: 615/329-0884 email: tnankervis@tnumc.org
  Web site: http://tnumc.org

RICHMOND AREA

Virginia Conference
VIRGINIA ADVOCATE (bi-weekly)
Editor — **vacant**
POB 1719 (10220 Staples Mill Road, 23060-3251), Glen Allen, VA
  23060-0659 804/521-1100 FAX: 804/521-1179
  Web site: www.vaumc.org

WESTERN JURISDICTION

DENVER AREA

Rocky Mountain Conference
THE ROCKY MOUNTAIN VISION (monthly)
Editor — **Veal, Faye**
2200 S. University Blvd., Denver, CO 80210-4797 303/733-3736
  FAX: 303/733-1730 email: FayeVeal@rmcumc.com
  Web site: www.rmcumc.org

Yellowstone Conference
YELLOWSTONE CONFERENCE CONNECTION (monthly)
Editor — **Morton, Kama Hamilton**
POB 108, Choteau, MT 59422 406/466-2641 FAX: 406/759-5967
email: kdmorton@earthlink.net
Web site: www.gbgm-umc.org/Yellowstone

LOS ANGELES AREA

California-Pacific Conference
***CIRCUIT WEST UM REVIEW** (biweekly)
Editor — **Steinman, Edna** (Interim)
1111 Cedar Ave., Redlands, CA 92373 909/793-1870 FAX: 909/793-
1870 email: ednaprsa@juno.com Web site:
www.cal-pac.org/circuit/index.html

PHOENIX AREA

Desert Southwest Conference
OPEN LINE (monthly)
Editor: **Athey, Wally**
1550 E. Meadowbrook Ave., Suite 200, Phoenix, AZ 85014-4040
800/229-8622 FAX: 602/266-5343 or 266-2196
email: wally@desertsw.org Web site: www.desertsw.org.

PORTLAND AREA

Alaska Missionary Conference
AURORA WITNESS (monthly)
Editor: **Wingfield, Brenda K.**
6037 Prosperity Drive, Anchorage, AK email: bscalaska@gci.net
Web site: www.aphids.com/alaska

Oregon-Idaho Conference
UNITED METHODIST (monthly)
Editor — **Sullivan, Linda**
1505 SW 18th Ave., Portland, OR 97201 800/593-7539 or 503/226-7931
FAX: 503/226-4158 email: linda@umoi.org
Web site: www.umoi.org

SAN FRANCISCO AREA

California-Nevada Conference
CALIFORNIA NEVADA UNITED METHODIST REVIEW (bi-weekly)
Editor — **Jones, Jeneane**
POB 980250 (1276 Halyard Dr.—95691), W. Sacramento, CA 95798-0250
916/374-1516 FAX: 916/372-5544 email: jeneanej@calnevumc.org
Web site: www.cnumc.org

SEATTLE AREA

Pacific Northwest Conference
CHANNELS (monthly)
Editor — **Schug, Tricia**
P.O. Box 3189, Kent, WA 98032 253/854-3722 FAX: 206/728-8442
email: tschug@attbi.com Web site: www.pnw-umc.org

JURISDICTIONAL NEWSPAPERS

Southeastern Jurisdiction

Jurisdictional Newspapers

SEJ UNITED METHODIST (quarterly)
Editor — **Smith, Jerome**
POB 237, Lake Junaluska, NC 28745 828/452-2881 ext. 645
FAX: 828/4562-4040 email: jerome@sejac-umc.com
Web site: www.sejac-umc.org

UNITED METHODIST CAUCUS PUBLICATIONS
(See also Caucuses, pp. 203-205)

AFFIRMATION NEWSLETTER

Editor —**Hagan, R. Wesley** or **Peck, Amory,** POB 1021, Evanston, IL
60201 360/734-5574

ASIAN AMERICAN NEWS (quarterly, National Federation of
Asian American UMs)

Editor — **Day, Inday Larot**

300 27th St., Oakland, CA 94612 510/836-0993 FAX: 510/836-0995
email: nfaaum@earthlink.net

BOLETIN DE MARCHA - (MARCHA-Metodistas Metodistas Associados Representando la Causa de Hispano-Americanos

Executive Director — **Rivera, José Orlando**
POB 1045, Lakewood, CA 90714

ECHO OF THE FOUR WINDS (Native American)

Editor — **Deer, Alvin**
616 SW 70th St., Oklahoma City, OK 73139 405/634-2005
FAX: 405/634-2181

METOHISPANO (quarterly, Florida Conference Committee on Hispanic Ministry)

Editor — **Montes, Francisco, Jr.**
2821 SW 38th Ave., Miami, FL 33134

NOW (Black Methodists for Church Renewal)

Contact — **Harris, Sandy**
601 W. Riverview Ave., Dayton, OH 45406-5543 937/227-9460
FAX: 937/227-9463 email: bmcr@bmcr-umc.org

SOCIAL QUESTIONS BULLETIN (bi-monthly, Methodist Federation for Social Action)

Editor — **Johnson, Kathryn J.**
212 E. Capitol St., NE, Washington, DC 20003 202/546-8806
FAX: 202/546-6811 email: mfsa@mfsaweb.org

"THE UNITED METHODIST MONITOR" A Newsletter of the General Commission on Religion and Race

Editor: **Pupo-Ortiz, Yolanda**
100 Maryland Ave., Suite 400, Washington, DC 2000-5620 202/547-2271 FAX: 202/547-0358 email: gcorr@erols.com

ECUMENICAL PERIODICALS

CHRISTIAN CENTURY (ecumenical)

Editor/Publisher — **Buchanan, John M.**
104 S. Michigan Ave., Chicago, IL 60603-5901 312/263-7510
  FAX: 312/263-7540 Web site: www.christiancentury.org

CHRISTIANITY TODAY (published May, June, July, Aug., Dec., Jan., evangelical)

Executive Editor — **Neff, David**
465 Gundersen Dr., Carol Stream, IL 60188 630/260-6200
  FAX: 630/260-0114 email: ctedit@aol.com

CHURCHWOMAN (quarterly, Church Women United)

Editor — **Sangko, Annie,**
475 Riverside Dr., Rm. 1626, New York, NY 10115 212/870-2343 FAX:
  212/870-2338 email: allamoso@churchwomen.org

DOVETAIL (Christian/Jewish bi-monthly newsletter)

Editor — **Rosenbaum, Mary**
775 Simon Greenwell Ln., Boston, KY 40107 800/530-1596
  FAX: 502/549-3543 email: di-ifr@bardstown.com

ECUMENICAL COURIER (U.S. Office of the World Council of Churches)

Editor — **Jenks, Philip E.**
475 Riverside Dr., Rm. 915, New York, NY 10115 212/870-3193
  FAX: 212/870-2528

ECUMENICAL TRENDS (Graymoor Ecumenical and Interreligious Institute)

Editor — **McMorrow, Kevin**
POB 306, Garrison, NY 10524-0306 914/424-3458 FAX: 914/424-3473

FIRST THINGS: *A Monthly Journal of Religion and Public Life* (The Institute on Religion and Public Life)

Editor-in-Chief — **Neuhaus, Richard John**
156 Fifth Ave., Suite 400, New York, NY 10010 212/627-1985
  FAX: 212/627-2184 email: rjn@firstthings.com

LIFEWATCH: *A Pro-Life Ministry* (quarterly, Taskforce of United Methodists on Abortion and Sexuality)

Editor — **Stallsworth, Rev. Paul T.**
111 Hodges St., Morehead City, NC 28557-2528 252/726-2175 or
  252/726-0491

THE OTHER SIDE (bi-monthly, evangelical)

Editors — **Davidson, Doug** and **Risher, Dee Dee**
300 W. Apsley, Philadelphia, PA 19144 215/849-2178
  FAX: 215/849-3755 email: editors@theotherside.org

SOJOURNERS (monthly)

Editor — **Wallis, Jim**
2401 15th St., NW, Washington, DC 20009 202/328-8842
  FAX: 202/328-8757 email: sojourners@sojo.net

AFFILIATED CAUCUSES AND ECUMENICAL GROUPS

CAUCUSES

(See also Caucus Publications, pp. 201-202)

Affirmation: UMs for Lesbian, Gay, and Bisexual Concerns

Spokesperson — **Hagan, R. Wesley** or **Peck, Amory,** POB 1021,
  Evanston, IL 60201 360/734-5574 or 703/824-8716 email:
  AmoryPeck@aol.com or Randy.Hagan@zzapp.org

Association of Physically Challenged Ministers of UM Churches

Executive Director - **Carr, John A.**, 1249 Yale Ave., Wallingford, CT 06492 203/284-8278 email: jcarr01@snet.net

Black Methodists for Church Renewal

Interim Executive Director - **Harris, Sandy,** 601 W. Riverview Ave., Dayton, OH 45406 937/227-9460 FAX: 937/227-9463 email: bmcr@bmcr-umc.org

Chairperson - **Williams, Anne Fleming,** 3857 N. Sydenham St., Philadelphia, PA 19140-3627 215/223-1391 FAX: 215/223-0898 email: awilli904@aol.com

Good News: Forum for Spiritual Christianity, Inc.

Editor - **Beard, Steve,** 308 E. Main St., Wilmore, KY 40390 859/858-4661 FAX: 606/858-4972 email: gnmag@aol.com

Metodistas Associados Representando la Causa de Hispano-Americanos (MARCHA)

Executive Director - **Silva, Mary,** P.O. Box 1067, San Mrcos, TX 78666 512/558-4534 FAX: 512/558-4540 email: marcha2000@centurytel.net

Chair - **Silva, Mary,** 13914 Anchorage Hill, San Antoniom TX 78217

Methodist Federation for Social Action

Executive Director - **Johnson, Kathryn J.,** 212 E. Capitol St., NE, Washington, DC 20003 202/546-8806 FAX: 202/546-6811 email: kj@mfsaweb.org

Methodists United for Peace with Justice

Board Chair - **Hallman, Howard W.,** 1500 16th St. NW, Washington, DC 20036 301/896-0013 email: mupwj@mupwj.org www.mupwj.org

Mission Society for United Methodists

President - **Granger, Philip R.,** 6234 Crooked Creek Rd., Norcross, GA 30092-8347 770/446-1381 FAX: 770/446-3044 email: pgranger@msum.org

National Federation of Asian American United Methodists

Executive Director - **Day, Inday Larot,** 1001 Holly Stream Ct., Brewster, NY 10509 845/279-8943 FAX: 845/279-8943 email: indayday01@aol.com

CA office: 436 14th St., Suite 1216, Oakland, CA 94612 510/836-0993 FAX: 510/836-0995 email: nfaaum@sbcglobal.net

Chair - **Nakagawa, Mark M.,** 300 S. Central Ave., Los Angeles, CA 90031 213/617-9097 FAX: 213/617-7688 email: revmmn@aol.com

Native American International Caucus

Executive Director - **Deer, Alvin,** 615 SW 70th St., Oklahoma City, OK 73139 405/634-2005 FAX: 405/634-2181
Chair - **Metoxen, Gary,** 5129 Old Randellman Rd., Greensboro, NC 27406 336/333-2890

Pacific Islander National Caucus of United Methodists
Executive Director - **Lauti, Pita,** 2990 Delta Ave., Long Beach, CA 90810 562/424-5780 FAX: 562/492-6183 email: tql@gte.net
Co-President - **Kelemeni, Eddie,** 4425 Kipling St., Wheat Ridge, CO 80033 303/424-0463 Home: 720/748-9090 FAX: 303/424-0950 email: EKELMENI@JUNO.COM
Co-President - **Aumua, Chester,** 253/272-6591

Reconciling Congregations Program

Executive Director - **Plummer, Rev. Troy**
www.rcp.org
3801 N. Keeler Ave., Chicago, IL 60641 773/736-5526
FAX: 773/736-5475 email: rmn@rmnetwork.org

Southern Asian National Caucus of UM Church

President - **Das, Man Lingh,** 11 Fernilee Ct., Aurora, IL 60506-9138 630/466-7544 or 815/753-6423 FAX: 630/466-7544

Taskforce of United Methodists on Abortion and Sexuality

www.lifewatch.org
Publications & Outreach Coordinator - **Evans, Cindy,** 1564 Sky View Dr., Holts Summit, AL 65043 573/896-9680
email: lwcindy@mchsi.com
Newsletter President - **Stallsworth, Rev. Paul T.,** 111 Hodges St., Morehead City, NC 28557 252/726-2175

Transforming Congregations Movement

Executive Director - **Booth, Rev. Karen,** POB 580, Millsboro, DE 19966 302/945-9650 email: transcong@aol.com

UM Action

www.ird-renew.org

Director - **Tooley, Mark,** 1521 16th St. NE, Suite 300, Washington, DC 20036-1466 202/986-1440 FAX: 202/986-3159 email: mail@ird-renew.org

United Methodist Rural Fellowship

President - **Eichler, Wanda Hayes,** 7218 Geiger Rd., Pigeon, MI 48755 517/453-3342 for administrative and presidential matters FAX: 517/453-4313

Contact - **West, Melvin,** field rep., 108 Balow Wynd, Columbia, MO 65203 573/445-9397 for materials and program matters FAX: 573/445-3788 email: melwest@aol.com

AFFILIATED GROUPS

Aldersgate Renewal Ministries (ARM)

www.aldersgaterenewal.org

Executive Director - **Moore, Gary L.,** POB 1205, Goodlettsville, TN 37070-1205 615/851-9192 FAX: 615/851-9372 email: armwork@concentric.net

Appalachia Service Project

Executive Director - **Crow, Susan,** 4523 Bristol Hwy., Johnson City, TN 37601-2937 423/854-0 FAX: 423/854-9771 email: asp@asphome.org Web site: www.asphome.org

Appalachian Development Committee (UMADC)

Executive Coordinator, **Letterman, N. Sharon,** POB 2231 (108 E. Franklin St.), Hagerstown, MD 21741-2231 301/791-7355 (FAX and Phone same number)

Association of United Methodist Conference Pensions & Benefits Officers

Contact - **Wilbur, Reuben L.,** 4800 Santana Cir., Suite 500, Columbia, MO 65203-7138 573/441-1770 email: rwilbur@moumethodist.org

Christian Educators Fellowship

www.cefumc.org
Director of CEF Services - **Van Buren, Corinne**, POB 24930,
Nashville, TN 37202 615/749-6870. FAX: 615/749-6871
email: cef@cefumc.org Office located on the first floor of The
United Methodist Publishing House.

Commission on Hispanic Ministry

Chair - **Kammerer, Charlene P.**, POB 18750, Charlotte, NC 28218
704/535-2260 FAX: 210/408-4502 email: bishop@umcswtx.org

Commission on Religion in Appalachia

Executive Director, **Willemsma, Tena**, POB 52190, Knoxville,
TN 37950-2910 885/584-6133 FAX: 615/554-8114
email: cora@kormet.org

The Conflict Transformation Center

Directors - **Lepley, L. M.**, and **Lepley, R. J.**, 373 Turnersburg Hwy.,
Statesville, NC 28625 704/873-9888 or cell: 828/381-9556
email: rllepley@aol.com

Council on Evangelism

Director - **Wesley, Daniel**, GBOD, POB 30003, Nashville, TN 37203
615/340-7049 FAX: 615/340-7015 email: wdaniel@gbod.org

Disciplined Order of Christ

www.geocities.com
Administrative Secretary - **Landrum, Marybelle**, PO Box 753,
Ashland, OH 44805 419/281-3932 email: maryboc@juno.com

Fellowship of United Methodists in Music and Worship Arts

Administrator - **Bone, David**, POB 24787, Nashville, TN 37202-4787
Voice: 800/952-8977 FAX: 615/749-6874 email: Fummwa@aol.com.
Office located on the first floor of The United Methodist Publishing
House.
President (1999–2001) - **Francabandiero, Daniel**, 4163 Shirley Ave.,
Jacksonville, FL 32210-2229 904/355-5491 email: dfffl@aol.com

Forum of Adults in Youth Ministry

Contact - **Trimmer, Edward,** 3081 Columbus Pk., Box 1204 MTSO, Delaware, OH 43015 740/362-3445 FAX: 740/362-3381 email: etrimmer@mtso.edu

Foundation for Evangelism

President - **Looney, Richard C.,** (551 Lakeshore Dr.), POB 985, Lake Junaluska, NC 28745 800/737-8333 or 828/456-4312 FAX: 828/456-4313 email: info@evangelize.org

International Christian Youth Exchange

Coordinator - **Hutchens, Heather C.,** 134 W. 26th St., New York, NY 10001

Marriage Encounter - UM

Contact - **Robey, Jerry** and **Robey, Donna,** 2635 Royal Oaks Dr., Freeport, IL 61032 815/232-8218 email: bmgb95a@prodigy.com
Contact - **Cross, Jim** and **Cross, Laura,** 1204 Davinbrook Dr., Oklahoma City, OK 73118-1010 405/842-0756 email: jimcross@ionet.net

National Association of Annual Conference Lay Leaders

President - **Holt, Gloria E.,** 6740 Clear Creek Cir., Trussville, AL 35173 205/661-9292 FAX: 205/856-8788 email: Gholt@umcna.bsc.edu

National Association of Annual Conference Treasurers

GCFA Contact: **Lackore, Sandra Kelley,** 1200 Davis St., Evanston, IL 60201 847/869-3345 FAX: 847/869-6972

National Association of Commissions on Equitable Compensation

President - **Clarke, Keith,** First UMC, 304 W. 5th St., Williamstown, KY 26187 304/342-0192

National Association of Directors of Connectional Ministries

Contact - **Huntington, Marilynn M.**, POB 6006, Pasadena, CA 91102-6006 626/568-7351 FAX: 626/796-7927
email: mhuntington@cal-pac.org

National Association of Conference Presidents of UM Men

President - **Hanke, Gilbert,** 803 Wildwood, Nacogdoches, TX 75961
936/560-1618 FAX: 936/560-3554 email: ghanke@sfasu.edu

National Association of Schools, Colleges and Universities of the UMC

Contact - **Yamada, Ken,** POB 871, Nashville, TN 37202 615/340-7399
FAX: 615/340-7379 email: kyamada@gbhem.org

National Association of UM Evangelists

President — **Nelson, Bob,** POB 4578, Lexington, KY 40544-4578
877/277-7547 FAX: 606/277-1766 email: bnelsonmin@aol.com
Executive Director— **Whittle, Charles,** NAUME Hdqtrs., POB 24241,
Ft. Worth, TX 76124 800/658-6569 FAX: 817/451-4409
email: charleswhittle@juno.com
Vice President of Council on Evangelism - **Barnett, Rod,** POB 88,
Winfield, WV 25213 304/586-3837 (also FAX)
email: rebeminc@aol.com

National Association of UM Foundations

President - **Crooch, Dr. John,** 4201 Classen Blvd., Oklahoma City,
OK 73118-2400 405/525-6863 FAX: 405/521-1429
email: jcrooch@okumf.com
Contact - **Joiner, Rev. Donald W.,** GBOD, Section on Stewardship,
POB 840, Nashville, TN 37202 615/340-7075 FAX: 615/340-7015
email: djoiner@gbod.org

National Association of UM Scouters

President - **Cash, Robert,** 8008 Slide Rd., #28, Lubbock, TX 79424
806/794-1145 or 806/794-7418 FAX: 806/794-7425 email:
Lindseysr@door.net Web site: SCOUTS-UMC@home.ease.lsoft.com

National Fellowship of Associate Members and Local Pastors

President - **Royer, Fred D.,** POB 329, Stockton, MO 65785
417/276-4717

National United Methodist Camp and Retreat Committee

Contact - **Thomas, Jon,** 329 Wesley Woods Rd., Townsend, TN 37082

National United Methodist Native American Center

Executive Director - **Noley, Homer,** c/o Claremont School of
Theology, 1325 N. College Ave., Claremont, CA 91711 909/447-2550
email: numnac@cst.edu

Order of Saint Luke

Contact - **Crouch, Nancy,** POB 22279, Akron, OH 44302-0079
330/535-8656 (also FAX) email: mail@Saint-Luke.org
Web site: www.Saint-Luke.org
Contact - **Vogel, Dwight,** Garrett-Evangelical Theological Seminary
Contact - **Pettus, Joanne,** GBOD, Discipleship Ministries Unit, POB
840, Nashville, TN 37202 615/340-7070 email: jpettus@gbod.org

Professional Association of UM Church Secretaries

GCFA Contact: **Haralson, Cynthia J.,** 1200 Davis St., Evanston, IL
60201 847/425-6548 FAX: 847/425-6569
President: **Rexrode, Deborah,** 5 Whiteoak Dr., Culloden, WV 25510
304/342-8843 email: raumcsv@aol.com

United Christian Ashrams

General Secretary - **Pyles, Rev. Jimmie,** 901 S. Vienna St., Ruston, LA
71720 318/232-0004 FAX: 310/232-0300 email: una@chris-
tianashram.org

UM Association of Church Business Administrators

GCFA Contact: **McKinsey, Linda S.,** 1200 Davis St., Evanston, IL
60201 847/425-6557 FAX: 847/425-6570 email: lmckinse@gcfa.org
GCFA Contact: **Kimble, Sheri Tyler,** 1200 Davis St., Evanston, IL
60201 847/425-6555 FAX: 847/425-6570 email: skimble@gcfa.org

President: **Klemann, Diane,** Bridgewater UMC, 651 Country Club
  Lane, Bridgewater, NJ 08807 908/526-1414 FAX: 908/429-8665
  email: dklemann@aol.com

UM Association of Communicators

President - **Horton, Alvin J.,** POB 11367 (4016 Broad St.), Richmond,
  VA 23230 804/359-9451 FAX: 804/359-5904
  email: al.horton@viaumc.org

UM Association of Health and Welfare Ministries

President - **Griffith, Mearle L.,** 601 W. Riverview Ave., Dayton,
  OH 45406 800/411-9901 or 937/227-9494 FAX: 937/222-7364
  email: uma@umassociation.org, mgriffith@umassociation.org

UM Association of Scholars Christian Education

Contact - **Slater, Nell,** 2120 Wynnedale Rd., Indianapolis, IN 46228
  317/299-5823 email: ngs@iquest.net

UM Higher Education Foundation

President - **Miller, George M.,** POB 871, Nashville, TN 37202
  615/340-7386 FAX: 615/340-7330 email: gmiller@gbhem.org

UM Men Foundation

Executive Director - **Coppock, Larry,** POB 34006, Nashville, TN
  37203 615/340-7145 FAX: 615/340-1770 email: lcppock@gcumm.org

United Methodist Youth Organization

Contact—**Seibert, Ronna,** POB 340003, Nashville, TN 37203-0003
  615/340-7181 FAX: 615/340-1764 email: rseibert@gbod.org
  Web site: www.umyouth.org

University Senate

President - **Tisdale, Henry N., send information to Yamada, Ken**
Contact - **Yamada, Ken,** POB 871, Nashville, TN 37202 615/340-7399
  FAX: 615/340-7379 email: kyamada@gbhem.org

ECUMENICAL GROUPS

American Bible Society

Contact - **London, Denise,** 1865 Broadway, New York, NY 10023
212/408-1330 FAX: 212/408-1456 FAX: 212/408-1456
email: dlondon@americanbible.org
Customer Service 212/408-8723 or Switchboard 212/408-1200

Associated Church Press

Executive Director - **Roos, Joe,** POB 21749, Washington,
DC 20009-1749 202/322-5544 FAX: 202/332-4559
email: jroos@erols.com

Commission on Pan Methodist Cooperation and Union

Administrative Secretary - **Love, Mary A.,** POB 44305, Charlotte,
NC 28215-0047 704/599-4630, ext. 324 FAX: 704/688-2548
email: mjet64@aol.com

Churches United in Christ

Director - **Wood, Bertrice Y.,** 700 Prospect Ave., Cleveland,
OH 44115-1100 216/736-3295 FAX: 216/736-3296
email: woodcuic@ucc.org

Council for Ecumenical Student Christian Ministry

Contact - **TBA,** 475 Riverside Dr., New York, NY 10115

The Council of Latin American Evangelical Methodist Churches in Latin America (CIEMAL)

President - **Gutierrez, Isaias,** Casilla 67, Santiago, CHILE 562 556 6074

Higher Education Ministries Arena

Contact - **Felder, Luther B.,** Campus Ministry Section, POB 871,
Nashville, TN 37202 615/340-7404 ext. 7420

Institute on Religion and Democracy

President - **Knippers, Diane,** 1521 16th St. NW, Suite 300,
Washington, D.C. 20036 202/986-1440 FAX: 202/986-3159
email: mail@ird-renew.org

National Council of the Churches of Christ in the USA

General Secretary - **Edgar, Robert,** 475 Riverside Dr., Rm. 880, New
York, NY 10115 212/870-2141 FAX: 212/870-2817
Web site: www.ncccusa.org
President - **Hoyt, Bishop Thomas,** Christian Methodist Episcopal
Church, Web site: www.ncccusa.org

Odyssey Channel (formerly Faith & Values Channel: formerly VISN)

74 Trinity Pl., 9th Floor, New York, NY 10006 212/964-1663
FAX: 212/964-5966

Project Equality, Inc.

President - **Perucca, Kirk P.,** 7132 Main St., Kansas City,
MO 64114-1406 816/361-9222 FAX: 816/361-8997
Web site: www.projectequality.org

Religion in American Life

President - **van Dyck, Nicholas,** 2 Queenston Pl., Princeton, NJ 08540
609/921-3639 FAX: 609/921-0551 email: rial@unadial.com

World Council of Churches, USA Office, worldcoun@mail.wcc-coe.org

General Secretary - **Kobia, Samuel,** POB 2100, CH 1211, Geneva, 2
SWITZERLAND (41) (22) 791-6111 FAX: (41) (22) 791-0361
Director, U.S. Office - **DeWinter, Deborah,** 475 Riverside Dr.,
Rm. 915, New York, NY 10115 212/870-2533 FAX: 212/870-2528
Communications Director - **Jenks, Philip E.,** 475 Riverside Dr., Rm.
915, New York, NY 10115 212/870-3193

World Methodist Council

General Secretary - **Freeman, George H.,** POB 518, 575 Lakeshore Dr.,
Lake Junaluska, NC 28745 828/456-9432 FAX: 828/456-9433
email: wmc6@juno.com Web site: www.worldmethodistcouncil.org

UM Study Committees/Mission Initiatives

UM Annual Conference Computer Administrators

President: **Taggart, Karen A.,** So. N.J. Conference, 1995 Marlton Pk. E., Cherry Hill, NJ 08003 609/424-1700 FAX: 609/424-9282 email: snjconfoff@aol.com

UMC Engaged in Seven Churchwide Mission Initiatives

The United methodist Church is now engaged in eight churchwide mission initiatives:
1) **Shared Mission Focus on Young People, Dyson, Drew,** director
2) **Bishops Initiative on Children & Poverty**
3) **Communities of Shalom, Byrd, Lynda R.,** director
4) **Restorative Justice Ministries**
5) **Strengthening the Black Church for the 21st Century, Stevenson, Cheryl,** coordinator
6) **Native American Comprehensive Plan, Saunkeah, Ann A.,** director
7) **Program on Substance Abuse and Related Violence,** and
8) **National Plan for Hispanic Ministries, Palos, José L.,** coordinator

Committee on Correlation and Editorial Revision

Chairperson - **Bartle, Naomi,** 3910 25th St. S., Fargo, ND 58104
  701/232-2241 FAX: 701/232-2615
Vice Chairperson - **Evans, Richard,** 6105 W. Douneray Loop,
  Crystal River, FL 34429-7507 352/563-5833
Secretary - **Valverde, Eradio,** 6800 Wurzbach, San Antonio, TX 78240
  210/684-0261 email: evalve@ix.netcom.com
Member - **Hendrix, Clelia,** 309 Arundel Rd., Greenville, SD 29615
  864/244-4359 (phone and FAX)
Secretary of the General Conference - **Marshall, Carolyn M.,** 204 N.
  Newlin St., Veedersburg, IN 47987 317/636-3328 FAX: 317/636-0073

SCHOOLS, COLLEGES, UNIVERSITIES, AND SEMINARIES

SCHOOLS OF THEOLOGY

Boston University School of Theology
  Hart, Ray L., interim dean, 745 Commonwealth Ave., Boston, MA
  02215 617/353-3050 FAX: 617/353-3061 email: rayhart@bu.edu

Candler School of Theology, Emory University
  Richey, Russell E., dean, 202 Bishops Hall, Atlanta, GA 30322
  404/727-6324 FAX: 404/727-3182 email: rrichey@emory.edu

Claremont School of Theology
  Amerson, Philip A., president, 1325 N. College Ave., Claremont,
  CA 91711-3199 909/447-2552 FAX: 909/621-3437
  email: pamerson@cst.edu

Drew University, The Theological School
  Beach, Maxine Clarke, dean and vice president, 36 Madison Ave.,
  Madison, NJ 07940 973/408-3258 FAX: 973/408-3534
  email: mbeach@drew.edu

Duke University, The Divinity School
  Jones, L. Gregory, dean, 107 New Divinity, Box 90968, Durham,
  NC 27708-0968 919/660-3434 FAX: 919/660-3474
  email: greg.jones@div.duke.edu

Gammon Theological Seminary
McKelvey, Walter H., president, POB 92426, 653 Beckwith St. SW, Atlanta, GA 30314 404/581-0300 FAX: 404/581-0305 email: wmckelvey@itc.edu

Garrett-Evangelical Theological Seminary
Campbell, Ted A., president, 2121 Sheridan Rd., Evanston, IL 60201 847/866-3900 FAX: 847/866-3884 email: ted.campbell@garrett.edu

Iliff School of Theology
Maldonado, David, Jr., president, 2201 S. University Blvd., Denver, CO 80210 303/765-3102 FAX: 303/777-3387 email: dmaldonado@iliff.edu

Methodist Theological School in Ohio
Dewire, Norman E., president, 3081 Columbus Pk., POB 8004, Delaware, OH 43015-8004 740/362-3122 FAX: 740/362-3122 email: ndewire@mtso.edu

Perkins School of Theology, Southern Methodist University
Lawrence, William B., dean, POB 750133, Dallas, TX 75275-0133 214/768-2534 FAX: 214/768-2966 email: blawren@smu.edu

Saint Paul School of Theology
McCoy, Myron F., president, 5123 Truman Rd., Kansas City, MO 64127 816/245-4801 FAX: 816/483-9605 (UPS Mail: 1515 Denver Ave., 64127) email: myron@spst.edu

United Theological Seminary
Zeiders, G. Edwin, president, 1810 Harvard Blvd., Dayton, OH 45406-4539 937/278-5817, ext. 2210 FAX: 937/278-1218 email: ezeiders@united.edu

Wesley Theological Seminary
McAllister-Wilson, David, president, 4500 Massachusetts Ave. NW, Washington, DC 20016-5632 202/885-8601 FAX: 202/885-8605 email: president@wesleysem.edu

PROFESSIONAL SCHOOL

Meharry Medical College
Maupin, John E., Jr., president, 1005 Dr. D.B. Todd, Jr. Blvd., Nashville, TN 37208 615/327-6904 FAX: 615/327-5590 email: jmaupin@mmc.edu

SENIOR COLLEGES AND UNIVERSITIES

Adrian College
Caine, Stanley P., president, 110 S. Madison, Adrian, MI 49221
517/265-5161 FAX: 517/264-3331

Alaska Pacific University
North, Douglas McKay, president, 4101 University Dr.,
Anchorage, AK 99508 907/564-8201 FAX: 907/562-2337

Albion College
Mitchell, Peter T., president, 611 E. Porter St., Albion, MI 49224
517/629-0210 FAX: 517/629-0619

Albright College
Zimon, Henry A., president, 13th and Bern St., POB 15234,
Reading, PA 19612-5234 610/921-7600 FAX: 610/921-7737

Allegheny College
Cook, Richard J., president, 520 N. Main St., Meadville, PA 16335
814/332-5380 FAX: 814/724-6032

American University
Ladner, Benjamin, president, 4400 Massachusetts Ave. NW,
Washington, DC 20016-8060 202/885-2121 FAX: 202/885-3265

Baker University
Lambert, Daniel M., president, POB 65, Baldwin City, KS 66006-
0065 785/594-8311 FAX: 785/594-8425

Baldwin-Wallace College
Collier, Mark H., president, 275 Eastland Rd., Berea, OH 44017-
2088 440/826-2424 FAX: 440/826-3777

Bennett College
Cole, Johnnetta B., president, 900 E. Washington St., Greensboro,
NC 27401-3239 336/273-4431 FAX: 336/370-8653

Bethune-Cookman College
Bronson, Oswald P., Sr., president, 640 Dr. Mary McLeod Bethune
Blvd., Daytona Beach, FL 32114-3099 386/481-2001 FAX: 386/481-
2010

Birmingham-Southern College
Berte, Neal R., president, 900 Arkadelphia Rd., Box 549002,
Birmingham, AL 35254 205/226-4620 FAX: 205/226-7020

Boston University
Chobanian, Aram V., president ad interim, One Sherborn St.,
Boston, MA 02215 617/353-2000 FAX: 617/353-9674

Brevard College
Van Horn, Drew L., president, 400 N. Broad St., Brevard, NC 28712-3306 828/884-8264 FAX: 828/884-3790

Centenary College
Hoyt, Kenneth L., president, 400 Jefferson St., Hackettstown, NJ 07840 908/852-1400, ext. 2201 FAX: 908/850-9508

Centenary College of Louisiana
Schwab, Kenneth L., president, POB 41188, Shreveport, LA 71134-1188 318/869-5101 FAX: 318/869-5010

Central Methodist College
Inman, Marianne E., president, 411 Central Methodist Square, Fayette, MO 65248 660/248-6221 FAX: 660/248-2287

Claflin University
Tisdale, Henry N., president, 400 Magnolia St., Orangeburg, SC 29115 803/535-5412 FAX: 803/535-5402

Clark Atlanta University
Broadnax, Walter D., president, 223 James P. Brawley Dr., SW, Atlanta, GA 30314 404/880-8000 FAX: 404/880-8995

Columbia College
Whitson, Caroline B., president, 1301 Columbia College Dr., Columbia, SC 29203 803/786-3178 FAX: 803/754-3178

Cornell College
Garner, Leslie H., Jr., president, 600 First St. W., Mount Vernon, IA 52314-1098 319/895-4324 FAX: 319/895-5237

Dakota Wesleyan University
Duffett, Robert G., president, 1200 W. University Ave., Mitchell, SD 57301 605/995-2601 FAX: 605/995-2723

DePauw University
Bottoms, Robert G., president, POB 37, Greencastle, IN 46135-0037 765/658-4220 FAX: 765/658-4224

Dickinson College
Durden, William G., president, POB 1773, Carlisle, PA 17013-2896 717/245-1322 FAX: 717/245-1941

Dillard University
Lomax, Michael L., president, 2601 Gentilly Blvd., New Orleans, LA 70122 504/816-4640 FAX: 504/288-8663

Drew University
Kean, Thomas H., president, 36 Madison Ave., Madison, NJ 07940 973/408-3100 FAX: 973/408-3080

Duke University
  Keohane, Nannerl O., president, 207 Allen Bldg., Box 90001,
  Durham, NC 27708-0001 919/684-2424 FAX: 919/684-3050

Emory & Henry College
  Morris, Thomas R., president, POB 947, Emory, VA 24327-0947
  540/944-6107 FAX: 540/944-6598

Emory University
  Wagner, James W., president, 408 Administration Bldg., Atlanta,
  GA 30322 404/727-6013 FAX: 404/727-5997

Ferrum College
  Braaten, Jennifer L., president, POB 1000, Ferrum, VA 24088
  540/365-4202 FAX: 540/365-4269

Florida Southern College
  Reuschling, Thomas L., president, 111 Lake Hollingsworth Dr.,
  Lakeland, FL 33801 863/680-4100 FAX: 863/680-5096

Green Mountain College
  Brennan John F., president, One College Cir., Poultney, VT 05764-
  1199 802/287-8201 FAX: 802/287-8097

Greensboro College
  Williams, Craven E., president, 815 W. Market St., Greensboro, NC
  27401-1875 336/272-7102 FAX: 336/217-7230

Hamline University
  Osnes, Larry G., president, 1536 Hewitt Ave., St. Paul, MN 55104
  651/523-2202 FAX: 651/523-2030

Hendrix College
  Cloyd, J. Timothy, president, 1600 Washington Ave., Conway, AR
  72032-3080 501/450-1351 FAX: 501/450-3821

High Point University
  Martinson, Jacob C., president, University Station, 833 Montlieu
  Ave., High Point, NC 27262-3598 336/841-9000 FAX: 336/841-4599

Huntingdon College
  West, J. Cameron, president, 1500 E. Fairview Ave., Montgomery,
  AL 36106-2148 334/833-4409 FAX: 334/833-4314

Huston-Tillotson College
  Earvin, Larry L., president, 900 Chicon St., Austin, TX 78702-2795
  512/505-3001 FAX: 512/505-3195

Illinois Wesleyan University
  McNew, Janet M., acting president, POB 2900, Bloomington, IL
  61702 309/556-3151 FAX: 309/556-3970

Iowa Wesleyan College
Johnston, William N., president, 601 N. Main St., Mount Pleasant, IA 52641 319/385-6204 FAX: 319/385-6296

Kansas Wesleyan University
Kerstetter, Philip P., president and CEO, 100 E. Claflin Ave., Salina, KS 67401-6196 785/827-5541, ext. 1227 FAX: 785/827-0927

Kendall College
Tullman, Howard A., president, 2408 Orrington Ave., Evanston, IL 60201 847/866-1300, ext. 2010 FAX: 847/866-6842

Kentucky Wesleyan College
Poling, Wesley H., president, 3000 Frederica St., POB 1039, Owensboro, KY 42302-1039 270/852-3104 FAX: 270/852-3190

LaGrange College
Gulley, F. Stuart, president, 601 Broad St., LaGrange, GA 30240 706/880-8230 FAX: 706/880-8358

Lambuth University
Arnold, W. Ellis, III, president, 705 Lambuth Blvd., Jackson, TN 38301 731/425-3201 FAX: 731/988-7000

Lebanon Valley College
Pollick, G. David, president, 101 N. College Ave., Annville, PA 17003-0501 717/867-6211 FAX: 717/867-6910

Lindsey Wilson College
Luckey, William T., Jr., president, 210 Lindsey Wilson St., Columbia, KY 42728 270/384-8001 FAX: 270/384-8009

Lycoming College
Douthat, James E., president, 700 College Pl., Williamsport, PA 17701-5192 570/321-4101 FAX: 570/321-4307

MacMurray College
Bryan, Lawrence D., president, 447 E. College Ave., Jacksonville, IL 62650 217/479-7025 FAX: 217/479-7201

Martin Methodist College
Brown, Ted, president, 433 W. Madison St., Pulaski, TN 38478 931/363-9802 FAX: 931/363-9892

McKendree College
Dennis, James M., president, 701 College Rd., Lebanon, IL 62254 618/537-6936 FAX: 618/537-6417

McMurry University
Russell, John W., president, Box 98, McMurry Station, Abilene, TX 79697-0098 325/793-3801 FAX: 325/793-4628

Methodist College
Hendricks, M. Elton, president, 5400 Ramsey St., Fayetteville, NC
28311-1420 910/630-7005 FAX: 910/630-7317

Millsaps College
Lucas, Frances, president, 1701 N. State St., Jackson, MS 39210-0001
601/974-1001 FAX: 601/974-1004

Morningside College
Reynders, John C., president, 1501 Morningside Ave., Sioux City,
IA 51106 712/274-5100 FAX: 712/274-5358

Mount Union College
Ewing, John L., Jr., president, 1972 Clark Ave., Alliance, OH 44601
330/823-6050 FAX: 330/829-2811

Nebraska Methodist College
Joslin, Dennis A., president, 8501 W. Dodge Rd., Omaha, NE
68114-3403 402/354-4918 FAX: 402/354-8893

Nebraska Wesleyan University
Watson, Jeanie, president, 5000 Saint Paul Ave., Lincoln, NE 68504-
2794 402/465-2217 FAX: 402/465-2103

North Carolina Wesleyan College
Newbould, Ian D. C., president, 3400 N. Wesleyan Blvd., Rocky
Mount, NC 27804 252/985-5140 FAX: 252/985-5199

North Central College
Wilde, Harold R., president, 30 N. Brainard St., Naperville, IL
60540 630/637-5454 FAX: 630/637-5457

Ohio Northern University
Baker, Kendall L., president, 525 S. Main St., Ada, OH 45810
419/772-2031 FAX: 419/772-1932

Ohio Wesleyan University
Courtice, Thomas B., president, 61 S. Sandusky St., Delaware, OH
43015 740/368-3000 FAX: 740/368-3007

Oklahoma City University
McDaniel, Tom J., president, 2501 N. Blackwelder, Oklahoma City,
OK 73106-1493 405/521-5032 FAX: 405/521-5264

Otterbein College
DeVore, C. Brent, president, Westerville, OH 43081 614/823-1420
FAX: 614/823-3114

Paine College
Lewis, Shirley A.R., president, 1235 Fifteenth St., Augusta, GA
30901-3182 706/821-8230 FAX: 706/821-8333

Pfeiffer University
Ambrose, Charles M., president, POB 960, Misenheimer, NC 28109-0960 704/463-1360 ext. 2050 FAX: 704/463-1363
Philander Smith College
Reed, Trudie Kibbe, president, One Trudie Kibbe Reed Dr., Little Rock, AR 72202 501/370-5275 FAX: 501/370-5277
Randolph-Macon College
Martin, Roger H., president, POB 5005, Ashland, VA 23005-5505 804/752-7211 FAX: 804/752-3129
Randolph-Macon Woman's College
Bowman, Kathleen G., president, 2500 Rivermont Ave., Lynchburg, VA 24503 434/947-8140 FAX: 434/947-8139
Reinhardt College
Isherwood, J. Thomas, president, 7300 Reinhardt College Cir., Waleska, GA 30183-2981 770/720-5500 FAX: 770/720-5887
Rocky Mountain College
Oates, Thomas R., president, 1511 Poly Dr., Billings, MT 59102 406/657-1015 FAX: 406/238-7253
Rust College
Beckley, David L., president, 150 Rust Ave., Holly Springs, MS 38635 662/252-2491 FAX: 662/252-8863
Shenandoah University
Davis, James A., president, 1460 University Dr., Winchester, VA 22601 540/665-4506 FAX: 540/665-5481
Simpson College
LaGree, R. Kevin, president, 701 North C St., Indianola, IA 50125-1297 515/961-1566 FAX: 515/961-1623
Southern Methodist University
Turner, R. Gerald, president, POB 750100, Dallas, TX 75275 214/768-3300 FAX: 214/768-3844
Southwestern College
Merriman, W. Richard, Jr., president, 100 College St., Winfield, KS 67156-2499 620/229-6223 FAX: 620/229-6224
Southwestern University
Schrum, Jake B., president, POB 770, Georgetown, TX 78627-0770 512/863-6511 FAX: 512/819-9911
Syracuse University
Shaw, Kenneth A., chancellor and president, 300 Tolley Administration Bldg., Syracuse, NY 13244-1100 315/443-2235 FAX: 315/443-3503

Tennessee Wesleyan College
  Armstrong, Thomas F., president, POB 40, Athens, TN 37371-0040
  423/746-5202 FAX: 423/746-5302
Texas Wesleyan University
  Jeffcoat, Harold G., president, 1201 Wesleyan St., Fort Worth, TX
  76105 817/531-4401 FAX: 817/531-4496
Union College
  de Rosset, Edward D., president, 310 College St., Barbourville, KY
  40906 606/546-1211 FAX: 606/546-1609
University of Denver
  Ritchie, Daniel L., chancellor, 2199 S. University Blvd., Denver, CO
  80208-2111 303/871-2111 FAX: 303/871-4101
University of Evansville
  Jennings, Stephen G., president, 1800 Lincoln Ave., Evansville, IN
  47722 812/479-2151 FAX: 812/474-4017
University of Indianapolis
  Israel, Jerry, Jr., president, 1400 E. Hanna Ave., Indianapolis, IN
  46227 317/788-3211 FAX: 317/788-6152
University of Puget Sound
  Thomas, Ronald R., president, 1500 N. Warner, Tacoma, WA 98416-
  0094 253/879-3201 FAX: 253/879-3938
University of the Pacific
  DeRosa, Donald V., president, 3601 Pacific Ave., Stockton, CA
  95211 209/946-2223 FAX: 209/946-2652
Virginia Wesleyan College
  Greer, William T., Jr., president, 1584 Wesleyan Dr., Norfolk, VA
  23502-5599 757/455-3204 FAX: 757/455-3139
Wesley College
  Miller, Scott D., president, 120 N. State St., Dover, DE 19901
  302/736-2364 FAX: 302/736-2312
Wesleyan College
  Knox, Ruth A., president, 4760 Forsyth Rd., Macon, GA 31210-4462
  478/757-5212 FAX: 478/757-2485
West Virginia Wesleyan College
  Haden, William R., president, 59 College Ave., Buckhannon, WV
  26201 304/473-8181 FAX: 304/473-8187
Wiley College
  Strickland, Haywood, president, 711 Wiley Ave., Marshall, TX
  75670 903/927-3200 FAX: 903/938-8100

Willamette University
Pelton, M. Lee, president, 900 State St., Salem, OR 97301 503/370-6209 FAX: 503/370-6148

Wofford College
Dunlap, Benjamin B., president, 429 N. Church St., Spartanburg, SC 29303-3663 864/597-4000 FAX: 864/597-4018

TWO-YEAR COLLEGES

Andrew College
Palmer, David A., president, 413 College St., Cuthbert, GA 39840-1395 229/732-5928 FAX: 229/732-5994

Hiwassee College
Philip, W. Chuck, president, 225 Hiwassee College Dr., Madisonville, TN 37354 423/420-1225 FAX: 423/420-1896

Lon Morris College
Lee, Clifford M., president, 800 College Ave., Jacksonville, TX 75766-2900 903/589-4000 FAX: 903/586-8562

Louisburg College
Ponder, Reginald W., president, 501 N. Main St., Louisburg, NC 27549 919/496-2521 FAX: 919/496-0247

Oxford College of Emory University
Greene, Dana, dean, POB 1328, Oxford, GA 30054 770/784-8300 FAX: 770/784-8440

Spartanburg Methodist College
Teague, Charles P., president, 1200 Textile Rd., Spartanburg, SC 29301-0009 864/587-4236 FAX: 864/587-4379

Wood College
Lowdermilk, Robert E., III, president, POB 289, Mathiston, MS 39752-0289 662/263-5352, ext. 110 FAX: 662/263-8148

Young Harris College
Yow, Thomas S., III, president, POB 98, Young Harris, GA 30582 706/379-3111 FAX: 706/379-4319

COLLEGE PREPARATORY SCHOOLS

Carrollton Christian Academy
Dunagin, Richard, interim superintendent, 2201 E. Hebron Pkwy. 75010 Carrollton, TX 75006 972/242-6688

Kents Hill School
Bonnefond, Rist, headmaster, POB 257, Kents Hill, ME 04349-0257 207/685-4914 ext. 120 FAX: 207/685-9529

Lydia Patterson Institute
  de Anda, Socorro Brito, president, POB 11, El Paso, TX 79940
  915/533-8286 FAX: 915/533-5236
McCurdy School
  Womack, Pamela, superintendent, 261 McCurdy Rd., Española,
  NM 87532 505/753-7221 FAX: 505/753-7830
The Pennington School
  Rigg, Lyle D., headmaster, 112 W. Delaware Ave., Pennington, NJ
  08534 609/737-1838 FAX: 609/737-9269
Randolph-Macon Academy
  Hobgood, Henry M., president, 200 Academy Dr., Front Royal, VA
  22630 540/636-5201 FAX: 540/636-5344
Red Bird Mission School
  Haggard, Fred, executive director, HC69 Box 700, Beverly, KY
  40913 606/598-3155 FAX: 606/598-3151
Robinson School
  Quintana, Gilberto, executive director, 5 Nairn St., San Juan,
  PUERTO RICO 00907 787/728-6767 FAX: 787/727-7736
Tilton School
  Clements, James R., head of school, 30 School St., Tilton, NH 03276
  603/286-4342 FAX: 603/286-3137
Wyoming Seminary College Preparatory School
  Packard, H. Jeremy, president, 201 N. Sprague Ave., Kingston, PA
  18704-3593 570/270-2150 FAX: 570/270-2154

PROGRAMS AND RESOURCES
(For complete contact information,
see general directory listing.)

Program	Agency	Contact Person
Abingdon Press	UMPH	**Academic/Bible/Reference/ Professional Resources Russell, Michael,** mrussell@umpublishing.org **Adult/General Interest Resources Dean, Mary Catherine,** mdean@umpublishing.org www./abingdonpress.com **Children's Resources Pon, Marjorie,** mpon@umpublishing.org **Congregational Resources Johannes, Mary,** mjohannes@umpublishing.org **Korean & Spanish Resources Won, Dal Joon,** djwon@umpublishing.org **Electronic Resources & Software Franklyn, Paul,** pfranklyn@umpublishing.org **Music Resources Gnegy, Bill,** bgnegy@umpublishing.org **Youth Resources Shell, Bob,** bshell@umpublishing.org
Abortion	GBCS	**Bales, Linda,** 202/488-5649 lbales@umc-gbcs.org
	GBGM	**Dauway, Lois,** ldauway@gbgm-umc.org
Academic Books, Editorial	UMPH	**Ratcliff, Bob,** rratcliff@umpublishing.org
Academy for Spiritual Formation	GBOD	**Haas, Jerry,** jerry-haas@gbod.org
Accreditation for Teacher Training/Development	GBOD	**Krau, Carol,** ckrau@gbod.org
Acts of Repentance for Racism	GCCUIC	**Marshall, Anne,** amarshall@gccuic-umc.org
Addresses-Clergy	GCFA	**Haralson, Cynthia J.,** charalso@gcfa.org
Addresses-Local Church Diaconal and Clergy	UMCom	**InfoServ,** 800/251-8141 infoserv@umcom.umc.org
Addresses-General	UMCom	**InfoServ,** 800/251-8140 general, infoserv@umcom.org

Administrative Board Council	GBOD	**Dick, Dan,** ddick@gbod.org
Adult Education Publications	UMPH	**Curric-U-Phone,** 800/251-8591 curricuphone@cokesbury.com
Advance for Christ and His Church	GBGM	**Carter, William T.,** wcarter@gbgm-umc.org
Advance for Christ and His Church Marketing	UMCom	**Dunlap-Berg, Barbara,** bdunlapberg@umcom.org
Advertising Media	UMCom	**Igniting Ministry,** 877/281-6535 im@umcom.org
Connectional Giving Interpretation		**McNish, Kent,** 615/742-5142 kmcnish@umcom.org
Advocacy for Women	GCSRW	**Burton, Garlinda,** gburton@gcfa.org
	GBCS	**Bales, Linda,** 202/488-5649 lbales@umc-gbcs.org
	GBGM	**Dauway, Lois,** ldauway@gbgm-umc.org
Advocacy in Public Policy	GBCS	**All program staff,** 202/488-5600
	GBHEM	**Bigham, Wanda D.,** wbigham@gbhem.org
	GBGM	**Johnson, Susie,** 202/488-5660
Affirmative Action	GCFA	**Bowen, Gary K.,** gbowen@gcfa.org
	GCSRW	**Burton, Garlinda,** gburton@gcfa.org
	GBOD	**Taylor-Thirus, Francine,** ftaylorthirus@gbod.org
	GBCS	**Fealing, Kenrick,** 202/488-5637 kfealing@umc-gbcs.org
Africa Advocacy Policy	GBCS	**Harrison, Mark,** 202/488-5645 mharrison@umc-gbcs.org
Africa, Central & Eastern	GBGM	**Anderson, Clyde,** canderson@gbgm-umc.org
Africa, Western & Southern	GBGM	**Marewangepo, Zebediah,** zmarewan@gbgm-umc.org
Africa, North	GBGM	**Siegfried, Peter,** psiegfri@gbgc-umc.org
Africa Church Growth	GBGM	**Nugent, Randolph,** rnugent@gbgm-umc.org
Africa University	GBHEM	**Del Pino, Jerome King,** mbsartain@gbhem.org
Development	GBHEM	**Salley, James,** 615/340-7438
Journal	GBHEM	**Hiers, Terri J.,** 615/340-7382
Staff Liaison	GBHEM	**Current-Felder, Angella P.,** 615/340-7342
Marketing/AVF	UMCom	**Hughes, Celinda,** chughes@umcom.org
Apportionment World Service	GBHEM	**Treasurer, CFO,** 615/340-7359
African American	GCRR	**Hawkins, Erin,** 202/547-2271

Ministries/Affairs	GBOD	**Taylor-Thirus, Francine** ftaylorthirus@gbod.org
	GBGM	**Lawson, Ruth,** rlawson@gbgm-umc.org
Agency Review Committee	GCRR	**Taylor, James,** 202/547-2271
Age-level Ministries	GBOD	**Norton, MaryJane Pierce,** mnorton@gbod.org
Curriculum Resources	UMPH	**Curric-U-Phone,** 800/251-8591 curricuphone@cokesbury.com
Aging Ministries with Older Adults	GBOD	**Gentzler, Richard,** rgentzler@gbod.org
Aging Social Policy	GBCS	**Day, Jackson,** 202/488-5608 jday@umc-gbcs.org
Health Issues	GBGM	**Njuki, Caroline** cnjuki@gbgm-umc.org
	GBCS	**Day, Jackson,** 202/488-5608 jday@umc-gbcs.org
Church Programs	GBOD	**Gentzler, Richard,** rgentzler@gbod.org
AIDS	GBCS	**Day, Jackson,** 202/488-5608 jday@umc-gbcs.org
	GBGM	**Gittens, Betty,** bgittens@gbgm-umc.org
Global HIV-AIDS	GBCS	Bales, Linda, 202/488-5649 lbales@umc-gbcs.org
Alcohol/Drug Concerns	GBCS	**vacant**
	GBGM	**Norfleet, Wilma,** 202/488-5626
Alive Now Magazine	GBOD	**Tidwell, Melissa,** mtidwell@upperroom.org
		Fisher, Eli, efisher@upperroom.org
Standing Orders		800/972-0433
Subscriptions		800/925-6847
American Indian Affairs	GBCS	**Valentin-Castañon, Eliezer,** 202/488-5637 evalentin@umc-gbcs.org
	GBCS	**Hanson, Jaydee,** 202/488-5650 jhanson@umc-gbcs.org
	GBCS	**Harrison, Mark,** 202/488-5645 mharrison@umc-gbcs.org
	GBGM	**Kent, Cynthia,** ckent@gbgm-umc.org
	GCRR	**Ware-Diaz, Suanne,** 202/547-2271
Annual Conference Relations	GBCS	**Childers, Clayton,** 202/488-5642 cchilders@umc-gbcs.org
	GBCS	**Williams, Annette,** 817/460-2573 awilliams@umc-gbcs.org
	GBGM	**Nuessle, John,** jnuessle@gbgm-umc.org
	GBHEM	**Felder, Luther B.,** lfelder@gbhem.org

	GBOD	**Ruach, Susan,** sruach@gbod.org
	UMCom	**Communications Resourcing Team,** 888/278-4862 crt@umcom.org
Anti-Racism Training	GCRR	NEJ - **Taylor, James,** 202/547-2271
	GCRR	SEJ - **Hawkins, Erin,** 202/547-2271
	GCRR	SCJ - **Pupo-Ortiz, Yolanda,** 202/547-2271
	GCRR	NCJ - **Ware-Diaz, Suanne,** 202/547-2271
	GCRR	WJ - **Thomas-Sano, Kathy,** 202/547-2271
	GBCS	**Christie, Neal,** 202/488-5611 nchristie@umc-gbcs.org
Apuntes Hispanic Journal	UMPH	**Gonzales, Justo,** 404/378-7651
Arab Israeli Conflict	GBCS	**Horman, Janet,** 202/488-5647 jhorman@umc-gbcs.org
Architecture for Worship	GBOD	**Benedict, Dan,** dbenedict@gbod.org
Asbury Awards	GBHEM	**Felder, Luther B.,** lfelder@gbhem.org
Asian American Ministries	GBCS	**Bautista, Librato,** 212/682-3633 lbautista@umc-gbcs.org
	GBCS	**Christie, Neal,** 202/488-5611 nchristie@umc-gbcs.org
	GBGM	**Kim, Jong Sung,** jskim@gbgm-umc.org
	GBOD	**Choi, Sungnam,** schoi@gbod.org
	GCRR	**Thomas-Sano, Kathy,** 202/547-2271
Asia/Pacific	GBGM	**Rodriguez, David,** drodriguez@gbgm-umc.org
Assessment:	GBGM	**Coulson, Gail,** gcoulson@gbgm-umc.org
How Do We Do It?	GBHEM	**Purushotham, Gwen,** gpurushotham@gbhem.org
Giving and Receiving Feedback	GBHEM	**Purushotham, Gwen,** gpurushotham@gbhem.org
Pastor/Staff	GBHEM	**Purushotham, Gwen,** gpurushotham@gbhem.org
Parish Relations Committee	GBOD	**Heavner, Betsey,** bheavner@gbod.org
Congregational Leaders	GBOD	**Dick, Dan,** ddick@gbod.org
Clergy and	GBHEM	**Purushotham, Gwen,** gpurushotham@gbhem.org
Congregations	GBOD	**Wallace, Julia,** jwallace@gbod.org
Clergy	GBHEM	**Purushotham, Gwen** gpurushotham@gbhem.org
Self-Reflection	GBOD	**Wallace, Julia,** jwallace@gbod.org
Team Ministry	GBHEM	**Purushotham, Gwen,** gpurushotham@gbhem.org
District Committee on Superintendency	GBHEM	**Purushotham, Gwen,** gpurushotham@gbhem.org

Association of Annual Conference Lay Leaders	GBOD	**Ziegler, Sandy,** sziegler@bgod.org
Association of Directors of Connectional Ministries	GCUMM	**Pickering, J. Delton,** 818/244-8622
Association UM Theological Schools	GBHEM	**Moman, Mary Ann,** mmoman@gbhem.org
Audio Production Facilities	UMCom	**Nelson, Larry,** lnelson@umcom.org
Audio Visual Materials	GBOD	**Discipleship Resources,** 800/685-4370
Church & Society	GBCS	**Service Department,** 800/967-0880
Deacon & Diaconal Ministry	GBHEM	**Heist, Linda,** lheist@gbhem.org
Missions	GBGM	**Obando, Jorge,** jobando@gbgm-umc.org
Production Consultation	UMCom	**Alexander, Leslie,** 615/742-5429
Production Facilities	UMCom	**Nelson, Larry,** lnelson@umcom.org
Sales	UMCom	**EcuFilm,** 888/346-3862 **Customer Service Center** 888/346-3862 (888/FINDUMC)
Igniting MinistryTraining	UMCom	**Reece, Emily,** 615/742-5134 ereece@umcom.org
Audit, Local Church	GCFA	**Belton, Dennis,** 615/329-3393 dbelton@gcfa.org
Baptism Resources	GBOD UMPH	**Benedict, Dan,** dbenedict@gbod.org 800/672-1789
Basic Protection Plan	GBOPHB	**Anderson, Daryl,** 800/851-2201
Bible Study Resources	UMPH	**Curric-U-Phone,** 800/257-8591 curricuphone@cokesbury.com
Bibliographic/Research Information	GCAH	**Rowe, Kenneth E.,** 973/408-3590
Bi-lateral Dialogues UMC/Roman Catholic	GCCUIC	**Gamble, Rev. Betty,** bgamble@gccuic-umc.org
UMC/Evangelical Lutheran Church in America	GCCUIC	
Bilingual Education	GBCS	**Valentin-Castañon, Eliezer,** evalentin@umc-gbcs.org
Biomedical Ethics	GBCS	**Hanson, Jaydee,** 202/488-5650 jhanson@umc-gbcs.org
	GBGM	**Dirdak, Paul,** pdirdak@gbgm-umc.org
Bishops		See pages 4-13
Bishops Award of Excellence	GCUMM	**Coppock, Larry,** lcoppock@gcumm.org

Black College Fund	GBHEM	**Capers, Joreatha,** bcfumc@gbhem.org
Apportionment Marketing	UMCom	**Hughes, Celinda,** chughes@umcom.org
Board of Ordained Ministry	GBHEM	**Rubey, Sharon,** srubey@gbhem.org
Resources	GBHEM	**Rubey, Sharon,** srubey@gbhem.org
Board of Trustees of UMC	GCFA	**Allen, Jim,** jallen@gcfa.org
	GCFA	**Howard, Irene,** 847/869-3345
Board of Trustees - Local Church	GBOD	**Joiner, Don,** djoiner@gbod.org
Book Editor of the UMC	UMPH	**Olson, Harriet Jane,** holson@umpublishing.org
Book of Discipline	UMPH	**Cropsey, Marvin,** mcropsey@umpublishing.org
Book of Resolutions	UMPH	**Cropsey, Marvin,** mcropsey@umpublishing.org
Book of Worship	GBOD	**Benedict, Dan,** dbenedict@gbod.org
Booktable Ministry	UMPH	**Barnes, Jeff,** jbarnes@umpublishing.org
Buddhist - Christian Relations	GCCUIC	**Marshall, Anne M.,** amarshall@gccuic-umc.org
Business Education Initiative	GBHEM	**Bigham, Wanda D.,** wbigham@gbhem.org
Calendar, Conference Program	UMCom	**Carey, Lladale,** lcarey@umcom.umc.org
Camp/Retreats, Christian Education, Evangelism, Music, Older Adults, Spiritual Formation	GBHEM	**Wood, Anita,** awood@gbhem.org
	GBCS	**Christie, Neal,** 202/488-5611 nchristie@umc-gbcs.org
Camping/Retreat Ministry	GBOD	**Witt, Kevin,** kwitt@gbod.org
Camping/Retreat Certification	GBHEM	**Wood, Anita,** awood@gbhem.org
Campus Ministry	GBHEM	**Felder, Luther B.,** lfelder@gbhem.org
Campus Ministry	GBCS	**Burton, Susan,** 202/488-5609 sburton@umc-gbcs.org
Justice Education	GBCS	**Burton, Susan,** 202/488-5609 sburton@umc-gbcs.org
Campus Ministry Publications	GBHEM	**Felder, Luther B.,** campmin@gbhem.org
Candidacy-Deacon	GBHEM	**Rubey, Sharon,** srubey@gbhem.org
Candidacy-Diaconal Ministry	GBHEM	**Rubey, Sharon,** srubey@gbhem.org
Candidacy-Elders and Local Pastors	GBHEM	**Rubey, Sharon,** srubey@gbhem.org
Capital Punishment	GBCS	**Fealing, Kenrick,** 202/488-5637 kfealing@umc-gbcs.org
Caribbean Church Dev't	GBGM	**Rae, Keith,** krae@gbgm-umc.org
Caribbean Relationships	GBGM	**Guerrero, Frank,** fguerrero@gbgm-umc.org

Caring Community Program (Mental Illness Network)	GBCS	**Day, Jackson,** 202/488-5608 jday@umc-gbcs.org
Caring Couples Network	GBOD	**Norton, MaryJane Pierce,** mnorton@gbod.org
Cassette Edition, *The Upper Room* magazine	GBOD	615/340-7252
Standing Orders		800/972-0433
Subscriptions		800/925-6847
Central America	GBGM	**Perez-Salgado, Lyssette,** lperez@gbgm-umc.org
Central America, Public Policy	GBCS	**Horman, Janet,** 202/488-5647 jhorman@umc.gbcs.org
Central Conference	GBCS	**Bautista, Liberato C.,** 212/682-3633 **Childers, Clayton,** 202/488-5642 cchilders@umc-gbcs.org
Central Conference Communications	UMCom	**Nissen, Barbara,** 888/278-4862 bnissen@umcom.org
Central Conference Social Justice Education	GBCS	**Christie, Neal,** 202/488-5611 nchristie@umc-gbcs.org
Certification of: Bus. Administrators	GCFA	**McKinsey, Linda,** lmckinse@gcfa.org
Certification of Welcoming Congregations	UMCom	**Igniting Ministry,** im@umcom.org
Chapel, The Upper Room	GBOD	**Kimball, Kathryn,** 877/899-2780, ext. 7206, kkimball@upperroom.org
Chaplains (Institutional and Military)	GBHEM	**Barrett, Pat,** 615/340-7411 pbarrett@gbhem.org
Endorsement	GBHEM	**Hill, Greg,** 615/340-7411 ghill@gbhem.org
Retreats/Recruitment	GBHEM	**Espino, Saul,** 615/340-7411 sespino@gbhem.org
Child Abuse	GBCS	**Valentín-Castañon, Eliezer,** 202/488-5657 evalentin@umc-gbcs.org
Child Advocacy	GBGM GBCS	**Taylor, Julia,** jtaylor@gbgm-umc.org **Valentín-Castañon, Eliezer,** 202/488-5657 evalentin@umc-gbcs.org
Child Pornography	GBCS	**Valentín-Castañon, Eliezer,** evalentin@umc-gbcs.org
Children/Youth Services	GBGM	**Halsey, Peggy,** phalsey@gbgm-umc.org
Children's Fund for Christian Mission	GBOD GBGM	**Gran, Mary Alice,** mgran@gbod.org **Dominques, Jorge,** jdominiqu@gbgm-umc.org
Children's Magazine, *Pockets*	GBOD	615/340-7333
Standing Orders		800/972-0433
Subscriptions		800/925-6847

Children's Ministries	GBGM	**Halsey, Peggy,** phalsey@gbgm-umc.org
	GBGM	**Taylor, Julia,** jtaylor@gbgm-umc.org
	GBOD	**Gran, Mary Alice,** mgran@gbod.org
	UMPH	**Curric-U-Phone,** curricuphone@cokesbury.com
Curriculum Resources	UMPH	800-251-8591
Children's Ministries Outside US	GBGM	**Calvin, Elizabeth,** ecalvin@gbgm-umc.org
Children's Teacher Magazine	UMPH	**Stickler, LeeDell,** lstickler@umpublishing.org
China Program	GBGM	**Coulson, Gail,** gcoulson@gbgm-umc.org
Christian Communication Certification	UMCom	**Noble, Kathy,** knoble@umcom.org
Christian Education	GBCS	**Hanson, Jaydee,** 202/488-5650 jhanson@umc.gbcs.org
	GBCS	**Christie, Neal,** 202/488-5611 nchristie@umc-gbcs.org
Local Church	GBOD	**Hynson, Diana,** dynson@gbod.org
Conference	GBOD	**Krau, Carol,** ckrau@gbod.org
Christian Education Certification	GBHEM	**Wood, Anita,** awood@gbhem.org
Christian Educators Fellowship		**Van Buren, Corinne,** 615/749-6870 chedfel@cs.com
Christian Initiation	GBOD	**Benedict, Dan,** dbenedict@gbod.org
Christian Mission	GBGM	**Nugent, Randolph,** rnugent@gbgm-umc.org
Christian Social Action Magazine	GBCS	**Hakola, Gretchen,** 202/488-5630 ghakola@umc-gbcs.org
Subscriptions	GBCS	**Moore, Terry,** 800/967-0880 tmoore@umc-gbcs.org
Chrysalis - Youth Emmaus	GBOD	
Church School Supplies	UMPH	800/672-1789
Curriculum	UMPH	**Curric-U-Phone,** 800/251-8591 curricuphone@cokesbury.com
Church and Community Workers	GBGM	**Clark, Kathleen,** kclark@gbgm-umc.org
Church Development Planning	GBGM	**Rivera, Eli,** erivera@gbgm-umc.org
Church Extension Loans,	GBGM	**Workman, Anna Gail,** aworkman@gbgm-umc.org
Church/Government Relations	GBCS	**Valentín-Castañon, Eliezer,** 202/488-5657 evalentin@umc-gbcs.org
	GBGM	**Johnson, Susie,** sjohnson@gbgm-umc.org

Church Growth	GBOD	**Miller, Craig,** cmiller@gbod.org
Church Office Systems	UMPH	800/672-1789
Church in Racially Changing Community	GCRR	NEJ-**Taylor, James,** 202/547-2271
		SCJ-**Pupo-Ortiz, Yolanda,** 202/547-2271
		SEJ-**Hawkins, Erin,** 202/547-2271
		NCJ-**Deere, Kenneth,** 202/547-2271
		WJ-**Thomas-Sano, Kathy,** 202/547-2271
Church School Curriculum	UMPH	**Curric-U-Phone,** 800/251-8591 curricuphone@cokesbury.com
Church School Development	GBOD	**Hynson, Diana,** dhynson@gbod.org
		Krau, Carol, ckrau@gbod.org
Church Transformation	GBGM	**Ruffle, Douglas,** druffle@gbgm-umc.org
Church World Service	GBGM	**Whiteside, Wendy,** wendyw@gbgm-umc.org
Churches Uniting in Christ	GCCUIC	**Marshall, Anne,** amarshall@gccuic-umc.org
CIC Companions in Christ	GBOD	**Helms, Cindy,** chelms@upperroom.org
Circuit Rider		
Managing Editor	UMPH	**Reddig, Jill S.,** jreddig@umpublishing.org
Stewardship Materials	UMPH	800/672-1789
Subscriptions	UMPH	subservies@umpublishing.org
CIS	GBGM	**Siegfried, Peter,** psiegfri@gbgm-umc.org
Civic Youth Ministry	GCUMM	**Coppock, Larry,** lcoppock@gcumm.org
Civil Rights/Civil Liberties	GBCS	**Fealing, Kenrick,** 202/488-5637 kfealing@umc-gbcs.org
Clergy Enlistment	GBHEM	**Hartley, Hal,** hhartley@gbhem.org
Clergy Mentoring Manual	GBHEM	**Wood, Anita,** awood@gbhem.org
Clergy Mentoring Tool Kit	GBHEM	**Wood, Anita,** awood@gbhem.org
Clergy Sexual Ethics	GBHEM	**Jackson, Marion,** mjackson@gbhem.org
	GBHEM	
Clergy Support Systems	GBHEM	**Purushotham, Gwen,** gpurushotham@gbhem.org
Clergywomen-Deacons	GBHEM	**Rubey, Sharon,** srubey@gbhem.org
Clergywomen-Elders	GBHEM	**Jackson, Marion,** mjackson@gbhem.org
Cokesbury Academy (online courses)	UMPH	www.cokesburyacademy.com **Kidd, Ron,** rkidd@umpublishing.org
Cokesbury	UMPH	800/672-1789
Stores	UMPH	See pages 90-95

Cokesbury Church Library Services	UMPH	**Briese, Shirley,** sbriese@umpublishing.org
Cokesbury's Church Office Network (CCON)	UMPH	800/672-1789
College Bound	GBHEM	**Bigham, Wanda D.,** wbigham@gbhem.org
College Handbook of UM-Related Schools, Colleges, Universities & Theological Schools	GBHEM	**Bigham, Wanda D.,** wbigham@gbhem.org
College Student Ministries	GBHEM	**Hartley, Hal,** hhartley@gbhem.org
College Student Seminars	GBCS	**Burton, Susan,** 202/488-5609 sburton@umc-gbcs.org
Committee on Older Adult Ministries	GBOD	**Gentzler, Richard,** rgentzler@gbod.org
Comprehensive Protection Plan	GBOPHB	**Anderson, Daryl,** 800/851-2201
Comm. Religion/Race Annual Conference	GCRR	NEJ- **Taylor, James,** 202/547-2271
	GCRR	SEJ - **Hawkins, Erin,** 202/547-2271
	GCRR	SCJ - **Pupo-Ortiz, Yolanda,** 202/547-2271
	GCRR	NCJ - **Ware-Diaz, Suanne,** 202/547-2271
	GCRR	WJ - **Thomas-Sano, Kathy,** 202/547-2271
Comm. Status & Role of Women	GCSRW	**Burton, Garlinda,** gburton@gcfa.org
Comm. on Theological Education	GBHEM	**Moman, Mary Ann,** mmoman@gbhem.org
Communications Audit, Conferences	UMCom	**Communications Resourcing Team,** 888/278-4862 crt@umcom.org
Communications Certification	UMCOM	**Noble, Kathy,** 888/278-4862, knoble@umcom.org
Communications, Conference Commission	UMCom	**Communications Resourcing Team,** 888/278-4862, crt@umcom.org
Communications, Conference Director of	UMCom	**Communications Resourcing Team,** 888/278-4862, crt@umcom.org
Communications Resources Annual Conference Local Church	UMCom	**Communications Resourcing Team,** 888/278-4862 crt@umcom.org
Communications Resourcing Team	UMCom	**Nissen, Barbara,** crt@umcom.org
Communications/Mission	GBGM	**Wilbur, Lorene,** lwilbur@gbgm-umc.org

Communications Training	UMCom	**Communications Resourcing Team,** 888/278-4862 crt@umcom.org
Communion Resources	GBOD	**Benedict, Dan,** dbenedict@gbod.org
Communion Sales	UMPH	800/672-1789
Community Action Organization	GBGM	**Lawson, Ruth,** rlawson@gbgm-umc.org
Community Economic Development	GBGM	**Lawson, Ruth,** rlawson@gbgm-umc.org
Community Ministries	GBGM	**Byrd, Lynda,** lbyrd@gbgm-umc.org
	GBOD	**Wallace, Julia,** jwallace@gbod.org
Companions in Christ	GBOD	**Helms, Cindy,** chelms@upperroom.org
Computer Information Systems	GCFA	**McGorry, Peter,** 507/263-7331 pmcgorry@gcfa.org
Computer Software and Hardware	UMCom	**McAtee, Sean,** 615/742-5417 smcatee@umcom.org
Sales	UMCom	**Customer Service Center,** 888/346-3862
Computerized AIDS Ministerial Network	GBGM	**Gittens, Betty,** bgittens@gbgm-umc.org
Concordats with Churches Methodist Origins	GBGM	**Hutchison, Peggy,** phutchinson@gbgm.org
	GCCUIC	**Chapman, Clare,** cchapman@gccuic-umc.org
Conference Boards of Church and Society	GBCS	**Childers, Clayton,** 202/488-5642 childers@umc-gbcs.org
	GBCS	**Williams, Annette,** 817/460-2573 awilliams@umc-gbcs.org
	GBCS	**Christie, Neal,** 202/488-5611 nchristie@umc-gbcs.org
Conference Board of Laity	GBOD	**Ziegler, Sandy,** sziegler@gbod.org
Conference Committee on Christian Education	GBOD	**Krau, Carol,** ckrau@gbod.org
Conference Committees on Mission Personnel	GBGM	**Goldstein, Stephen,** sgoldste@gbgm-umc.org
Conference Communications Resources	UMCom	**Communications Resourcing Team,** 888/278-4862 crt@umcom.org
Conference Council on Ministries	GCOM	**Church, Daniel K.,** dchurch@gcom-umc.org
	GBOD	**Ruach, Susan,** sruach@gbod.org
Conference Council Directors	GBOD	**Ruach, Susan,** sruach@gbod.org
Conference Evangelism Chairs	GBOD	**Daniel, Wesley S. K.,** wdaniel@gbod.org
Conference Higher Education Relationship	GBHEM	**Felder, Luther B.,** lfelder@gbhem.org
Conference Lay Leaders	GBOD	**Ziegler, Sandy,** sziegler@gbod.org
Conference Leadership Development	GBOD	**Ziegler, Sandy,** sziegler@gbod.org **Ruach, Susan,** sruach@gbod.org
Conference Spiritual Leadership Networks	GBOD	**Ruach, Susan,** sruach@gbod.org

Conference Newspaper	UMCom	**Tanton, Tim,** ttanton@umcom.org
Conference Prayer Advocate	GCUMM	**Malone, Larry,** lmalone@gcumm.org
Conference Program Calendar	UMCom	**Carey, Lladale,** lcarey@umc.umc.org
Conf. Research/Planning	GBGM	**Rivas, Michael,** mrivas@gbgm-umc.org
	GCOM	**This, Craig,** cthis@gcom.org
Communications Resourcing Team	UMCom	**Nissen, Barbara,** crt@umcom.org
	GBOD	**Pace, Kimberly,** kpace@gbod.org
Conference Secretaries		See pages 148-52
Conference Scouting	GCUMM	**Coppock, Larry,** lcoppock@gcumm.org
Conference Scouting Coordinator	GCUMM	**Coppock, Larry,** lcoppock@gcumm.org
Conf. Stewardship Chairs	GBOD	**Bell, David,** dbell@gbod.org
Conference Staff	GBOD	**Ruach, Susan,** sruach@gbod.org See pages 135-40
Conference UMMen	GCUMM	**Malone, Larry,** lmalone@gcumm.org
Conference Web Sites	UMCom	**Downey, Steve,** 615/742-5434 sdowney@umcom.org
Confirmation Resources	UMPH	**Curric-U-Phone,** 800/251-8591 curricuphone@cokesbury.com
Conflict Mediation and Transformation	JUSTPEACE	**Porter, Tom,** 874/425-6526 justpeace@JUSTPEACEumc.org
Conflict Resolution	GBCS	**Christie, Neal,** 202/488-5611 nchristie@umc-gbcs.org
	GBCS	**Baustista, Liberato,** 212/682-3633 lbaustista@umc.gbcs.org
Congregational Development	GBGM	**Day, Randy,** rday@gbgm-umc.org
Congregational Ministry and Leader Development	GBOD	**Dick, Dan,** ddick@gbod.org
Congregational Ministry Social Justice	GBCS	**Christie, Neal,** 202/488-5611 nchristie@umc-gbcs.org
	GBCS	**Gale, Shenandoah,** 202/488-5612 sgale@umc-gbcs.org
Congregational Studies	GBOD	**Miller, Craig,** cmiller@gbod.org **Heavner, Betsey,** bheavner@gbod.org
Congress on Evangelism	GBOD	**Daniel, Wesley S. K.,** 615/340-7049 wdaniel@gbod.org
Conscientious Objectors	GBCS	**Hanson, Jaydee,** 202/488-5650 jhanson@umc-gbcs.org
	GBCS	**Horman, Janet,** 208/488-5647 jhorman@umc-gbcs.org
Connectional Giving	UMCom	**McNish, Kent,** 615/742-5142 kmcnish@umcom.org

Continuing Ed. - Elders	GBHEM	**Jackson, Marion,** mjackson@gbhem.org
Deacons & Diaconal Ministers	GBHEM	**Wood, Anita,** awood@gbhem.org
Coop. Parish Development	GBGM	**Byrd, Lynda,** lbyrd@gbgm.org
	GBOD	**Wallace, Julia,** jwallace@gbod.org
Coordinated Calendar	GCOM	**Rife, Judy,** 717/699-4982 rife@attglobal.net
Coor. Adult Ministries	GBOD	**Gentzler, Richard,** rgentzler@gbod.org
Coor. Children's Ministries	GBOD	**Gran, Mary Alice,** mgran@gbod.org
Coor. Family Ministries	GBOD	**Norton, MaryJane Pierce,** mnorton@gbod.org
	GBOD	**Sa, Soozung,** ssa@gbod.org
Coor. Older Adult Ministries	GBOD	**Gentzler, Richard,** rgentzler@gbod.org
Coor. Singles Ministries	GBOD	**Sa, Soozung,** ssa@gbod.org
Coor. Conf. Youth Ministries	GBOD	**Carty, Terry,** tcarty@gbod.org
Coor. Congregational Youth Ministries	GBOD	**Hay, Susan,** shay@gbod.org
Coor. Young Adult Ministries	GBOD	**Crenshaw, Bill,** bcrenshaw@gbod.org
Copyright Permission	GBGM	**Scott, Catherine,** cscott@gbgm-umc.org
	GBOD	**Schaller-Linn, Sarah,** slinn@upperroom.org
Corporate Responsibility	GBGM	**Takamine, Connie,** ctakamin@gbgm-umc.org
	GBCS	**Hanson, Jaydee,** 202/488-5650 jhanson@umc-gbcs.org
	GBOPHB	**Mixon, Vidette Bullock,** 800/851-2201, ext. 5293
Council of Presidents of Black Colleges	GBHEM	**Capers, Joreatha,** jcapers@gbhem.org
Council on Ministries - Local Church	GBOD	**Dick, Dan,** ddick@gbod.org
Council on Ministries-Sales	UMPH	800/672-1789
Course of Study For Ordained Ministry	GBHEM	**Daye, Lynn,** ldaye@gbhem.org
Covenant Discipleship	GBOD	**Manskar, Steve,** smanskar@gbod.org
Covenant Relationship	GBGM	**Herring, MaeOla,** mherrin@gbgm-umc.org
Covenanting, Acts of	GCCUIC	**Chapman, Clare,** cchapman@gccuic-umc.org
Criminal Justice and Repression	GBCS	**Fealing, Kenrick,** 202/488-5637 kfealing@umc-gbcs.org
Crisis Management	UMCom	**Drachler, Stephen,** 615/742-5411 sdrachler@umcom.org

Crisis Communications Training	UMCom	**Nissen, Barbara,** bnissen@umcom.org
Cross and Flame Award	GCUMM	**Coppock, Larry,** lcoppock@gcumm.org
Cross and Flame	GCFA	**Perrone, Christine,** 847/869-3345 cperrone@gcfa.org
Cross Cultural Communication	GCORR	**Thomas-Sano, Kathy,** 205/547-2291
	GCORR	**Pupo-Ortiz, Yolanda,** 202/547-2271
Crusade Scholarships	GBGM	**Fitzgerald, James,** jfitzgerald@gbgm-umc.org
Cumulative Pension and Benefit Fund	GBOPHB	**Success, Daphne,** 800/851-2201 ext. 4282
Curriculum	UMPH	**Curric-U-Phone,** 800/251-8591 curricuphone@cokesbury.com
Daily Christian Advocate	UMPH	**Cropsey, Marvin,** mcropsey@umpublishing.org
Data Processing Info.	GCFA	**McGorry, Peter,** 507/263-7331 pmcgorry@gcfa.org
Systems, Church	UMPH	**Franklyn, Paul,** pfranklyn@umpublishing.org
Deaconesses	GBGM	**Purkey, Betty,** bpurkey@gbgm-umc.org
Deaf Ministries	GBGM	**Fuentes, Noemi,** nfuentes@gbgm-umc.org
Death with Dignity	GBCS	**Day, Jackson,** jday@umc-gbcs.org
Deferred Gifts	GBGM	**Bibbee, Barbara,** bbibbee@gbgm-umc.org
	GBGM	**Park, James,** jpark@gbgm-umc.org
	GBGM	**Conner, Mark,** mconnor@gbgm-umc.org
	GBGM	**McNabb, Anna Beth,** amcnabb@gbgm-umc.org
	GBOD	**Joiner, Don W.,** djoiner@gbod.org
	GBCS	**Harvin, David,** 202/488-5659 dharvin@umc-gbcs.org
Demographic Data	GCOM	**This, Craig,** cthis@gcom-umc.org
	GBGM	**Rivas, Michael,** mrivas@gbgm-umc.org
Dempster Graduate F'ship	GBHEM	**Kohler, Robert F.,** rkohler@gbhem.org
Devotional Literature	GBOD	**Miller, JoAnn,** jmiller@upperroom.org
	UMPH	**Cokesbury,** 1-800-672-1789
Devo'Zine Magazine	GBOD	**Miller, Sandy,** 615/340-7089 smiller@upperroom.org **Corlew, Nicole,** 615/340-1778 ncorlew@upperroom.org
Standing Orders		800/972-0433
Subscription		800/925-6847
Deacons and Diaconal Ministries	GBHEM	**Heist, Linda,** lheist@gbhem.org

	GBOPHB	**Vargas, Manuel,** 800/851-2201
Devotional Magazine	GBOD	**The Upper Room magazine,** 615/340-7252
Standing orders		800/972-0433
Subscriptions		800/925-6847
Diet & Fitness	UMPH	800/672-1789
Dimensions for Living	UMPH	**Dean, Mary Catherine,** mdean@umpublishing.org
Direct Sales Call Center	UMPH	800/672-1789
Directory of Chief Exec. Officers of UM Schools, Colleges, Universities, and Theological Schools	GBHEM	**Bigham, Wanda D.,** wbigham@gbhem.org
Disabilities, Persons with	GBHEM	**Espino, Saul,** sespino@gbhem.org
	GBCS	**Day, Jackson,** 202/488-5608 jday@umc-gbcs.org
	GBGM	**Fuentes, Noemi,** nfuentes@gbgm-umc.org
	GBOD	**Hynson, Diana,** dhynson@gbod.org
Curriculum Resources	UMPH	**Curric-U-Phone,** 800/251-8591 curricuphone@cokesbury.com
Resource Ordering	UMPH	**Cokesbury,** 800/672-1789
Disability and Survivor Benefit Programs	GBOPHB	**Anderson, Daryl,** 800/851-2201 ext. 4265
Disarmament	GBCS	**Horman, Janet,** 202/488-5647 jhorman@umc-gbcs.org
	GBCS	**Bautista, Liberato,** 212/682-3633 lbautista@umc-gbcs.org
Disaster Relief	GBGM	**Sachen, Kristin,** ksachen@gbgm-umc.org
Disaster Updates	GBGM	**UMCOR,** 800/841-1235
Discernment	GBOD	**Haas, Jerry,** jerry_haas@gbod.org
Disciple Bible Study	UMPH	**Grizzle, Wini,** wgrizzle@umpublishing.org
Discipline, Book of	UMPH	**Cropsey, Marvin,** mcropsey@umpublishing.org
Discipleship Resources Editorial Planning	GBOD	**Whited, Linda,** lwhited@gbod.org
Discipleship Resources	GBOD	**Gregory, Mary,** mgregory@gbod.org
Disciplined Order of Christ	GBOD	513/274-2189
District Directors Religion/Race	GCRR	NEJ-**Taylor, James,** 202/547-2271
		SEJ-**Hawkins, Erin,** 202/547-2271
		SCJ-**Pupo-Ortiz, Yolanda,** 202/547-2271
		NCJ - **Deere, Kenneth,** 202/547-2271
		WJ - **Thomas-Sano, Kathy,** 202/547-2271
District Lay Leaders	GBOD	**Ziegler, Sandy,** sziegler@gbod.org

District Mission Secy.	GBGM	**Nuessle, John,** njuessle@gbgm-umc.org
District Prayer Advocate	GCUMM	**Malone, Larry,** lmalone@gcumm.org
District Scouting Coor.	GCUMM	**Coppock, Larry,** lcoppock@gcumm.org
District Superintendents Meeting for Pastors	GBOD	**Ruach, Susan,** sruach@gbod.org
District Superintendents Spouses	GBHEM	**Purushotham, Gwen,** gpurushotham@gbhem.org
Supervision/Assessment	GBHEM	**Purushotham, Gwen,** gpurushotham@gbhem.org
Web site	GBHEM	**Purushotham, Gwen,** gpurushotham@gbhem.org
District UM Men	GCUMM	**Malone, Larry,** lmalone@gcumm.org **Kena, Kwasi,** kkena@gcumm.org
Divorce and Remarriage	GBOD	**Norton, MaryJane Pierce,** mnorton@gbod.org **Sa, Soozung,** ssa@gbod.org
Divorce/Pension Assets	GBOPHB	**Geiger-Wojtal, Sue,** 800/851-2201 ext. 4643
Domestic Surveillance	GBCS	**Valentín-Castañon, Eliezer,** 202/488-5657 evalentin@umc-gbcs.org
Domestic Violence	GBGM	**Halsey, Peggy,** phalsey@gbgm-umc.org
	GBCS	**Fealing, Kenrick,** 202/488-5637 kfealing@umc-gbcs.org
Drug/Alcohol Concerns	GBGM	**Norfleet, Wilma,** 202/488-5626
Eco Justice	GBCS	**Hill, John,** 202/488-5654 jhill@umc-gbcs.org
Ecology	GBCS	**Hill, John,** 202/488-5654 jhill@umc-gbcs.org
Economic Development	GBGM	**Dirdak, Paul,** pdirdak@gbgm-umc.org
Economic Justice	GBCS	**Harrison, Mark,** 202/488-5645 mharrison@umc-gbcs.org
	GBGM	**Clement, Marilyn,** mclement@gbgm-umc.org
EcuFilm Marketing	UMCom	**Clark, Carrol,** cclarrk@umcom.org
Sales	UMCom	**Customer Service,** 888/346-3862
Ecumenical-Church World Service	NCCCUSA	**Bautista, Liberato,** 212/682-3633 lbautista@umc-gbcs.org
Ecumenical Programs	GCCUIC	**Gamble, Elizabeth,** bgamble@gccuic-umc.org
Ecumenical Programs Outside US	GBGM	**Asedillo, Rebecca,** rasedill@gbgm.org
Ecumenical Shared Ministries	GCCUIC	**Gamble, Rev. Betty,** bgamble@gccuic-umc.org

Editorial		
Books	UMPH	See Abingdon Press
Curriculum Res.	UMPH	**Curric-U-Phone,** 800/251-8591
		curricuphone@cokesbury.com
Discipleship Res.	GBOD	**Bock, Gail,** 877/899-2780, ext. 7061
		www.discipleshipresources.org
Resources	GBCS	**Hakola, Gretchen,** 202/488-5630
		ghakola@umc-gbcs.org
Upper Room Books	GBOD	**Miller, JoAnn E.,**
		jmiller@upperroom.org
Education	GBOD	**Krau, Carol,** ckrau@gbod.org
	GBCS	**Christie, Neal,** 202/488-5611
		nchristie@umc-gbcs.org
	GBCS	**Burton, Susan,** 202/488-5609
		sburton@gbcs.org
	GBCS	**Valentin-Castañon, Eliezer,**
		202/488-5657
		evalentin@umc-gbcs.org
	GBGM	**Kang, Youngsook,**
		ykang@gbgm-umc.org
	GBHEM	**Bigham, Wanda D.,**
		wbigham@gbhem.org
Education: Gift of Hope	GBHEM	**Bigham, Wanda D.,**
		wbigham@gbhem.org
Education Materials	UMPH	**Curric-U-Phone,** 800/251-8591
		curricuphone@cokesbury.com
EIIA	GBHEM	**Yamada, Ken,**
		kyamada@gbhem.org
El Aposento Alto magazine	GBOD	**Gaud, Carmen M.,**
		cgaud@upperroom@org
		Berrios, Jorge, jberrios@upperroom.org
Standing Orders		800/972-0433
Subscriptions		800/964-3730
El Intérprete	UMCom	**Bachus, Amanda,** 615/742-5115
(Hispanic Journal)		abachus@umcom.org
Subscription Fulfillment		888/346-3862 (888/FINDUMC)
Elders and Local Pastors	GBHEM	**Kohler, Robert,**
		bkohler@gbhem.org
Electronic Products	UMPH	**Franklyn, Paul,**
		pfranklyn@umpublishing.org
Electronic Publishing	GBOD	**Richardson, Beth,** 877/899-2780,
		ext. 7242, brichardson@upperroom.org
		Capshaw, Cheryl,
		ccapshaw@gbod.org
		Teague, Martha, mteague@gbod.org
Electronic Worship	UMCom	**Igniting Ministry,**
Resources		877/281-6535 im@umcom.org
Emergency Relief	GBGM	**Sachen, Kristin,**
		ksachen@gbgm-umc.org

Emmaus Walk	GBOD	**Gilmore, Dick,** dgilmore@upperroom.org
		Johnson Green, Jean johnsongreen@upperroom.org
Endorsement, Ecclesiastical	GBHEM	**Barrett, Patricia,** Endorsing Agent pbarrett@bghem.org
		Hill, Greg, Director of Endorsement ghill@gbhem.org
Energy Development and Conservation	GBCS	**Hill, John,** 202/488-5654 jhill@umc-gbcs.org
English Lang. Amendment	GCRR	**Thomas-Sano, Kathy,** 202/488-5654
Environmental Justice	GBCS	**Hill, John,** 202/488-5650 jhill@umc-gbcs.org
	GBGM	**Salter, Andris,** asalter@gbgm-umc.org
Episcopal Fund	GCFA	**Okayama, Elizabeth T.,** 847/869-3345, lokayama@gcfa.org
Marketing	UMCom	**Wood, Tracy,** twood@umcom.org
Equal Rights for Women	GBCS	**Bales, Linda,** 202/488-5649 lbales@umc-gbcs.org
Equitable Compensation	GCFA	**Borst, Beth Babbitt,** bbabbitt@gcfa.org
Ethnic Campus Ministry	GBHEM	**Smith, Lillian,** lsmith@gbhem.org
Ethnic Church Resources	GBOD	**Choi, Sungham,** schoi@gbod.org
Ethnic Clergywomen	GBHEM	**Jackson, Marion,** mjackson@gbhem.org
Ethnic Communications	UMCom	**Communications Resourcing Team** 888/278-4862, crt@umcom.org
Ethnic Concerns	GCRR	**Pupo-Ortiz, Yolanda,** 202/547-2271
	GBOD	**Choi, Sungham,** schoi@gbod.org
	GBCS	**Christie, Neal,** 202/488-5611 nchristie@umc-gbcs.org
Ethnic Caucuses		See pages 205-208
Ethnic Churches	GBOD	**Choi, Sungnam,** schoi@gbod.org
Ethnic Clergy Concerns	GBHEM	**Barrett, Patricia,** pbarrett@gbhem.org
Ethnic Curriculum	UMPH	Korean - **Won, Dal Joon,** djwon@umpublishing.org
	UMPH	Spanish - **Clark, John,** jclark@umpublishing.org
Ethnic Fellowship	UMCom	**Tucker-Shaw, Amelia,** 888/278-4862 http://crt.umc.org/REM
Ethnic Local Church	GCOM	**Hayashi, Donald L.,** dhayashi@gcom-umc.org

	GBOD	**Choi, Sungnam,** schoi@gbod.org
Coordination	GBGM	**Day, R. Randy,** rday@gbgm-umc.org
Coordination	GBCS	**Christie, Neal,** 202/488-5611 nchristie@umc-gbcs.org
	GCRR	NEJ - **Taylor, James,** 202/547-2271
		SEJ - **Hawkins, Erin,** 202/547-2271
		SCJ - **Pupo-Ortiz, Yolanda,** 202/547-2271
		NCJ - **Ware-Diaz, Suanne,** 202/547-2271
		WJ - **Thomas-Sano, Kathy,** 202/547-2271
African American	GBOD	**Taylor-Thirus, Francine,** ftaylorthirus@gbod.org
	GBGM	**Lawson, Ruth M.,** rlawson@gbgm-umc.org
Asian American	GBOD	**Choi, Sungnam,** schoi@gbod.org
Hispanic American	GBOD	**Chamberlain, Marigene,** mchamberlain@gbod.org
		Perez, Alma, aperez@gbod.org
		Longhurst, Blanca, blonghurst@gbod.org
	GBGM	**Avitia, Edgar,** cavitia@gbgm-umc.org
Korean American	GBOD	**Choi, Sungnam,** schoi@gbod.org
	GBGM	**Kim, Jong Sung,** jskim@gbgm-umc.org
Native American	GBOD	
	GBGM	**Kent, Cynthia,** ckent@gbgm-umc.org
	UMCom	**Buckley, Ray,** rbuckley@umcom.org
Pacific Islander	GBOD	**Choi, Sungnam,** schoi@gbod.org
Ethnic Local Church Resources		**Miller, JoAnn,** 615/340-7239 jmiller@gbod.org
Cokesbury		**Spanish Resources,** 800/251-8591
	UMPH	Spanish-**Clark, John,** jclark@umpublishing.org
	UMPH	Korean-**Won, Dal Joon,** djwon@umpublishing.org
Ethnic Local Church Workshops	GCRR	NEJ - **Taylor, James,** 202/547-2271
		SEJ - **Hawkins, Erin,** 202/547-2271
		SCJ - **Pupo-Ortiz, Yolanda,** 202/547-2271
		NCJ - **Ware-Diaz, Suanne,** 202/547-2271
		WJ - **Thomas-Sano, Kathy,** 202/547-2271

	GBCS	**Christie, Neal,** 202/488-5611
		nchristie@umc-gbcs.org
Ethnic History	GCAH	**Yrigoyen, Charles,**
		cyrigoyen@gcah.org
Ethnic Scholarships	GBHEM	**Current-Felder, Angella P.,** 615/340-7342
	UMCom	**Communications Resourcing Team,**
		888/278-4862
		scholarships@umcom.org
	GBGM	**Fitzgerald, James,**
		jfitzger@gbgm-umc.org
Ethnic Young Adult	GBCS	**Christie, Neal,** 202/488-5611
Summer Interns		nchristie@umc-gbcs.org
	GBCS	**Toledo, Ana,** 202/488-5651
		atoledo@umc-gbcs.org
Europe/CIS	GBGM	**Siegfried, Peter,**
		psiegfri@gbgm-umc.org
Euthanasia	GBCS	**Day, Jackson,** 202/488-5608
		jday@umc-gbcs.org
Evaluation - Gen. Agencies	GCOM	**Hayashi, Donald,**
		dhayashi@gcom-umc.org
		Long, Cecelia M.,
		clong@gcom-umc.org
Evangelism Certification	GBHEM	**Wood, Anita,** awood@gbhem.org
Evangelism-Conference	GBOD	**Daniel, Wesley S. K.,**
Resource Training		wdaniel@gbod.org
Evangelism, Council on	GBOD	**Daniel, Wesley S. K.,**
		wdaniel@gbod.org
Evangelism (Ecumenical)	GCCUIC	**GCCUIC Staff,** 212/749-3553
Evangelism, Mission	GBGM	**Kimbrough, ST,**
		skimbrou@gbgm-umc.org
Evangelism Resources	GBOD	**Evangelism Staff,** 615/340-7049
Program		**Daniel, Wesley S. K.,**
		wdaniel@gbod.org
Evangelism Resources	GBOD	**Discipleship Resources,**
		615/340-7068
Evangelization		
Training	GBGM	**Ruffle, Douglas,**
		druffle@gbgm-umc.org
Programs	GBGM	**Rae, Keith,** krae@gbgm-umc.org
	GBOD	**Daniel, Wesley S. K.,**
		wdaniel@gbod.org
Every Man Shares	GCUMM	**Kena, Kwasi,** kkena@gcumm.org
		615/340-7146
Executives in Church-	GBHEM	**Bigham, Wanda D.,**
Related Higher Education		wbigham@gbhem.org
Exemplary Teacher Awards	GBHEM	**Bigham, Wanda D.,**
		wbigham@gbhem.org
Exploration in Ordained	GBHEM	**Hartley, Hal,** hhartley@gbhem.org
Ministry		**Rubey, Sharon,** srubey@gbhem.org

		Espino, Saul, sespino@gbhem.org
FaithQuest	GBOD	Heavner, Betsey,
		bheavner@gbod.org
Faith Sharing Initiative	GBOD	Wesley, Daniel S.K.,
		wdaniel@gbod.org
Families in Crisis	GBGM	Halsey, Peggy,
		phalsey@gbgm-umc.org
Family Issues, Advocacy	GBCS	Valentin-Castañon, Eliezer,
		evalentin@umc-gbcs.org
Family Life Committee	GBOD	Norton, MaryJane Pierce,
		mnorton@gbod.org
Family Ministries	GBOD	Norton, MaryJane Pierce,
		mnorton@gbod.org
		Sa, Soozung, ssa@gbod.org
Family Planning	GBCS	Bales, Linda, 202/488-5636
		lbales@umc-gbcs.org
Family Resources		Miller, JoAnn,
		jmiller@upperroom.org
	GBOD	Norton, MaryJane Pierce,
		mnorton@gbod.org
		Sa, Soozung, ssa@gbod.org
Farm Crisis	GBCS	Harrison, Mark, 202/488-5645
		mharrison@umc-gbcs.org
Fellowship UMs in Worship	GBOD	McIntyre, Dean,
Music and Other Arts		dmcintyre@gbod.org
		Bone, David, fummwa@aol.com
Films - Missions	GBGM	Obando, Jorge,
		jobando@gbgm-umc.org
Finance Committee	GBOD	Joiner, Donald, djoiner@gbod.org
Fin. Commitment Booklet	GCFA	Fishel, Robert, rfishel@gcfa.org
Fin./Retirement Seminars	GBOPHB	Figueredo, Mary, 800/851-2201
Benefits Education		ext. 2738
Five Day Academy	GBOD	Haas, Jerry, jerry_haas@gbod.org
Flyer, The (Newsletter)	GCSRW	Burton, Garlinda, gburton@gcfa.org
		Kim, Soomee,
Forecast	UMPH	800/672-1789
Foreign Policy	GBCS	Bautista, Liberato, 212/682-3633
		lbautista@umc-gbcs.org
		Horman, Janet, 202/488-5647
		jhorman@umc-gbcs.org
	GBGM	Adjali, Mia, EAdjali@gbgm-umc.org
Foundation for Evangelism		Ervin, Paul, paulervin@prodigy.net
Funding Church's Prog.	GBOD	Joiner, Donald, djoiner@gbod.org
Funeral Resources	GBOD	Benedict, Dan, dbenedict@gbod.org
	UMPH	800/672-1789
Gambling	GBCS	Harrison, Mark, 202/488-5645
		mharrison@umc-gbcs.org
GBG Musik	GBGM	Kimbrough, ST, Jr.,
		skimbrou@gbgm-umc.org

Genetics	GBCS	**Hanson, Jaydee,** 202/488-5650 jhanson@umc-gbcs.org
Gender Inclusiveness	GCSRW	**Burton, Garlinda,** gburton@gcfa.org
General Adm. Fund- Apportionment Marketing	UMCom	**Wood, Tracy,** twood@umcom.org
General Agency Group	GCFA	**Manous, Rhonda,** 615/329-3393 rmanous@gcfa.org
General Conference Secretary		**Marshall, Carolyn M.,** cmarshall@gccuic-umc.org
Gen. Conf. Business Mgr.		**Bowen, Gary K.,** gbowen@gcfa.org
General Council on Ministries	GCOM	**Church, Daniel K.,** dchurch@gcom-umc.org See pages 24-30
GCOM Research	GCOM	**This, Craig,** cthis@gcom-umc.org
General Funds	GCFA	**Fishel, Robert,** 847/869-3345 rfishel@gcfa.org
General Minutes	GCFA	**Borst, Beth Babbitt,** bbabbitt@gcfa.org
Genetic Science	GBCS	**Hanson, Jaydee,** 202/488-5650 jhanson@umc-gbcs.org
Georgia Harkness Scholarship	GBHEM	**Jackson, Marion A.,** mjackson@gbhem.org
Giving and the Local Congregation	GBOD	**Bell, David,** dbell@gbod.org
Global Justice Ministries	GBGM	**Hutchison, Peggy,** phutchinson@gbgm.org
	GBCS	**Horman, Janet,** 202/488-5047 jhorman@umc-gbcs.org
	GBCS	**Hanson, Jaydee,** 202/488-5650 jhanson@umc-gbcs.org
Global Praise	GBGM	**Kimbrough, ST, Jr.,** skimbrou@gbgm-umc.org
God and Country	GCUMM	**Coppock, Larry,** lcoppock@gcumm.org
Golden Cross Sunday	GBGM	**Fuentes, Noemi,** nfuentes@gbgm-umc.org
Grants, Media (TV) Igniting Ministry Campaign	UMCom	**Vaughan, Jackie,** 888/281-6535 imgrants@umcom.org
Grants, Leadership/ Scholarship	GBGM	**Fitzgerald, James,** jfitzger@gbgm-umc.org
Grants, Ethnic Local Church	GBCS	**Christie, Neal,** 202/488-5611 nchristie@umc-gbcs.org
Grants, Peace with Justice	GBCS	**Horman, Janet,** 202/488-5647 jhorman@umc-gbcs.org
Grants, Shared Mission Focus on Young People	GBCS	**Christie, Neal,** 202/488-5611 nchristie@umc-gbcs.org
Grave Markers for UM Clergy		**Cokesbury,** 800/672-1789
Guidelines for Local Church		**McGee, Sheila W.,** smcgee@umpublishing.org

Gun Control	GBCS	**Fealing, Kenrick,** 202/488-5637
		kfealing@umc-gbcs.org
HANA (Hispanic, Asian,	GBHEM	**Yamada, Ken,** kyamada@gbhem.org
Native American)		
Curriculum Resources	UMPH	**Curric-U-Phone,** 800/251-8591
		curricuphone@cokesbury.com
Resource Ordering	UMPH	**Cokesbury,** 800/672-1789
Hate Groups	GBCS	**Fealing, Kenrick,** 202/488-5637
		kfealing@umc-gbcs.org
	GBGM	**Dauway, Lois,**
		ldauway@gbgm-umc.org
	GCRR	**Taylor, James,** 202/547-2271
Health & Environment	GBCS	**Hill, John,** 202/488-5654,
		jhill@umc-gbcs.org
Health Benefit Programs	GBOPHB	**Glass, Mia,** 800/851-2201, ext. 2711
Health Care	GBGM	**Chand, Sarla,**
		schand@gbgm-umc.org
Health Care Policy	GBCS	**Day, Jackson,** 202/488-5608
		jday@umc-gbcs.org
Health Care Sabbath	GBCS	**Day, Jackson,** 202/488-5608
		jday@umc-gbcs.org
Health - International	GBGM	**Chand, Sarla,**
		schand@gbgm-umc.org
Health & Welfare Ministries	GBGM	**Dirdak, Paul,**
		pdirdak@gbgm-umc.org
Health Yourself	UMPH	800/672-1789
Heritage Landmarks	GCAH	**Yrigoyen, Charles,**
		cyrigoyen@gcah.org
Heritage Sunday	GCAH	**Yrigoyen, Charles,**
		cyrigoyen@gcah.org
High Potential Metro	GBOD	**Smith, Debra,** dsmith@gbod.org
Church Initiative		
Higher Education	GBHEM	**Yamada, Ken,** kyamada@gbhem.org
Hispanic Devotional	GBOD	**Gaud, Carmen M.,**
Magazine		elaposentoalto@upperroom.org
(*El Aposento Alto*)		
Standing Orders		800/972-0433
Subscription		800/964-3730
Hispanic Program	UMCom	**Bachus, Amanda,**
Magazine		abachus@umcom.org 615/742-5113
Hispanic Issues	GCRR	**Pupo-Ortiz, Yolanda,** 202/547-2271
	GBCS	**Valentin-Castañon, Eliezer,**
		202/488-5657
		evalentin@umc-gbcs.org
	GBOD	**Chamberlain, Marigene,**
		mchamberlain@gbod.org
Multi-Language Resources	GCOM	**Murraine, Nelda Barrett,**
		nmurrain@gcom-umc.org
	GBOD	**Chamberlain, Marigene,**
		mchamberlain@gnbod.org
		Perez, Alma, aperez@gbod.org

	GBOD	**Discipleship Resources,** www.discipleshipresources.com
	UMPH	**Cokesbury,** 800/251-8591
	GBOD	**Upper Room,** 877/899-2780
	GBGM	**Ferrari, Nilda,** nferrari@gbgm-umc.org
	GBHEM	**Espino, Saul,** sespino@gbhem.org
	GBHEM	**Capers, Joreatha,** jcapers@gbhem.org
Apuntes Journal	UMPH	**Gonzalez, Justo,** 404/378-7651
El Intérprete	UMCom	**Bachus, Amanda,** 615/742-5115 abachus@umcom.org
Hispanic Curriculum	UMPH	**Clark, John,** jclark@umpublishing.org
Hispanic Ministries	GBCS	**Valentín-Castañon, Eliezer,** 202/488-5657 evalentin@umc.gbcs.org
	GBHEM	**Espino, Saul,** sespino@gbhem.org
	GBOD	**Chamberlain, Marigene,** mchamberlain@gbod.org
		Perez, Alma, aperez@gbod.org
		Longhurst, Blanca, blonghurst@gbod.org
	GCRR	**Pupo-Ortiz, Yolanda,** 202/547-2271
	GBGM	**Avitia, Edgar,** eavitia@gbgm-umc.org
		Palos, Jose, jpalos@gbgm-umc.org
Hispanic Ministries, National Plan for	GBGM	**Palos, Jose,** jpalos@gbgm-umc.org
Historical/Research	GCAH	**Rowe, Kenneth,** 973/408-3590
Historical Society	GCAH	**Yrigoyen, Charles,** cyrigoyen@gcah.org
Historic Sites	GCAH	**Yrigoyen, Charles,** cyrigoyen@gcah.org
Holy Communion	GBOD	**Benedict, Dan,** dbenedict@gbod.org
Home Missionaries	GBGM	**Purkey, Betty,** bpurkey@gbgm-umc.org
Homosexuality Study	GCCUIC	**Gamble, Rev. Betty,** bgamble@gccuic-umc.org
Human Relations Day	GBCS	**Fealing, Kenrick,** 202/488-5637 kfealing@umc-gbcs.org
Grant	UMCom	**Dunlap-Berg, Barbara,** bdunlap-berg@umcom.org
Human Rights	GBCS	**Bautista, Liberato,** 212/682-3633 lbautista@umc-gbcs.org
	GBCS	**Horman, Janet,** 202/488-5647 jhorman@umc-gbcs.org
	GBGM	**Wildman, David,** dwildman@gbgm-umc.org
		Adjali, Mia, 212/682-3633
	GCCUIC	**Marshall, Anne M.,**

		amarshall@gccuic-umc.org
Human Sexuality Resources	UMPH	**Curric-U-Phone,** 800/251-8591
		curricuphone@cokesbury.com
Human Welfare	GBCS	**Valentin-Castañon, Eliezer,** 202/488-5657
		evalentin@umc-gbcs.org
Hunger-Relief	GBGM	**Kim, June,** jkim@gbgm-umc.org
Hunger/US Policy	GBCS	**Harrison, Mark,** 202/488-5645
		mharrison@umc-gbcs.org
Hymnal, editorial	UMPH	**Smith, Gary A.,** gsmith@umpublishing.org
Hymnal, interpretation	GBOD	**McIntyre, Dean,** dmcintyre@gbod.org
Hymnal, order copies	UMPH	800/672-1789
Hymnal, permission to reproduce		The Copyrite Co., 800/779-1177
I.E. Newsletter	GBHEM	**Bigham, Wanda D.,** wbigham@gbhem.org
Igniting Ministry Sales	UMCom	**Igniting Ministry,** 877/281-6535
		im@umcom.org
		Customer Service Center 888/346-3862 (888/FINDUMC)
Immigration/Naturalization	GBGM	**Fernandez, Lilia,** liliaf@gbgm-umc.org
	GBCS	**Horman, Janet,** 202/488-5647
		jhorman@umc-gbcs.org
Inclusiveness-Racial	GCRR	NCJ-**Diaz, Suanne,** 202/547-2271
		NEJ-**Taylor, James,** 202/547-2271
		SEJ-**Hawkins, Erin,** 202/547-2271
		SCJ-**Pupo-Ortiz, Yolanda,** 202/547-2271
		WJ-**Thomas-Sano, Kathy,** 202/547-2271
InfoServ, Information related to UMC	UMCom	800/251-8140
		infoserv@umcom.org
Insignia of UMC	GCFA	**Perrone, Christine,** 847/869-3345
		cperrone@gcfa.org
Institute of Higher Education	GBHEM	**Noseworthy, James A.,** jnose@gbhem.org
Institutions of Higher Education	GBHEM	**Yamada, Ken,** kyamada@gbhem.org
Institutions - Health and Welfare	GBGM	**Dirdak, Paul,** pdirdak@gbgm-umc.org
Institutional Ministries	GBGM	**Scott, Jerald,** jscott@gbgm-umc.org
Insurance-Property/Casualty Local Churches, Conferences Conferences	GCFA	**Cholak, Linda C.,** 847/869-3345 lcholak@gcfa.org

Agencies, Unit Plans, D&O, AD&D		
Interagency Task Force/Legislation	GCOM	**Church, Daniel K.,** dchurch@gcom-umc.org **Long, Cecelia M.,** clong@gcom-umc.org
Interchurch Aid	UMCOR	**Dirdak, Paul,** pdirdak@gbgm-umc.org
Interdenom. Cooperation Fund-Apportionment	GCCUIC	**Chapman, Clare J.,** cchapman@gccuic-umc.org
Marketing	UMCom	**Dunlap-Berg, Barbara,** bdunlap-berg@umcom.org
International Affairs	GBCS	**Bautista, Liberato,** 212/682-3633 lbautista@umc-gbcs.org
	GBCS	**Hanson, Jaydee,** 202/488-5650 jhanson@umc-gbcs.org
	GBGM	**Adjali, Mia,** eAdjali@gbgm-umc.org
International Association Methodist-related Schools, Colleges, Universities (IAMSCU)	GBHEM	**Yamada, Ken,** kyamada@gbhem.org
International Ministries, *The Upper Room*	GBOD	**Bryant, Stephen D.,** sbryant@upperroom.org
International Health Ministries	GBGM	**Chand, Sarla,** schand@gbgm-umc.org
International New Church Development	GBOD	**Daniel, Wesley S. K.,** wdaniel@gbod.org
International Seminars	GBCS	**Christie, Neal,** 202/488-5611 nchristie@umc-gbcs.org
Internet	UMCom	**Downey, Steve,** 615/742-5434 sdowney@umcom.org
Internet Gambling	GBCS	**Harrison, Mark,** 202/488-5645 mharrison@umc-gbcs.org
Interpreter	UMCom	**Burton, Garlinda,** 615/742-5107 gburton@umcom.org
Advertising and Marketing	UMCom	**Carey, Lladale,** lcarey@umcom.org
Subscription Fulfillment		**Customer Service Center,** Subscriptions@umcom.org 888/346-3862 (888/FINDUMC)
Interreligious Relationships	GCCUIC	**Marshall, Anne M.,** amarshall@gccuic-umc.org
Investment Guidelines	GCFA	**Soo Hoo, Frank,** 847/869-3345 fsoohoo@gcfa.org
Irish-American Scholars Program	GBHEM	**Bigham, Wanda D.,** wbigham@gbhem.org
Jewish Christian Relationships	GCCUIC	**Gamble, Rev. Betty,** bgamble@gccuic-umc.org
John Wesley Fellows	GCUMM	**Coppock, Larry,** lcoppock@gcumm.org

Jurisdictional Field Staff	GBGM	NC-**Rhodes, Wayne,** 630/357-0170
		NE-**Conklin, Elizabeth,**
		518/884-8456
		SC-**Hawkins, Rick,** 214/373-1554
		SE-**Magnus, Joy,** 404/584-6222
		W-**Hanson, Heather,** 213/386-5335
Judicial Council		**Matheny, Tom,** 504/345-3367
Justice Education	GBGM	**Dharmaraj, Glory,** 212/682-3633
	GBCS	**Christie, Neal,** 202/488-5611
		nchristie@umc-gbcs.org
JUSTPEACE	GCFA	**Porter, Tom,** 847/425-6526
		justpeace@justpeaceumc.org
Kendall Fund	GBGM	**Dirdak, Paul,**
		pdirdak@gbgm-umc.org
Key Event Celebration	GBOD	615/340-7053
Kingswood Books	UMPH	**Armistead, Kathy,**
		karmistead@umpublishing.org
Korean Clergy Issues	GBHEM	**Barrett, Patricia,**
		pbarrrett@gbhem.org
Korean Curriculum	UMPH	**Won, Dal Joon,**
		djwon@umpublishing.org
Korean Ministries	GBOD	**Choi, Sungnam,** schoi@gbod.org
Resources	GBGM	**Chung, Jungrea,**
(Mission)		jchung@gbgm-umc.org
Korean Program Magazine	UMCom	**Cho, Sang Yean,** scho@umcom.org
(UMs in Service)		
Korean Lang. Mission	UMPH	**Won, Dal Joon,**
Resources		djwon@umpublishing.org
	GBGM	**Chung, Jungrea,**
		jchung@gbgm-umc.org
Labor Mgment. Relations	GBCS	**Harrison, Mark,** 202/488-5645
		mharrison@umc-gbcs.org
Laity Conferences,	GBOD	**Ziegler, Sandy,** sziegler@gbod.org
Retreats and Laity Sunday		
	GBCS	**Childers, Clayton,** 202/488-5642
		cchilders@umc-gbcs.org
Laity Resources	GBOD	**Miller, JoAnn,**
		jmiller@upperrroom.org
		Ziegler, Sandy, sziegler@gbod.org
Language and Racism	GCRR	**Pupo-Ortiz, Yolanda,**
		Thomas-Sano, Kathy, 202/547-2271
Large Membership Church	GBOD	**Daniel, Wesley S. K.,**
Initiatives		wdaniel@gbod.org
Large Print, *Upper Room*	GBOD	**Redding, Mary Lou,**
magazine		mredding@upperroom.org
Standing Orders (bulk)		800/972-0433
Subscriptions		800/925-6847
Latin America	GBGM	**Guerrero, Frank,**
		fguerrer@gbgm-umc.org

Latin American Public Policy	GBCS	**Horman, Janet,** 202/488-5650 jhorman@umc-gbcs.org
Law of the Sea	GBCS	**Hill, John,** 202/488-5654 jhill@umc-gbcs.org
Lay Leaders	GBOD	**Ziegler, Sandy,** sziegler@gbod.org
Lay Members of Conference	GBOD	**Ziegler, Sandy,** sziegler@gbod.org
Lay Speaking Ministry	GBOD	**Ziegler, Sandy,** sziegler@gbod.org
Leader Formation		
Annual Conference	GBOD	**Ruach, Susan,** sruach@gbod.org
Local Church	GBOD	**Dick, Dan,** ddick@gbod.org
Leader in Christian Education Ministries magazine		**Kidd, Ron,** rkidd@umpublishing.org
Leadership Development	GBCS	**All Program Staff,** 202/488-5600
	GBOD	**Dick, Dan,** ddick@gbod.org
Leadership Development Local Church	GBOD	**Ruach, Susan,** sruach@gbod.org
Congregational	GBOD	**Dick, Dan,** ddick@gbod.org
Leadership Development Grants	GBGM	**Fitzgerald, James,** jfitzger@gbgm-umc.org
Leadership Dev't	GBOD	**Wallace, Julia,** jwallace@gbod.org
(UM Women)	GBGM	**Needham, Ann,** annedham@gbgm-umc.org
Leadership Resources		**Miller, JoAnn,** 877/899-2780, ext. 7239
Leadership Training for Elimination of Sexism	GCSRW	**Burton, Garlinda,** gburton@gcfa.org,
Leadership Training for Elimination of Racism	GCRR	NCJ-**Ware-Diaz, Suanne,** 202/547-2271 NEJ-**Taylor, James,** 202/547-2271 SEJ-**Hawkins, Erin,** 202/547-2271 SCJ-**Pupo-Ortiz, Yolanda,** 202/547-2271 WJ-**Thomas-Sano, Kathy,** 202/547-2271
Leader in the Church School	UMPH	**Kidd, Ron,** rkidd@umpublishing.org
Leading from the Center	GBOD	**Ruach, Susan,** sruach@gbod.org
Learning Center	GBOD	**Gaither, Donna,** dgaither@gbod.org
Lectionary Resources	GBOD	**Benedict, Dan,** dbenedict@gbod.org
	UMPH	**Cokesbury,** 800/672-1789
Legal Consultation	GCFA	**Howard, Irene,** 847/869-3345 email: ihoward@gcfa.org
	GCFA	**Allen, Jim,** jallen@gcfa.org **Gary, Dan,** dgary@gcfa.org
Legal Counsel Higher Education	GBHEM	**Yamada, Ken,** kyamada@gbhem.org
Legislative Affairs	GBCS	**Hanson, Jaydee,** 202/488-5650 jhanson@umc-gbcs.org
Legislative Hotline		866/862-4226

	GBOPHB	**Hirsen, Sarah,** 800/851-2201, ext. 4644
Lenten/Easter Resources	UMPH	800/672-1789
Curriculum	UMPH	**Curric-U-Phone,** 800/251-8591
		curricuphone@cokesbury.com
	GBOD	**Benedict, Dan,** dbenedict@gbod.org
	GBOD	**Upper Room Books,**
		800/972-0433 (orders)
Lex Collegii	GBHEM	**Jarman, Lisa,** ljarman@gbhem.org
Living into the Future	GCOM	**Church, Daniel K.,**
		dchurch@gcom-umc.org
Living Prayer Center	GBOD	**Benedict, Mary O.,**
		mbenedict@gbod.org
Loans (Church Extension)	GBGM	**Workman, Anna Gail,**
		aworkman@gbgm-umc.org
Loans from the Personal	GBOPHB	**Success, Daphne,** 800/851-2201, ext. 4282
Investment Plan		
Loans (Student)	GBHEM	**Harding, James,** jharding@gbhem.org
Local Church Audit Guide	GCFA	**Belton, Dennis,** 615/329-3393
		dbelton@gcfa.org
Local Church Organization	GBOD	**Dick, Dan,** ddick@gbod.org
Local Church Planning	GBOD	**Dick, Dan,** ddick@gbod.org
Local (lay) Pastors	GBHEM	**Dave, Lynn,**
		ldave@gbhem.org
Male-Female Dynamics	GCSRW	**Burton, Garlinda,**
		gburton@gcfa.org
Marriage Enrichment	GBOD	**Norton, MaryJane Pierce,**
		mnorton@gbod.org
Mature Years Magazine	UMPH	**Cropsey, Marvin W.,**
		mcropsey@umpublishing.org
Media Advertising	UMCom	**Igniting Ministry,**
		877/281-6535 im@umcom.org
Medical Work	GBGM	**Dirdak, Paul,**
		pdirdak@gbgm-umc.org
Method X	GBOD	**Stephens, Kathleen,**
		kstephens@upperroom.org
Ministerial Education Fund	GBHEM	**Moman, MaryAnn,**
Administration,		mmoman@gbhem.org
Seminaries and Elders		
MEF Fund for Deacons		
and Diaconal		
Ministry		
Membership-UMW	GBGM	**Bass, Ressie,** rbass@gbgm-umc.org
Men's Congress	GCUMM	**Harris, Joseph,** jharris@gcumm.org
MensNews	GCUMM	**Kena, Kwasi,** kkena@gcumm.org
Men's Work	GCUMM	**Malone, Larry,** lmalone@gcumm.org
Mental Illness	GBCS	**Day, Jackson,** 202/488-5608
		jday@umc-gbcs.org
Methodist History Journal	GCAH	**Yrigoyen, Charles,**
		cyrigoyen@gcah.org

Metropolitan Ministries	GBGM	**Byrd, Lynda,** lbyrd@gbgm-umc.org
Microfilm - Service & Sales	GCAH	**Patterson, L. Dale,** 973/408-3189
Middle East	GBCS	**Bautista, Liberato,** 212/682-3633
		lbautista@umc-gbcs.org
	GBCS	**Horman, Janet,** 202/488-5647
		jhorman@umc-gbcs.org
	GBGM	**Hutchison, Peggy,**
		phutchinson@gbgm.org
Migrant Labor	GBCS	**Harrison, Mark,** 202/488-5645
		mharrison@umc-gbcs.org
Militarism	GBCS	**Horman, Janet,** 202/488-5647
		jhorman@umc-gbcs.org
MINDS[21] Methodist	GBHEM	**Bigham, Wanda D.,**
Interactive		wbigham@gbhem.org
Database System		**Cherry, Tommye,**
		tcherry@gbhem.org
Ministerial Educ. Fund	UMCom	**Wood, Tracy,** twood@umcom.org
Apportionment Marketing		
Ministerial Enlistment -	GBHEM	**Hartley, Hal,** hhartley@gbhem.org
Elders		
Ministerial Enlistment -	GBHEM	**Rubey, Sharon,** srubey@gbhem.org
Deacons & Diaconal		
Ministerial Pension Plan	GBOPHB	**Vargas, Manuel,** 800/851-2201,
		ext. 4565
Ministry with Children	GBOD	**Gran, MaryAlice,** mgran@gbod.org
Minority Group - Self	GCRR	**Bennett, Telina L.,** 202/547-4828
Determination Fund		
Minority In-Service Training	GBHEM	**Barrett, Patricia,** pbarrett@gbhem.org
Minority Rights	GBCS	**Fealing, Kenrick,** 202/488-5637
		kfealing@umc-gbcs.org
Minority Women's Issues	GCRR	**Hawkins, Erin,** 202/547-2271
Missions	GBGM	**Nugent, Randolph,**
		rnugent@gbgm-umc.org
Missions Communications	GBGM	**Wilbur, Lorene,**
		lwilbur@gbgm-umc.org
Mission Education	GBOD	**Krau, Carol,** ckrau@gbod.org
	GBOD	**Daniel, Wesley S. K.,**
		wdaniel@gbod.org
	GBCS	All Program Staff 202/488-5600
	GBGM	**McLean, Roderick,**
		rmclean@gbgm-umc.org
Mission Evangelism	GBGM	**Kimbrough, S.T., Jr.,**
		stkimbrou@gbgm-umc.org
Mission Interns	GBGM	**Jones, Una,**
		ujones@gbgm-umc.org
Mission Interpreters'	GBGM	**Jones, Una,**
Training		ujones@gbgm-umc.org
Mission Leadership	GBGM	**Jones, Una,**
		ujones@gbgm-umc.org
Mission Service -	GBGM	**Gleaves, Edith,**

Personnel		egleaves@gbgm-umc.org
Mission Magazine/Video	GBGM	**Obando, Jorge,**
		jobando@gbgm-umc.org
Mission Opportunity-UMW	GBGM	**Funk, Annette,**
		afunk@gbgm-umc.org
Mission Resources	GBGM	**DeGregorie, Frank,**
		fdegrego@gbgm-umc.org
Mission Studies	GBGM	**Gould, Ivan (Toby),**
		631/728-7689
Mission Travel/Study	GBGM	**Jones, Una,** ujones@gbgm-umc.org
	GBCS	**Christie, Neal,** 202/488-5611
		nchristie@umc-gbcs.org
Missional Priority,	GCOM	**Church, Daniel K.,**
Development		dchurch@gcom-umc.org
Missionary Support	GBGM	**Lee, Christine,** clee@gbgm-umc.org
The Monitor Newsletter	GCRR	**Pupo-Ortiz, Yolanda,** 202/547-2271
	GCRR	**Thomas-Sano, Kathy,** 202/547-2271
	GCRR	**Tello, Michelle,** 202/547-2271
Monitoring of Agencies	GCSRW	**Burton, Garlinda,** gburton@gcfa.org
	GCRR	**Taylor, James,** 202/547-2271
Monitoring Annual Conf.	GCRR	**Pupo-Ortiz, Yolanda,** 202/547-2271
Monitoring Theol. Schools	GCRR	**Pupo-Ortiz, Yolanda,** 202/547-2271
Multicultural Congregations	GBOD	**Magee, Marilyn,** mmagee@gbod.org
Multicultural Ministries	GCRR	SEJ - **Hawkins, Erin,**
		202/547-2271
	GCRR	NCJ - **Ware-Diaz, Suanne,**
		202/547-2271
	GCRR	SCJ - **Hawkins, Erin,** 202/547-2271
	GCRR	WJ - **Thomas-Sano, Kathy,**
		202/547-2271
	GCRR	NEJ - **Taylor, James,** 202/547-2271
	GBCS	**Christie, Neal,** 202/488-5611
		nchristie@umc-gbcs.org
Music Certification	GBHEM	**Wood, Anita,** awood@gbhem.org
Music Materials	UMPH	**Smith, Gary,**
		gsmith@umpublishing.org
		Tyree, Debi,
		dtyree@umpublishing.org
		Gnegy, Bill,
		bgnegy@umpublishing.org
	GBOD	**McIntyre, Dean,**
		dmcintyre@gbod.org
Music Resources	GBOD	**McIntyre, Dean,**
		dmcintyre@gbod.org
Muslim Christian	GCCUIC	**Marshall, Anne M.,**
Relationships		amarshall@gccuic-umc.org
Mutual Recognition of	GCCUIC	**Robbins, Bruce,**
Members (COCU)		brobbins@gccuic-umc.org

National Assn. of Annual Conf. Treasurers NAACT	GCFA	**Winkelmann, Jeri,** 402/464-5994
National Assn. of Commissions on Equitable Compensation (NACEC)	GCFA	**Borst, Beth Babbitt,** bbabbitt@gcfa.org
National Assn. Independent Colleges and Universities (NAICU)	GBHEM	**Bigham, Wanda D.,** wbigham@gbhem.org
National Assn. of Schools and Colleges of the UMC (NASCUMC)	GBHEM	**Yamada, Ken,** kyamada@gbhem.org
National Assn. of United Methodist Evangelists	GBOD	**Daniel, Wesley S. K.,** wdaniel@gbod.org
National Assn. Conference Presidents of UM Men	GCUMM	**Malone, Larry,** lmalone@gcumm.org
National Assn. UM Foundations	GBOD	**Joiner, Don,** djoiner@gbod.org
National Assn. UM Scouts	GCUMM	**Coppock, Larry,** lcoppock@gcumm.org
National Assn. of Stewardship Leaders	GBOD	**Bell, David,** dbell@gbod.org
National Council of the Churches of Christ	GCCUIC	**Chapman, Clare,** cchapman@gccuic-umc.org
National Plan for Hispanic Ministries	GBGM	**Palos, Jose,** jpalos@gbgm-umc.org
National Workshop on Christian/Jewish Relationships	GCCUIC	**Gamble, Rev. Betty,** bgamble@gccuic-umc.org
National Workshops on Christian Unity	GCCUIC	**Marshall, Anne,** amarshall@gccuic-umc.org
Native People Communications Office	UMCom	**Buckley, Ray,** 615/742-5414 rbuckley@umcom.org
Native American Comprehensive Plan	GBCS	**Harrison, Mark,** 202/488-5645 mharrison@umc-gbcs.org
	GBGM	**Saunkeah, Ann,** asaunke@gbgm-umc.org
Native American Ministries Sunday Marketing	UMCom	**Dunlap-Berg, Barbara,** bdunlap-berg@umcom.org
Communications	GCRR	**Ware-Diaz, Suanne,** 202/547-2271
	UMCom	**Buckley, Ray,** rbuckley@umcom.org 615/742-5414
	OIMC	**Kernell, Chebon,** 405/632-2006
Dialogue	GCCUIC	**Marshall, Anne M.,** amarshall@gccuic-umc.org
Interreligious		

Legislative	GBCS	**Hanson, Jaydee,** 202/488-5650
		jhanson@umc-gbcs.org
Grant Referral	GBGM	**Kent, Cynthia,** ckent@gbgm-umc.org
Ministries	GBGM	**Kent, Cynthia,**
		ckent@gbgm-umc.org
	NACP	**Saunkeah, Ann,**
		asaunke@gbgm-umc.org
	OIMC	**Wilson, David,** WEilson@oimc.org
NA Seminary Awards	GBHEM	**Zimmerman, Patti,** 615/340-7344
Resources	UMCom	**Buckley, Ray,** rbuckley@umcom.org
		615/742-5414
	GBGM	**Kent, Cynthia,** ckent@gbgm-umc.org
School of Evangelism	GBOD	**Daniel, Wesley S. K.,**
		wdaniel@gbod.org
New Church Development	GBGM	**Day, R. Randy,**
		rday@gbgm-umc.org
New Congregational	GBOD	**Miller, Craig,**
Development		cmiller@gbod.org
New Interpreter's	UMPH	**Russell, Michael R.,** 615/749-6217
Bible		mrussell@umpublishing.org
New Solutions	GBOD	**Pippin, Robin,**
		rpippin@upperroom.org
		Peterson, Tony,
		stpeterson@upperroom.org
New World Outlook	GBGM	**House, Christie,**
		chouse@gbgm-umc.org
New Perspectives	GBHEM	**Bigham, Wanda D.,**
		wbigham@gbhem.org
News Service	UMCom	**Underwood, Ginny,** 615/742-5124
		newsdesk@umcom.org
Newscope Editor	UMPH	**Chamberlain, Dow,**
		dchamberlain@umpublishing.org
Subscriptions	UMPH	subservices@umpublishing.org
News Media Relations	UMCom	**Drachler, Stephen,** 615/742-5411
		sdrachler@umcom.org
New Visions Summer	GBHEM	**Smith, Lillian,**
Companies		lsmith@gbhem.org
News in the Pews	UMCOM	**Tanton, Tim,** 615/742-5473
Local Church Newsletter		
Nominations & Personnel	GBOD	**Dick, Dan,** ddick@gbod.org
in Local Church		
North Africa	GBGM	**Siegfried, Peter,**
		psiegfried@gbgm-umc.org
"Off the Front Page"	GBCS	**Hakola, Gretchen,** 202/488-5630
(newsletter)		ghakola@umc-gbcs.org
Offering Christ Today	GBOD	**Daniel, Wesley S. K.,**
		wdaniel@gbod.org,
		(Newsletter)
Official Forms & Records	GCFA	**Fishel, Robert,** rfishel@gcfa.org

Older Adult Certification	GBHEM	**Wood, Anita,** awood@gbhem.org
Older Adult Ministries	GBOD	**Gentzler, Richard,** rgentzler@gbod.org
	GBCS	**Day, Jackson,** 202/488-5608 jday@umc-gbcs.org
	GBHEM	**Espino, Saul,** sespino@gbhem.org
	GBGM	**Fuentes, Noemi,** nfuentes@gbgm-umc.org
One Great Hour of Sharing- Marketing	GBGM	**Dirdak, Paul,** pdirdak@gbgm-umc.org
	UMCom	**Dunlap-Berg, Barbara,** bdunlap-sberg@umcom.org
Open Itinerancy	GCRR	**Taylor, James,** 202/547-2271
Ordained Elders	GBHEM	**Kohler, Robert,** bkohler@gbhem.org
BOM Relations		**Rubey, Sharon,** srubey@gbhem.org
Continuing Education		**Jackson, Marion,** mjackson@gbhem.org
Course of Study		**Daye, Lynn,** ldaye@gbhem.org
Clergywomen		**Jackson, Marion,** mjackson@gbhem.org
Enlistment/		**Hartley, Hal,** hhartley@gbhem.org
Ethnic Concerns		**Barrett, Patricia,** pbarrrett@gbhem.org
Supervision and		**Purushotham, Gwen,** gpurushotham@gbhem.org
Support Systems Workshops		
	GBCS	**Christie, Neal,** 202/488-5611 nchristie@umc-gbcs.org
Order of Saint Luke	GBOD	**Benedict, Dan,** dbenedict@gbod.org
Order of Deacons	GBHEM	**Wood, Anita,** awood@gbhem.org
Order of Elders	GBHEM	**Kohler, Robert,** rkohler@gbhem.org
	GBHEM	**Rubey, Sharon,** srubey@gbhem.org
Orientation Magazine	GBHEM	
Editorial Issues		**Hiers, Terri J.,** 615/340-7383
Orders		**Upton, Billie,** bupton@gbhem.org
Staff		**Felder, Luther B.,** lfelder@gbhem.org
Outdoor Ministries	GBOD	**Witt, Kevin,** kwitt@gbod.org
Pacific Islander	GCRR	**Thomas-Sano, Kathy,** 202/547-2271
Issues/Ministries	GBGM	**Rodriguez, David,** drodriguez@gbgm-umc.org
	GBOD	**Choi, Sungnam,** schoi@gbod.org see Revival of Hope Resources
Pan-Methodist Coalition		
Parish Ministries	GBGM	**Byrd, Lynda,** lbyrd@gbgm-umc.org
Passages	UMCom	**Alexander, Leslie,** lalexander@umcom.org
Pastoral Care and	UMPH	**Cokesbury,** 800/672-1789
Counseling Resources	GBHEM	**Barrett, Patricia,** 615/340-7411

Endorsements	GBHEM	**Hill, Greg,** ghill@gbhem.org
Pathways Center for Christian Spirituality	GBOD	**Thompson, Marjorie,** mthompson@upperroom.org
Peace with Justice Program	GBCS	**Horman, Janet,** 202/488-5647 jhorman@umc-gbcs.org
	GBGM	**Hutchison, Peggy,** phutchinson@gbgm.org
Peace with Justice Sunday-Marketing	UMCom	**Dunlap-Berg, Barbara,** bdunlap-berg@umcom.org
	GBCS	**Horman, Janet,** 202/488-5647 jhorman@umc-gbcs.org
Pension Fund Investments	GBOPHB	**Zellner, Dave,** 800/851-2201 ext. 4698
Perryman Scholarship	UMCom	**Communication Resourcing Team,** scholarships@umcom.org
Personal Investment Plan	GBOPHB	**Success, Daphne,** 800/851-2201 ext. 4282
Personnel Policies & Practices Committee	GCFA	**Manous, Rhonda,** 615/329-3393 rmanous@gcfa.org
	GBCS	**Ruiz, Evelyn,** 202/488-5628 eruiz@umc-gbcs.org
Persons with Disabilities	GBCS	**Day, Jackson,** 202/488-5608 jday@umc-gbcs.org
	GBOD	**Hynson, Diana,** dhynson@gbod.org
	GBGM	**Fuentes, Noemi,** nfuentes@gbgm-umc.org
Curriculum Resources	UMPH	**Curric-U-Phone,** 800/251-8591 curricuphone@cokesbury.com
Resource Ordering	UMPH	**Cokesbury,** 800/672-1789
Photographer, News	UMCom	**DuBose, Mike,** mdubose@umcom.org
Photographic Services	GBGM	**Moultrie, Edward,** emoultrie@gbgm-umc.org
	UMPH	**Dorris, Sid,** sdorris@umpublishing.org
Planned Giving Resources	GBOD	**Joiner, Don,** djoiner@gbod.org
	GBGM	**Takamine, Connie,** ctakamin@gbgm-umc.org
Pockets Magazine	GBOD	**Gilliam, Lynn,** lgilliam@upperroom.org
Standing Orders		800/972-0433
Subscriptions		800/925-6847
Political & Human Rights	GBCS	**Bautista, Liberato,** 212/682-3633 lbautista@umc-gbcs.org **Valentin-Castañon, Eliezer,** 202/488-5657 evalentin@umc-gbcs.org
Political Prisoners	GBCS	**Horman, Janet,** 202/488-5631 jhorman@umc-gbcs.org

Population & Development	GBCS	**Bales, Linda,** 202/488-5649
		lbales@umc-gbcs.org
Pornography/Sexual	GBCS	**Fealing, Kenrick,** 202/488-5634
Violence		kfealing@umc-gbcs.org
	GBCS	**Valentin-Castañon, Eliezer,**
		202/488-5657
		evalentin@umc-gbcs.org
	GBGM	**Halsey, Peggy,**
		phalsey@gbgm-umc.org
Prayer & Bible Conference	GBOD	**Albin, Tom,** 877/899-2780, ext. 7110
Prayer Calendar	GBGM	**Thomas, Susan,**
		sthomas@gbgm-umc.org
Prayer Center	GBOD	**Benedict, Mary O.,** 800/251-2468
Prayer Covenant Groups	GBOD	**Benedict, Mary O.,**
		mbenedict@upperroom.org
Prayer in Public Schools	GBCS	**Valentin-Castañon, Eliezer,**
		202/488-5657
		evalentin@umc-gbcs.org
Prayer, Telephone Ministry	GBOD	615/340-7215
Preaching Clinic	GBOD	**Fosua, Safiya,** sfosua@gbod.org
Preaching Resources	GBOD	**Fosua, Safiya,** sfosua@gbod.org
Circuit Rider Sermon	UMPH	**Cokesbury,** 800/672-1789
Series		**Reddig, Jill, S.,**
		jreddig@umpublishing.org
Prejudice and Religion	GCRR	**Taylor, James,** 202/547-2271
Preschool Christian Ed.	GBOD	**Gran, Mary Alice,** mgran@gbod.org
Preschool Curriculum	UMPH	**Fleegal, Daphne,**
Resources		dfleegal@umpublishing.org
Presidential Papers	GBHEM	**Matthews, Graham P.,**
		gmatthews@gbhem.org
Professional Association	GCFA	**Rexrode, Deborah,** 304/342-8843
of UM Church Secretaries		**Haralson, Cynthia,**
		charalso@gcfa.org
Professional Books	UMPH	**Ratcliff, Robert,**
		rratcliff@umpublishing.org
Professional Church	GBHEM	**Moman, MaryAnn,**
Leadership-NCC		mmoman@gbhem.org
	GBHEM	**Kohler, Robert,** rkohler@gbhem.org
Product Development	UMPH	**Smith, Judy,** 615/749-6034
Executive Director		jsmith@umpublishing.org
Product Marketing	UMCom	**Niedringhaus, Chuck,** 615/742-5101
		cniedringhaus@umcom.org
Production - Video/Audio	UMCom	**Alexander, Leslie,** 615/742-5450
		lalexander@umcom.org
Program Calendar	UMCom	**Carey, Lladale,**
		lcarey@umcom.umc.org
Sales		**Customer Service Center**
		888/346-3862 (888/FINDUMC)
Project Equality	GCRR	**Taylor, James,** 202/547-2271

	GBCS	**Jett, Frances,** fjett@umc-gbcs.org
Promotion of Giving	UMCom	**McNish, Kent,**
		kmcnish@umcom.umc.org
Psychological Testing	GBHEM	**Howe, Debbie,**
for Elders		dhowe@gbhem.org
for Deacons		
Public Information Office	UMCom	**Drachler, Stephen,** 615/742-5411
		sdrachler@umcom.org
Public Policy in Higher	GBHEM	**Bigham, Wanda D.,**
Education		wbigham@gbhem.org
	GBCS	**Valentín-Castañon, Eliezer,**
		202/488-5657
		evalentin@umc-gbcs.org
Newsletter	GBHEM	**Bigham, Wanda D.**
(Public Policy Update)		wbigham@gbhem.org
Public Relations	GBGM	**Crosson, Lesley Y.,**
		lcrosson@gbgm-umc.org
Public Relations	UMCom	**Drachler, Stephen,** 615/742-5411
		sdrachler@umcom.org
Puerto Rican Political	GBCS	**Valentín-Castañon, Eliezer**
		202/488-5657
		evalentin@umc-gbcs.org
Quarterly Review Journal	GBHEM	**Pieterse, Hendrick R.,** 615/340-7334
		hpieterse@gbhem.org
Racial and Ethnic Pluralism	GBCS	**Fealing, Kenrick,** 202/488-5637
		kfealing@umc-gbcs.org
		Christie, Neal, 202/488-5611
		nchristie@umc-gbcs.org
	GCRR	**Thomas-Sano, Kathy,** 202/547-2271
		Pupo-Ortiz, Yolanda, 202/547-2271
Racial Ethnic Minority	UMCom	**Communications Resourcing Team,**
Fellowship		rem@umcom.umc.org
Racial Harassment	GCRR	**Pupo-Ortiz, Yolanda,** 202/547-2271
Racial Justice	GBCS	**Fealing, Kenrick,** 202/488-5637
		kfealing@umc-gbcs.org
Racial Justice Seminars	GBGM	**Williams, Suzanne,**
		swilliams@gbgm-umc.org
Racism Workshops	GCRR	NEJ-**Taylor, James,** 202/547-2271
		SEJ-**Hawkins, Erin,** 202/547-2271
		SCJ-**Pupo-Ortiz, Yolanda,**
		202/547-2271
		NCJ-**Ware-Diaz, Suanne,**
		202/547-2271
		WJ-**Thomas-Sano, Kathy,**
		202/547-2271
Radio Spots (PSA)	UMCom	**Alexander, Leslie,**
		lalexander@umcom.org
Radio Spots	UMCom	**Igniting Ministry,**
		im@umcom.org 877/281-6535

Raising Healing and Wholeness to a Lifestyle	GBOD	877/899-2780, ext. 7527
RASH (Racism, Ageism, Sexism, Handicappism)	GBCS	**Fealing, Kenrick,** 202/488-5637 kfealing@umc-gbcs.org
Records	GCFA	**Haralson, Cynthia,** charalso@gcfa.org
Refugee Resettlement	GBGM	**Fernandez, Lilia,** liliaf@gbgm-umc.org
Refugees	GBCS	**Horman, Janet,** 202/488-5647 jhorman@umc-gbcs.org
Regional Training Igniting Ministry	UMCom	**Reece, Emily,** ereece@umcom.org
Religion and Race	GCRR	NEJ-**Taylor, James,** 202/547-2271 SEJ-**Hawkins, Erin,** 202/547-2271 SCJ-**Pupo-Ortiz, Yolanda,** 202/547-2271 NCJ-**Ware-Diaz, Suanne,** 202/547-2271 WJ-**Thomas-Sano, Kathy,** 202/547-2271
Religious Freedom	GBCS	**Valentín-Castañon, Eliezer,** 202/488-5657 evalentin@umc-gbcs.org
Research	GBGM	**Rivas, Michael,** mrivas@gbgm-umc.org
	GCOM	**This, Craig,** cthis@gcom-umc.org
Research, Small Church	GBOD	**Wallace, Julia,** jwallace@gbod.org
Resolutions, Book of	GBCS	**Hakola, Gretchen,** 202/488-5630 ghakola@umc-gbcs.org
	UMPH	**Alsgaard, Erik,** ealsgaard@umpublishing.org
Response Magazine	GBGM	**Jones, Dana,** djones@gbgm-umc.org
Retirement Planning/ Seminars	GBOPHB	**Figueredo, Mary,** 800/851-2201 ext. 2738
Revitalization/Racial and Ethnic Congregational	GBOD	**Taylor-Thirus, Francine,** ftaylor@gbod.org
Risk Management	GCFA	**Cholak, Linda C.,** 847/869-3345 lcholak@gcfa.org
Roman Catholic Relations	GCCUIC	**GCCUIC Staff,** 212/749-3553
Rumbo a la Universidad	GBHEM	**Bigham, Wanda D.,** wbigham@gbhem.org
Rural Communities and Racism	GCRR	**Taylor, James,** 202/547-2271
	GBCS	**Harrison, Mark,** 202/488-5645 mharrison@umc-gbcs.org
Rural Issues	GBCS	**Harrison, Mark,** 202/488-5645 mharrison@umc-gbcs.org
Rural Life Sunday	GBGM	**Byrd, Lynda,** lbyrd@gbgm-umc.org

Rural Ministries	GBGM	Byrd, Lynda, lbyrd@gbgm-umc.org
	GBOD	Wallace, Julia Kuhn, jwallace@gbod.org
Rural/Town Evangelism	GBOD	Daniel, Wesley S. K., wdaniel2gbod.org
Russian Initiative	GBGM	Weaver, Bruce, 214/273-0330
Sam Taylor Fellowships	GBHEM	Bigham, Wanda D., wbigham@gbhem.org
Sanctuary/Refugees	GBCS	Horman, Janet, 202/488-5647 jhorman@umc-gbcs.org
Scholarships		
Communications	UMCom	Tucker-Shaw, Amelia atucker-shaw@umcom.org, 888/278-4862
Crusade Scholarships	GBGM	Fitzgerald, James, jfitzger@gbgm-umc.org
Dempster Fellowships	GBHEM	Kohler, Robert, bkohler@gbhem.org
Deacons & Diaconal	GBHEM	Wood, Anita, awood@gbhem.org
Graduate Fellowship	GBHEM	
Ethnic Minority	GBHEM	Zimmerman, Patti, 615/340-7344 pzimmerman@gbhem.org
General	GBHEM	Zimmerman, Patti, 615/340-7344 pzimmerman@gbhem.org
Georgia Harkness		Jackson, Marion, mjackson@gbhem.org
Gift of Hope	GBHEM	Zimmerman, Patti, 615/340-7344 pzimmerman@gbhem.org
HANA (Hispanic, Asian, Native Amer.)	GBHEM	Zimmerman, Patti, 615/340-7344 pzimmerman@gbhem.org
Native American Seminary Award	GBHEM	Zimmerman, Patti, 615/340-7344 pzimmerman@gbhem.org
Racial Ethnic Minority Fellowship	UMCom	Communications Resourcing Team, 888/278-4862 rem@umcom.org
Women of Color	GBHEM	Current-Felder, Angella P., 615/340-7342, acurrent@gbhem.org Jackson, Marion, mjackson@gbhem.org
Women's Division	GBGM	Sohl, Joyce, jsohl@gbgm-umc.org
School of Christian Mission	GBGM	Lyman, Mary Grace, mlyman@gbgm-umc.org
Schools, Colleges, Universities	GBHEM	Bigham, Wanda D., wbigham@gbhem.org
Irish Student Placement Project		
Korean Student Placement Project		
Scouting	GCUMM	Coppock, Larry, lcoppock@gcumm.org

Small Membership Church	GBOD	**Wallace, Julia Kuhn**,
Resources	UMPH	800/672-1789
	GBOD	800/485-4370
Social/Economic Justice	GBCS	**Harrison, Mark,** 202/488-5648
		mharrison@umc-gbcs.org
Social Issues	GBCS	All Program Staff, 202/488-5600
Global	GBCS	**Bautista, Liberato,** 212/682-3633
		lbautista@umc-gbcs.org
Resources	UMPH	800/251-8591
	GBCS	www.discipleshipresources.org
Social Justice Retreats	GBCS	**Childers, Clayton,** 202/488-5642
		cchilders@umc-gbcs.org
	GBCS	**Williams, Annette,** 817/460-2573
		awilliams@umc-gbcs.org
Social Principles	GBCS	**Moore, Terry,** 800/967-0880
Resources		tmoore@umc-gbcs.org
Society of John Wesley	GCUMM	**Coppock, Larry,**
Fellows		lcoppock@gcumm.org
Soul Feast	GBOD	**Bryant, Stephen,**
		sbryant@upperroom.org
		Helms, Cindy,
		chelms@upperroom.org
Southwest Border Issues	GBGM	**Avitia, Edgar,**
		eavitia@gbgm-umc.org
Spanish Lang. Materials	GBOD	**Peres, Alma,** aperes@gbod.org
	UMCom	**Bachus, Amanda,**
		615/742-5113, abachus@umcom.org
	GBCS	**Moore, Terry,** 800/967-0880
		tmoore@umc-gbcs.org
	GBGM	**Ferrari, Nilda,**
		nferrari@gbgm-umc.org
	GBHEM	**Espino, Saul,** sespino@gbhem.org
	UMPH	**Clark, John,**
		jclark@umpublishing.org
Special Sundays Promotion	UMCom	**Dunlap-Berg, Barbara,**
/Resources Marketing		bdunlap-berg@umcom.org
Spiritual Discernment in	GBOD	**Haas, Jerry,** jerry_haas@gbod.org
the Church	GBHEM	**Wood, Anita,** awood@gbhem.org
Spiritual Formation		
Certification		
Spiritual Formation	GBOD	**Albin, Tom,** 877/899-2780, ext. 7110
Resources		talbin@upperroom.org
	GBOD	**Miller, JoAnn,**
		jamiller@upperroom.com
	UMPH	800/251-8591
	GBHEM	**Jackson, Marion,**
		mjackson@gbhem.org
	GBCS	**Christie, Neal,** 202/488-5611
		nchristie@umc-gbcs.org

Spiritual Leadership Development	GBOD	**Ruach, Susan,** sruach@gbod.org
Spiritual Leadership Teams for Congregations	GBOD	**Dick, Dan,** ddick@gbod.org **Heavner, Betsey,** bheavner@gbod.org
Spiritual Leadership Journal Standing Orders Subscriptions	GBOD	*Weavings,* 615/340-7254 800/972-0433 800/925-6847
Staff Retirement Benefits Program	GBPHB	**Vargas, Manuel,** 800/851-2201 ext. 4565
Statistical Data	GCFA	**Borst, Beth Babbitt,** bbabbitt@gcfa.org
Step Forward	UMPH	800/672-1789
Stewardship Education	GBOD	**Bell, David,** dbell@gbod.org
Stewardship Resources Program	GBOD	**Bell, David,** dbell@gbod.org
Stoody/West Fellowship	UMCom	Communications Resourcing Team, scholarships@umcom.org
Strength for Service To God & Country	GCUMM	**Coppock, Larry,** lcoppock@gcumm.org
Strengthening the Black Church for the 21st Century Coordinating Committee	GCOM	**Stevenson, Cheryl,** cstevens@gcom-umc.org
United Methodist Student Day	GBHEM	**Current-Felder, Angella P.,** 615/340-7342, acurrent@gbhem.org
Marketing	UMCom	**Dunlap-Berg, Barbara** bdunlap-berg@umcom.org
Student Forum of The United Methodist Student Movement	GBHEM	**Hartley, Hal,** hhartley@gbhem.org
Suicide	GBCS	**Day, Jackson,** 202/488-5608 jday@umc-gbcs.org
Summer Intern Program, Black College Fund	GBHEM	**Capers, Joreatha,** jcapers@gbhem.org
Tax Exemptions	GCFA	**Perrone, Christine,** 847/869-3345 cperrone@gcfa.org
Teacher Development	GBOD	**Krau, Carol,** ckrau@gbod.org
Teacher Resources	UMPH	**Curric-U-Phone,** 800/251-8591 curricuphone@cokesbury.com
Teachers in Schools of Christian Mission	GBGM	**Lyman, Mary Grace,** mlyman@gbgm-umc.org
	GBOD	**Gran, Mary Alice,** mgran@gbod.org
	GBOD	**Krau, Carol,** ckrau@gbod.org
Technology Techshop	UMCom	**MacAtee, Sean,** smacatee@umcom.org
Customer Service	UMCom	Customer Service Center, 888/346-3862 techshop@umcom.org

Television Programming	UMCom	**Underwood, Ginny,** 615/742-5124
	UMTV	gunderwood@umcom.org
Training UMCom	UMCom	**Nissen, Barbara,** 615/742-5139 bnissen@umcom.org
Theological Education	GBHEM	**Moman, Mary Ann,** mmoman@gbhem.org
Tithe: Resources and Seminars	GBOD	**Bell, David,** dbell@gbod.org
Tobacco Issues	GBCS	**vacant**
Town/Country Ministries	GBOD	**Wallace, Julia,** jwallace@gbod.org
	GBGM	**Byrd, Lynda,** lbyrd@gbgm-umc.org
TQuest for Men	GCUMM	**Malone, Larry,** lmalone@gcumm.org
Transitional Communities	GCRR	**Jones, Chester R.,** 202/547-2271
		Taylor, James, 202/547-2271
	GBGM	**Byrd, Lynda,** lbyrd@gbgm-umc.org
UM Association of Church Business Administrators	GCFA	**McKinsey, Linda,** lmckinse@gcfa.org
UM Association of Communicators	UMAC	**Communications Resourcing Team,** 888/278-4862 crt@umcom.org
UM Association of Health and Welfare Ministries		**Dilgard, Charles,** 513/461-2354 **Pulliam, Dean,** uma@umassociation.org
UMC.org	UMCom	**Carlisle, Matt,** 615/742-5153 mcarlisle@umcom.org
UMCom.org	UMCom	**Downey, Steve,** 615/742-5434 sdowney@umcom.org
UM Committee on Relief	GBGM	**Dirdak, Paul,** pdirdak@gbgm-umc.org
UM Communications	UMCom	**Hollon, Larry,** 615/742-5410 lhollon@umcom.org
UM Development Fund	GBGM	**Dixon, Sam Jr.,** sdixon@gbgm-umc.org
UM Directory	UMPH	**Johannes, Mary,** mjohannes@umpublishing.org
UM Higher Education Foundation	GBHEM	**Miller, George M.,** gmiller@gbhem.org
UM Hymnal, permission to reproduce	UMPH	800/779-1177, 615/244-5588
UM Hymnal Resources	GBOD	**McIntyre, Dean,** dmcintyre@gbod.org
UM Men Foundation	GCUMM	**Coppock, Larry,** lcoppock@gcumm.org
UM Men Presidents	GCUMM	**Malone, Larry,** lmalone@gcummorg
UMMen Magazine	GCUMM	**Kena, Kwasi,** kkena@gcumm.org
UM Ministries in Higher Education	GBHEM	**Felder, Luther B.,** lfelder@gbhem.org
UM News Service	UMCom	**Underwood, Ginny,** gunderwood@umcom.org

UM Research Office	GCom	**This, Craig,** cthis@gcom-umc.org
UM Rural Fellowship		**Eichler, Wanda Hayes,** 517/453-3342
UM Rural Fellowship Bulletin		**Armstrong, Roger,** 501/373-5027
UM Scouters Newsletter	GCUMM	**Coppock, Larry,** lcoppock@gcumm.org
UM Seminars on Nat'l & Int'l Affairs	GBCS	212/682-3633 202/488-5651 **Burton, Susan,** 202/488-5609 sburton@umc-gbcs.org
UMs in Service (Korean Journal)	UMCom	**Cho, Sang Yean,** sch@umcom.umc.org
UM Student Day	GBHEM	**Current-Felder, Angella,** 615/340-7342, acurrent@gbhem.org
Marketing	UMCom	**Dunlap-Berg, Barbara,** bdunlap-berg@umcom.org
UM Student Movement	GBHEM	**Hartley, Hal,** hhartley@gbhem.org
UM Studies: History, Doctrine, Polity	GBHEM	**Kohler, Robert,** rkohler@gbhem.org
UM Voluntary Services	GBGM	**Lawson, Ruth,** rlawson@gbgm.-umc.org
UM Women	GBGM	**Sohl, Joyce D.,** jsohl@gbgm-umc.org
Advocacy for Women	GBGM	**Dauway, Lois,** ldauway@gbgm-umc.org
Anti-Racism Training	GBGM	**Williams, Ife,** swilliam@gbgm-umc.org
Child Advocacy	GBGM	**Taylor, Julie,** jtaylor@gbgm-umc.org
Child Labor	GBGM	**Taylor, Julie,** jtaylor@gbgm-umc.org
Children's Ministries	GBGM	**Taylor, Julie,** jytalor@gbgm-umc.org
Christian Social Resp.	GBGM	**Dauway, Lois M.,** ldauway@gbgm-umc.org
Church/Government Rel.	GBGM	**Johnson, Susie,** johnsons@gbgm-umc.org
Continuing Education Lay Women	GBGM	**Trent, Cheryl,** ctrent@gbgm-umc.org
Devotional Literature	GBGM	**Craig, J. Ann,** acraig@gbgm-umc.org
Economic Justice	GBGM	**Clement, Marilyn,** mclement@gbgm-umc.org
Environmental Justice	GBGM	**Salter, Andris,** asalter@gbgm-umc.org
Family Issues, Advocacy	GBGM	**Taylor, Julie,** jtaylor@gbgm-umc.org
Global Justice Ministries	GBGM	**Adjali, Mia,** eadjali@gbgm-umc.org
Hate Groups	GBGM	**Dauway, Lois M.,** ldauway@gbgm-umc.org
Human Rights	GBGM	**Adjali, Mia,** eadjali@gbgm-umc.org
Immigration/ Naturalization	GBGM	**Johnson, Susie,** johnsons@gbgm-umc.org
Inclusiveness-Racial	GBGM	**Williams, Ife,** swilliam@gbgm-umc.org
International Affairs	GBGM	**Adjali, Mia,** eadjali@gbgm-umc.org
Justice Education	GBGM	**Dharmaraj, Glory,**

		gdharma@gbgm-umc.org
		Christie, Neal, nchristie@umc-gbcs.org
Leadership Development	GBGM	**Needham, Ann,** aneedham@gbgm-umc.org
Leadership Training for Elimination of Racism	GBGM	**Williams, Ife,** swilliam@gbgm-umc.org
Middle East	GBGM	**Adjali, Mia,** eadjali@gbgm-umc.org
Mission Education	GBGM	**Trent, Cheryl,** ctrent@gbgm-umc.org
Program Resources	GBGM	**Trent, Cheryl,** ctrent@gbgm-umc.org
Racial Justice Seminars	GBGM	**Williams, Ife,** swilliam@gbgm-umc.org
Schools of Christian Mission	GBGM	**Lyman, Mary Grace,** mlyman@gbgm-umc.org
Sexism	GBGM	**Dauway, Lois M.,** ldauway@gbgm-umc.org
Social/Economic Justice	GBGM	**Clement, Marilyn,** mclement@gbgm-umc.org
United Nations	GBGM	**Adjali, Mia,** eadjali@gbgm-umc.org
	GBCS	**Bautista, Liberato,** 212/682-3633 lbautista@umc-gbcs.org
	GBCS	**Riddleberger, Kathleen,** 212/682-3633 kriddleberger@umc-gbcs.org
Women and Racism	GBGM	**Williams, Ife,** swilliam@gbgm-umc.org
Youth Ministries	GBGM	**Taylor, Julie,** jtaylor@gbgm-umc.org
UM Youth Fellowship	UMPH	ileadyouth.com
Resources	GBOD	**Hay, Susan,** shay@gbod.org
United Methodist Youth	UMYO	www.umyouth.org
Organization		**Seibert, Ronna,** rseibert@gbod.org
UNITEDMETHODIST.org	UMCom	**Igniting Ministry,** im@umcom.org
United Nations Church Center	GBCS	**Bautista, Liberato,** 212/682-3633 lbautista@umc-gbcs.org
	GBCS	**Riddleberger, Kathleen,** 212/682-3633 kriddleberger@umc-gbcs.org
	GBGM	**Nesbitt, Claretta,** cnesbitt@gbgm-umc.org
Universal Health Care	GBCS	**Day, Jackson,** 202/488-5608 jday@umc-gbcs.org
University Senate	GBHEM	**Yamada, Ken,** kyamada@gbhem.org
Upper Room Books	GBOD	**Collett, Rita,** rcollett@upperroom.org
	GBOD	**Miller, JoAnn,** jmiller@upperroom.org
Upper Room		**Book orders,** 800/972-0433
Upper Room Chapel/ Museum	GBOD	**Kimball, Kathryn,** kkimball@upperroom.org

Upper Room Fellowship		615/340-7024
Upper Room Magazine	GBOD	**Redding, Mary Lou**,
		mredding@upperroom.org
		Stafford, James T.,
		jstafford@upperroom.org
		Hines, Vicki,
		vhines@upperroom.org
		King, Susan, sking@upperroom.org
Standing Orders		800/972-0433
Subscriptions		800/925-6847
Urban Ministries	GBCS	**Harrison, Mark,** 202/488-5645
		mharrison@umc-gbcs.org
	GBOD	**Smith, Debra,** dsmith@gbod.org
Urban Ministries	GBGM	**Johnson, Diane,**
		djohnson@gbgm-umc.org
US-2 Program	GBGM	**Gleaves, Edith,**
		egleaves@gbgm-umc.org
Vacation Bible School	UMPH	**Salley, Susan,**
Resources		ssalley@umpublishing.org
		Curric-U-Phone, 800/251-8591
		curricuphone@cokesbury.com
Video Production	UMCom	**Alexander, Leslie,** 615/742-5450
		lalexander@umcom.org
Video-Sales	UMCom	**Customer Service Center,**
		888/346-3862 (888/FINDUMC)
Volunteer Building Teams	GBGM	**Blankenbaker, Jeanie,**
		jblanken@gbgm-umc.org
Volunteers in Mission	GBGM	**Blankenbaker, Jeanie,**
		jblanken@gbgm-umc.org
Walk to Emmaus	GBOD	**Gilmore, Dick,** 877/899-2780 ext. 7298
	GBOD	**Johnson-Green, Jean,**
		877/899-2780 ext. 7222
Washington Seminars	GBCS	**Burton, Susan,** 202/488-5609
		sburton@umc-gbcs.oprg
	GBCS	**Toledo, Ana,** 202/488-5651
		atoledo@umc-gbcs.org
Weavings Journal	GBOD	**Mogabgab, John,** 615/340-7254
		jmogabgab@upperroom.org
		Hawkins, Pamela,
		phawkins@upperroom.org
Standing orders		800/972-0433
Subscriptions		800/925-6847
Web Ministry	UMCom	**Downey, Steve,** 615/742-5434
		sdowney@umcom.org
Websites	UMCom	**Downey, Steve,** 615/742-5434
		sdowney@umcom.org
Web Site Administration	GBGM	**Obando, Jorge,**
		jobando@gbgm-umc.org
	GBOD	**Capshaw, Cheryl,**

		ccapshaw@gbod.org
		Richardson, Beth,
		877/899-2780 ext. 7242
		brichardson@upperroom.org
	UMCom	**Mai, Danny,** dmai@umcom.org
Web Site Development	UMCom	**Downey, Steve,** 615/742-5434
		sdowney@umcom.org
Web Site, District	GBHEM	**Gafke, Arthur,** agafke@gbhem.org
Superintendents		
Wedding Resources	GBOD	**Benedict, Dan,** dbenedict@gbod.org
Week of Prayer	GCCUIC	**Gamble, Elizabeth,** 212/749-3553
for Christian Unity		bgamble@gccuic-umc.org
Weekday Ministries for	GBOD	**Gran, Mary Alice,** mgran@gbod.org
Children		
Weekday Ministries	UMPH	**Curric-U-Phone,** 800/251-8591
Curriculum		curricuphone@cokesbury.com
Welcoming Ministry	UMCom	**Igniting Ministry,**
		877/281-6535
		im@umcom.org
Wellsprings Publication	GBHEM	**Jackson, Marion,**
Journal		mjackson@gbhem.org
White Constituency	GCRR	**Taylor, James,** 202/547-2271
Concerns (Anti-Racism)		
Wills, Trusts	GCFA	**Allen, Jim,** 615/329-3393
		jallen@gcfa.org
	GBOD	**Joiner, Don,** djoiner@gbod.org
Women and Addiction	GBCS	**Bales, Linda,** 202/488-5649
		lbales@umc-gbcs.org
Women and Health	GBCS	**Bales, Linda,** 202/488-5649
		lbales@umc-gbcs.org
	GBGM	**Halsey, Peggy,**
		phalsey@gbgm-umc.org
Women and Racism	GCRR	**Barnes, Constance N.,** 202/547-2271
Women - Campus Ministry	GBHEM	**Smith, Lillian,** lsmith@gbhem.org
Women Clergy	GBHEM	**Jackson, Marion,**
		mjackson@gbhem.org
Women in Crisis	GBGM	**Halsey, Peggy,**
		phalsey@gbgm-umc.org
Women's Advocacy		**Hixon, Stephanie Anna,**
		shixon@gcfa.org
	GBCS	**Bales, Linda,** 202-488-5649
		lbales@umc-gbcs.org
Women's Division	GBGM	**Sohl, Joyce,** jsohl@gbgm-umc.org
Women of Color	GBHEM	**Jackson, Marion,**
Scholarship		mjackson@gbhem.org
		Current, Angella P., 615/340-7344
Women's History	GCAH	**Yrigoyen, Charles,**
		cyrigoyen@gcah.org
Women's Issues Res.	GCSRW	**Burton, Garlinda,**
		gburton@gcfa.org

Women - Ministries to:	GBGM	**Halsey, Peggy,** phalsey@gbgm-umc.org
	GBGM	**Calvin, Elizabeth,** ecalvin@gbgm-umc.org
Women's Rights	GBCS	**Bales, Linda,** 202/488-5649 lbales@umc-gbsc.org
World Communion Sunday	GBHEM	**Current-Felder, Angella,** 615/340-7342
Marketing	UMCom	**Dunlap-Berg, Barbara,** bdunlap-berg@umcom.org
World Council of Churches	GCCUIC	**Chapman, Clare,** cchapman@gccuic-umc.org
World Hunger	GBGM	**Kim, June,** jkim@gbgm-umc.org
	GBCS	**Harrison, Mark,** 202/488-5645 mharrison@umc-gbcs.org
World Methodist Council		**Hale, Joseph,** umc6@juno.com
World Parish		**Hale, Joseph,** umc6@juno.com
World Service Contingency Fund	GCOM	**Hayashi, Donald L.,** dhayashi@gcom-umc.org
World Service Fund Apportionment Marketing	UMCom	**Wood, Tracy,** twood@umcom.org
World Service Special Gifts	GCOM	**Hayashi, Donald L.,** dhayashi@gcom-umc.org
World Service Special Gifts-Marketing	GCFA	**Zekoff, Steve,** 847/425-6506
	UMCom	**McNish, Kent,** kmcnish@umcom.umc.org
	GCOM	**Hayashi, Donald L.,** dhayashi@gcom-umc.org
World Student Christian Federation	GBHEM	**Hartley, Hal,** hhartley@gbhem.org
Worship, Book of	UMPH	
	GBOD	**Benedict, Dan,** dbenedict@gbod.org
Worship Resources	GBOD	**Benedict, Dan,** dbenedict@gbod.org
		McIntyre, Dean, dmcintyre@gbod.org
	GBGM	**Walker, Tamara,** twalker@gbgm-umc.org
	GBOD	**Fosua, Safiyah,** sfsosua@gbod.org
Adult	GBOD	**Crenshaw, Bill,** bcrenshaw@gbod.org
Children	GBOD	**Gran, Mary Alice,** mgran@gbod.org
Christian Education	GBOD	**Krau, Carol,** ckrau@gbod.org
Coordinators Age-level	GBOD	**Gran, Mary Alice,** mgran@gbod.org
Families	GBOD	**Sa, Soozung,** ssa@gbod.org
		Norton, MaryJane Pierce, mnorton@gbod.org
Local Church Education	GBOD	**Hynson, Diana,** dhynson@gbod.org
Older Adult	GBOD	**Gentzler, Rick,** rgentzler@gbod.org
Resources	UMPH	**Curric-U-Phone,** 800/251-8591 curricuphone@cokesbury.com

Scouting	GCUMM	**Coppock, Larry**, 615/340-7149
Single Adult	GBOD	**Sa, Soozung**, ssa@gbod.org
Young Adults	GBOD	**Crenshaw, Bill,** bcrenshaw@gbod.org
Youth	GBOD	**Carty, Terry**, tcarty@gbod.org **Hay, Susan,** shay@gbod.org
Youth Certification	GBHEM	**Wood, Anita,** awood@gbhem.org
Youth Curriculum Resources	UMPH	**Curric-U-Phone,** 800/251-8591 www.ileadyouth.com curricuphone@cokesbury.com
Youth Devotional Magazine (*Devo'Zine*)	GBOD	**Pippin, Robin,** 615/340-7247 **Miller, Sandy,** 615/340/7089 **Corlew, Nicole,** 615/340-1778
Standing Orders (Bulk)		800/972-0433
Subscriptions		800/925-6847
Youth Ministries	GBGM	**Walker, Tamara,** twalker@gbgm-umc.org
Women's Division	GBGM	**Hemmerle, Cheryl,** chemmerl@gbgm-umc.org
Youth Ministries:	GBOD	**Carty, Terry,** tcarty@gbod.org
Conference Adult Workers with Youth and Conference	GBOD	
Congregational Youth Ministries	GBOD	**Hay, Susan,** shay@gbod.org
Youth Programs	GBOD	**Carty, Terry,** tcarty@gbod.org
UMYO	UMYO	**Seibert, Ronna,** rseibert@gbod.org
Youth Offender Project	GBCS	**Fealing, Kendrick,** 202/488-5637 kfealing@umc-gbcs.org
Youth Seminar	GBCS	**Burton, Susan,** 202/488-5609 sburton@umc-gbcs.org
Youth Service Fund	UMYO	**Seibert, Ronna,** rseibert@gbod.org

INDEX

SUBSCRIPTION NOTICE

YES! I want to subscribe to **The United Methodist Directory and Index of Resources**. I understand that each year, beginning with this edition, I will receive the latest edition of the **Directory** as it is published and that my subscription will continue unless I change or cancel my order. I will be billed for each issue as it is shipped.

_____Charge to Cokesbury Account #_____
_____Open a new Cokesbury Account for me.

Send to: _____
Street: _____
City/State/Zip

_____

Bill to: _____
(if different from above)
Street _____
City/State/Zip _____
Ordered by: _____
Daytime Phone (if we have a question)_____

Send to:
The United Methodist Directory and Index of Resources
Nancy Provost, Editor
Post Office Box 801
Nashville, TN 37202
Phone: 615/749-6447
FAX: 615/749-6128